ADVANCES IN
INTERNATIONAL
ACCOUNTING

Supplement 1 • 1998

ADVANCES IN INTERNATIONAL ACCOUNTING

Editor: TIMOTHY S. DOUPNIK
School of Accounting
College of Business Administration
University of South Carolina

Volume Editors: VERNON K. ZIMMERMAN
ANDREW D. BAILEY, JR.
Center for International Education and Research in Accounting (CIERA)
University of Illinois, Urbana-Champaign

SUPPLEMENT 1 • 1998

JAI PRESS INC.

Stamford, Connecticut *London, England*

100 Prospect Street
Stamford, Connecticut 06901-1640

JAI PRESS LTD.
38 Tavistock Street
Covent Garden
London WC2E 7PB
England

ISBN: 0-7623-0461-8

Transferred to digital printing 2005

CONTENTS

LIST OF CONTRIBUTORS

Ziad K. Al-Rai	University of Jordan
Bhabatosh Banerjee	University of Calcutta
Maureen Berry	Department of Accounting University of Illinois at Urbana-Champaign
Nasuhi I. Bursal	University of Istanbul and The Ohio State University
Regis Cunningham	AGCO Corporation South America
Naim Dahmash	University of Jordan
John W. Eichenseher	University of Wisconsin, Madison
Naim A. Hassan	Department of Accounting and Finance The Birmingham Business School University of Birmingham, England
Sara York Kenny	International Finance Corporation
Victoria Krivorgorsky	University of Wisconsin, Madison
Robert K. Larson	School of Business Administration Pennsylvania State University, Harrisburg
Joëlle Le Vourc'h	ESCP Paris School of Management
Stanley C. Martens	DePaul University
Marc F. Massoud	Accounting and Finance Claremont McKenna College
John E. McEnroe	DePaul University

Mohamed Ali Mirghani King Fahad University of Petroleum and Minerals
Dhahran, Saudi Arabia

Ronald J. Points Washington Consulting Practice
PriceWaterhouse Coopers LLP

William H. Sholem Baltics/Belarus Team
European Bank for Reconstruction and Development

PREFACE

When Vern Zimmerman proposed the 1996 Center for International Education and Research in Accounting (CIERA) Conference, I was Head of the Department of Accountancy. As Head of the Department, it was clear to me that CIERA attracted an important group of international accounting researchers to our campus and reflected well on the University of Illinois' commitment to international education and research. Vern was kind enough to involve me in the activities of the center, including the planning for this conference in accounting and commerce. At the time, I had no idea that I would become the co-editor of the conference proceedings. When Vern's health declined and he was no longer able to carry the full responsibility of the center, he graciously asked me to assume editorship of the CIERA journal, *The International Journal of Accounting*, and later the directorship and management of CIERA itself. The editorial responsibility for this conference came with the CIERA directorship. I was honored by the request and have done my best to advance Vern's legacy in CIERA and, more specifically, to see his remaining projects through to publication.

The concept behind this conference, as well as its development and implementation, were all a part of Vern's vision. The conference was his last before his death. He was very proud of the quality of the research, the presenters and the attendees. My role, as the new director, was to carry out Vern's concept to completion. I hope Vern is pleased with the result.

We have published the papers in an only slightly different order than their appearance during the conference. The theme of transitional and developing economies struggling with the introduction and implementation of international accounting standards is evident throughout the papers. While current events often seem to outstrip our ability to keep up, I believe you will find that these papers continue to provide useful insights about current events in the adoption and application of the international accounting standards.

Andrew D. Bailey, Jr., Director
Center for International Education
and Research in Accounting

PART I

CONTRIBUTIONS TO THE DEVELOPMENT AND APPLICATION OF INTERNATIONAL ACCOUNTING STANDARDS IN TRANSITIONAL AND DEVELOPING ECONOMIES

THE APPLICATION OF INTERNATIONAL ACCOUNTING STANDARDS IN TRANSITIONAL SOCIETIES AND DEVELOPING COUNTRIES

Ronald J. Points and Regis Cunningham

INTRODUCTION

International accounting standards (IAS) issued by the International Accounting Standards Committee (IASC) have existed since the early 1970s. However, they have taken on unprecedented importance in recent years. The purpose of this paper is to discuss: (1) why the IAS have achieved a higher profile and greater relevance in recent years, (2) what factors impact the IAS adoption process, and (3) what practical problems are faced by transitional societies and developing countries in adopting IAS.

Advances in International Accounting, Supplement 1, pages 3-16.

ISBN: 0-7623-0461-8

PriceWaterhouse Coopers LLP has been in the forefront of efforts to adopt IAS in the republics of the former Soviet Union and other transitional societies and developing countries around the world. This paper builds on that experience.

WHY ARE IAS BECOMING MORE IMPORTANT?

IAS have taken on an importance in the 1990s not witnessed in the previous two decades of their existence. This section of the paper explores the reasons for this.

Globalization of Business Activities

In past decades, it was often enough for enterprises to produce and market their products and services within their national borders. For many enterprises, those days are gone. Competition has increased. Consequently, enterprises have been forced to seek ways to produce their products at lower costs, expand their markets, and provide greater customer satisfaction. As enterprises have sought ways to decrease costs, they have also sought overseas markets to increase sales. Fierce domestic competition, such as that between Coca-Cola and Pepsi, often makes less competitive international markets more attractive and lucrative. Shrinking domestic consumption caused by changes in demographic or social patterns may also make international expansion necessary for survival.

As enterprises expand operations internationally, the need for consistent financial reporting has increased. Headquarters needs financial information prepared on a consistent basis from all of its subsidiaries to consolidate financial reports, compare operating results, and make investment decisions among competing opportunities. The IAS provide a means of achieving comparable financial information. Moreover, accounting is the language of business. Businesspeople need financial information prepared on a consistent basis of accounting to communicate clearly their business activities.

Technology and Communication Advances

If economic, social, regulatory, and other events have been the drivers for enterprises to move operations overseas, technologic and communication advances have been the enablers for them to do so. Large multinational companies have had worldwide operations for decades. However, the technological and communications revolution of the last decade or so has made it increasingly possible for smaller companies to "go international." Enterprises can now mobilize their employees more quickly, safely, comfortably, and at less cost to respond to business needs overseas than ever before. However, the exciting and greatest impacts have been felt from the ongoing revolution in the computer and telecommunications industries.

Deregulation of the U.S. telecommunications industry and the creation of MCI, Sprint, and others to compete with AT&T have lowered costs and unleased a wave of new international calling services. The development and laying of fiber optic cables have improved the quality of telecommunication services and permitted a significant increase in the volume of international messages. Similarly, technological advances in telecommunication satellites, the launching of private satellites such as PANAMSAT, and competition in the satellite industry have greatly improved communication services and allowed capacity to keep pace with the surging demand. Powerful laptop computers; spreadsheet, graphic, and word processing software; electronic mail; the World Wide Web; mobile telephones; international conference calling; teleconferencing; and international call-home services are just a sample of the technological advances enabling companies to work more effectively and economically overseas. This, in turn, enables businesses to have proposals and reports sent in from overseas locations, edited, returned electronically in a matter of hours, and sent electronically to clients. Phone calls from one country to another can be forwarded automatically to any location in the world. Technological advances such as these enable companies to conduct business globally as never before. As business has become more international, the need to communicate financial information on a consistent basis across borders has increased.

Globalization of Capital Markets

Growth requires increasing amounts of working capital and capital investments. Companies are increasingly obtaining this capital beyond the borders of the country in which they are registered. The technological advances discussed above are making this possible by providing information on investment needs and availability around the world on an economical and timely basis. The reasons for these international financial flows are diverse. Financial investors may be merely attempting to obtain the highest return possible and, therefore, be indifferent to the country in which they make the investment as long as it matches their risk/return profile. Financial investors may also attempt to diversify their risk on a geographic basis. Strategic investors may be interested in developing a new geographic market for their products or services or developing a strategic alliance with a company in another geographic region. An oversupply of capital, such as that in Chile caused by the growth of the country's pension funds, also may cause capital to flow across national boundaries. The security of the U.S. market attracts capital from other countries and the burgeoning debt of the U.S. government makes capital inflows from overseas a necessity.

Regardless of the reason for these international capital flows, there is one constant: the need for reliable financial information that is understandable to the reader. However, as companies look to invest overseas, they often find that financial reports are prepared on a basis of accounting different from that of their own country. In some cases, the difference is so great that the financial reports are totally unintelligible or even misleading.

The clearest case of a different basis of accounting is that in the countries created out of the former Soviet Union. Russia, Kazakhstan, Kyrgyzstan, and the other new nations have adhered to the Russian model of accounting, which is significantly different from that used in the United States. Its focus is tax-based. Inventory is revalued for inflation, and taxes and certain other disbursements are not recorded as expenses. General administrative and selling costs (period costs) are capitalized as part of the inventory cost and flow through the statement of operations as an element of cost of sales. But even countries such as Germany, France, and Italy have significant accounting differences with those used in the United States.

Capital markets function efficiently only when information on investments is readily available to investors at little or no cost. In the case of the countries of the former Soviet Union, the financial information available is not understandable to Western investors. Moreover, the cost and time to convert the financial reports to a basis of accounting that is usable by Western investors is significant, further reducing the efficiency of the market. Thus, most countries are recognizing the need for a set of international accounting standards that is used consistently around the world. The lack of such standards hampers both investors and those seeking capital injections.

In the republics of the former Soviet Union, the need for capital is desperate. Cash flow from the government has stopped. Equipment requires replacement. Debt financing is exorbitant, and traditional suppliers and customers have disappeared. Western companies that might be interested in investing or supplying credit frequently do not do so because of the lack of reliable and understandable financial information. Economic and political instability in the former Soviet Union is a major deterrent to investment. The lack of reliable and understandable financial information, however, also prevents or delays otherwise executable investments.

Obviously, investments in the former Soviet Union are being made. However, these investments are often executed for strategic reasons or on the basis of "soft" data, not on the basis of carefully analyzed financial statements.

Many countries, including the republics of the former Soviet Union, are working toward adopting the international accounting standards. The process they are following and some of the problems encountered in adopting IAS are discussed below.

FACTORS IMPACTING THE IAS ADOPTION PROCESS

The process for setting standards and the extent to which the accounting standards adopted in a country are consistent with IAS depend on the political, legal, economic, and cultural environment of the country. This section discusses some of the more important factors.

Who Sets Accounting Standards?

The organization that researches, drafts, and promulgates accounting standards varies from country to country. Common forms of the standard-setting body include: (1) professional organizations, (2) independent private sector accounting standards boards, (3) independent government commissions, (4) government ministries, (5) intergovernmental agencies, and (6) some mixture of these.

In the United States, accounting standards used by the private sector were initially researched and promulgated by the American Institute of Certified Public Accountants (AICPA), a private sector, nonprofit professional association. To avoid potential conflicts of interest, an entirely independent, nonprofit private sector organization, the Financial Accounting Standards Board (FASB), was established in 1973. The Government Accounting Standards Board (GASB) was created in 1984 to promulgate accounting standards for state and local governments. Both the FASB and GASB report to the Financial Accounting Foundation (FAF). In 1990, the Federal Accounting Standards Advisory Board (FASAB) was established to set standards for the U.S. federal government, including government enterprises. The FASAB is an intergovernmental organization composed of representatives from the principal federal government financial management agencies and federal departments.

The Securities and Exchange Commission (SEC) actually has the authority to issue standards in the United States that must be applied by publicly traded companies. However, the SEC has delegated the function of issuing accounting standards for publicly traded companies to the FASB, although the SEC can decide not to accept standards that it does not agree with, thereby wielding unofficial veto power over FASB standards. The SEC rarely exercises this power but has done so in the past when it believed that the FASB was unduly influenced by industry.

In many states of the former Soviet Union, the accounting regulations inherited from the Russian model are in the process of being modified, updated, or replaced. In Russia, a large multi-institutional organization composed of government ministries, international organizations, academicians, and public accounting firms was established to promulgate standards. Competing interests have limited the results of this body to the adoption of one standard in approximately four years. This may be a case of too many cooks in the kitchen. It has proved nearly impossible to develop a consensus in Russia on new accounting standards.

In Kazakhstan, Kyrgyzstan, Uzbekistan, Ukraine, and Moldova, technical assistance for both public and private sector organizations is being funded by USAID, the World Bank, and UNDP. Lacking private sector professional accountancy associations, the Ministry of Finance has taken the lead in accounting reforms in these countries. The lack of professional accountancy associations and the traditional preeminent position of the Ministry of Finance for 70 years under Soviet administration make this an appropriate approach.

To understand this, it is necessary to remember that the accounting profession in the former Soviet Union is at a much lower level of development than those in the United States, England, and other Western industrialized countries. One frequently hears that there are no accountants, only bookkeepers, in the region. This may be something of an exaggeration and show a lack of appreciation of the Russian accounting model, but it is true that the accountancy profession is less developed than in the West.

One must also understand the culture of the region. Independent action was not fostered in the former Soviet Union. A commonly heard saying in the region is, "Revolutionaries are shot." Consistent with this mentality, we were told by chief accountants in the region that they would implement whatever reforms were handed down by the Ministry of Finance. To the Western mind, this may not seem totally democratic. However, it is an approach that works in the region and is a means of getting the reform wheel rolling and accomplishing some reform in a short period of time. There may be too many "old-school," vocal, and influential nonreformists to achieve accounting reform via democratic participation as we know it in the West. This conclusion appears to be borne out by the Russian experience.

One of the bilateral donor agencies is embarking on a different approach in the region. Technical assistance funding is being directed at implementing Western financial information systems in selected enterprises. The expectation is that the spark will spread across the country in a more Western-style, grassroots, bottom-up approach as opposed to a centrally directed reform.

Although consistent with the agency's private sector dogma, it remains to be seen: (1) how many of the region's enterprises take action independent of directives from the Ministry of Finance, (2) the effects of competing with an ongoing national government-led accounting reform, and (3) the legality of the enterprise-led reforms. In Russia, enterprises that have moved to the front on the national reform have been saddled with the weight of operating two accounting systems. With national statutory charts of accounts throughout the region, it is difficult and costly to deviate much from the accounting model sponsored by the Ministry of Finance. Also, empowering bookkeepers to be revolutionaries in a culture in which revolutionaries have been known to spend time in cold, remote areas or worse may be tough sledding.

What Is Beneath the Waters?

If accounting standards were written by machines in a vacuum, they would have the sole purpose of fair financial statement presentation and would probably be almost identical from country to country. Fortunately or unfortunately, as the case may be, accounting standards are written by individuals who are subject to pressures and forces extant in a particular country at a given point in time.

The IAS written in the 1970s provided many more alternative accounting treatments than are allowed currently. One might question why the earlier versions of the standards did not have more backbone to them. The answer may lie in the fact that it must have been very difficult to get signatory countries with widely different accounting practices and a strong dose of nationalistic pride to agree on anything. Some of the early standards indicate that the authors agreed not to agree and to get on with it. The result in some cases was warm, fuzzy, mom-and-apple-pie wording that did not appear to say much at all. Fortunately, after over two decades of work, the IASC member countries appear much more united in their attempt to harmonize accounting practices around the world.

The United States presents a litigious environment not found anywhere else in the world, although Europe appears to be catching the same malady. Disclosure in the United States has become so complex that even though no one understands the notes, they include all the information necessary for an investor to make an informed investment decision, provided that he or she has the number-crunching capability of the autistic brother in the movie Rain Man. The mode is highly defensive. The attitude is "let's disclose all the information that could possibly be desired by any potential investor for any possible reason. If we do so, we're probably safe from potential legal action."

The situation is totally different in Latin America, Central Asia, and most developing countries and transitional societies, where the norm is secrecy rather than full disclosure. In Latin America, for example, capital has traditionally been concentrated in the hands of a small number of wealthy families that operate groups of companies. Investment and working capital for the enterprises in the group are generally provided by internally generated earnings or by financial institutions in the group. These financial institutions channel financing to the enterprises whether the enterprises are creditworthy or not. Financing decisions are made not by professional management but by the owner of the group. This system obviates the need for outside financing and, therefore, for full or any other type of disclosure.

Tax avoidance and competition are strong motivators in this system. Ownership is distributed among trusted members of the extended family. The less disclosure as to who owns what, where financing comes from, and which operations are profitable, the better. Given the high-handed and sometimes politically motivated operation of government tax agencies and the poor administration of tax revenues by governments in these countries, secrecy and tax avoidance are understandable. This obsession with secrecy is also an important reason that stock markets in many countries of the region have little activity other than the trading of bank and government paper. Few companies are willing to disclose the information necessary to list their stocks on an exchange.

Accounting systems are generally designed to measure those things that are most important to management and the entity. In the former Soviet Union, taxes and production had prime importance, and the Russian accounting model was accordingly designed to measure those things. Enterprises did not need to demonstrate profitability to attract investment capital or secure working capital loans. Cash shortfalls were remedied by cash injections from the government.

With the adoption of market economies in the newly independent states, the rules of the game have changed. First and foremost, the government has stopped the cash spigot. Enterprises must now generate cash internally or turn to financial institutions and investors. Consequently, management must concentrate on cash flow, profitability, and financial position. These are precisely the elements measured by the international accounting standards model and the reason that the newly independent states are interested in adopting the IAS.

Many countries in the region appear inclined toward evolution, not revolution, in the reform of their national accounting systems. Consequently, it will not be surprising if certain vestiges of the former tax/production orientation are found in their adoption of the IAS. Also, adopting IAS is easier said than done. Some of the primary problems encountered by the new republics are discussed next.

Problems Adopting IAS

Adoption of the IAS is not a simple matter for the republics of the former Soviet Union. Success in overcoming the obstacles discussed below requires careful planning, patience, dogged perseverance, and a sense of humor.

Why Do We Need It?

Increasing international competition and cross-border capital flows are matters of record. The change from controlled to market economy is law in much of the former Soviet Union. Extremely low plant utilization and inventory and receivable turnovers, massive employee layoffs, severe liquidity situations, and plant shutdowns are common. Yet, those responsible for accounting reform often do not sense the urgency for it. In certain cases, it may be that the government employees responsible for reform do not have enough vision or are too risk-averse to take the bold actions necessary to implement it.

However, it would be unfair to judge the would-be reformers too harshly. A functioning market economy is not part of the life experiences of many of the reformers. They have never seen a functioning stock market. They do not fully comprehend the role of a securities and exchange commission or an accounting standards board. They do not understand Western investor mentality. While they may have seen such institutions briefly in other countries and understand the concepts on an intellectual level, they have not lived in a market economy. Therefore, they do not fully comprehend the complex interrelationships that exist and the fundamental and critical role that accounting standards play in making the entire market economy function properly.

The Russian bookkeeping system is ingenious. It may even provide a much better audit trail than Western accounting systems. However, it was designed to meet needs that are different than those of today's transitioning economies. Until the would-be reformers understand the functioning of the market economy, they may not be able to perceive the need to change the existing system. And this may take time. Again, it should be remembered: "Revolutionaries are shot."

OK, How Do We Learn It?

Once the need for change is understood and accepted, understanding Western accounting presents an equally challenging problem. The Western and Russian accounting models are similar in some ways but very different in others. General, administrative, and selling expenses are period, not production, costs. Taxes are period costs, not a use of profit. The differences go on and on.

The former Soviet Union was closed to Westerners. Therefore, accountants in the republics of the former Soviet Union have not had an opportunity to learn Western accounting for very long. There is also a shortage of Western accounting material that has been translated into Russian. Two Western accounting texts that have been translated into Russian are not readily available or widely distributed, despite their low cost (U.S.$3.50). And for some unknown reason, few Russian-speaking CPAs or chartered accountants in the United States and Europe are ready, willing, and able to teach in the former Soviet Union.

What Is a Professional Accounting Association?

In the United States and many other countries around the world, national accounting standards were first developed by a professional accounting association. This implies: (1) a high level of professionalization on the part of accountants and (2) an organization to research, promulgate, and ensure the application of the standards. In the former Soviet Union, private sector professional accounting associations generally have not existed.

As mentioned, accountants and their associations may be too close to their clients to provide the objectivity needed to issue accounting standards. Independent accounting standard boards, representing a diverse constituency of persons knowledgeable about financial reporting, have been created to research and write standards. There is a strong belief in the republics of the former Soviet Union that the authority for the issuance of accounting standards belongs in the domain of the government. Writing accounting standards in a country in which the accounting profession is not highly developed and in which few, if any, accountants understand IAS is a daunting task.

What Does Culture Have to Do with It?

Culture is an important element in setting standards. Accounting standards developed for this region will need to take account of the fact that local accountants and bookkeepers are accustomed to taking orders, not independent action. Initial standards may have to be very specific, leaving little opportunity for discretion and interpretation.

Authority for accounting standard-setting may have to remain in the government for some time because the would-be reformers believe that there is no tradition of pro bono activity. Board members would not attend meetings, we were told. Also, if a board were created, meetings would have to be closed to the public; there is no tradition of open, public debate in the republics of the former Soviet Union.

What Is in a Concept?

The concept of accrual accounting, for example, is known and accepted in the region. Other Western accounting concepts, however, are totally alien to accountants of the region. Fair value, for example, is a troublesome concept in Central Asia. It is not sufficiently determinate. There is no way to determine a priori what fair value might be in a given transaction. The response to the explanation that fair value is what two reasonable and knowledgeable persons would agree to pay in an arms-length transaction is that two other people might agree to pay something else. So what is the fair value? And how do we write standards that tell the accountants how to calculate it? Lacking a tradition of discretion and independent action, the Central Asian mind is always looking for a way to specify the exact accounting treatment or calculation to be used in every situation.

Terminology: A Land Mine

Interpreters are sometimes used in reform projects. One can imagine the difficulties in discussing a concept that does not yet exist in the region using terminology that does not yet exist or, worse yet, that has a different meaning in Russian than in English. Even Russian speakers who know Western accounting have difficulty translating certain Western terms into Russian. Measurement, for example, a seemingly benign Western accounting term, is understood in Russian in an engineering context. In an accounting context, it may be understood as counting. It is easy to see the potential problems of substituting counting for measurement when discussing the measurement of fair value.

Many Western accounting terms do not have accepted translations into Russian. For example, revenue, profit, and gain are all translated using the same Russian term. The same thing happens with depreciation, amortization, and depletion. With such difficulties, the mere translation of the IAS into Russian is a slow and laborious process fraught with pitfalls and unseen land mines.

The Russian Bookkeeping System

The Russian bookkeeping system is a marvel once it is understood by the Westerner. Unfortunately, it probably takes the Westerner as much time to understand the Russian bookkeeping system as it does the accountants of the former Soviet Union to understand IAS and our bookkeeping system. The Russian bookkeeping system accomplishes nearly the same thing as bookkeeping systems in the West; it just doesn't use a trial balance or general journal or post to general ledger revenue and expense accounts. In fact, the general ledger is a somewhat insignificant accounting record.

Equally unfortunate for would-be reformers and Western advisers alike, adjusting the Russian bookkeeping system is essential to being able to implement IAS. To take one example, if general administrative and selling expenses are to be recorded as expenses of the period, not as production costs, many changes will need to be made to the Russian ledgers and work sheets. Adopting IAS 2 on inventory requires more than just modifying the debits and credits that are recorded.

This is a problem. There is a significant reluctance on the part of the government officials in the region to modify the underlying bookkeeping system. Also, Western advisers may not have the interest or time to plow through the Russian bookkeeping system to determine which changes that are necessary. International funding agencies also have not shown the patience or understanding of the work necessary to carry out national accounting reforms in the former Soviet Union. Quick and demonstrable results are not consistent with national accounting reform efforts.

CONCLUSION

In the international environment, changes in the dynamics of global capital flows have augmented the demand for comparability in financial reporting among companies in different countries. Trends in technology brought increases in the flows of cross-border financing and investing, and the implications of events and transactions in international finance began to impact the accounting environment.

These drivers and enablers of international business guarantee that the trend toward increasing cross-border capital flows will continue. To ensure that investors make capital market decisions based on reliable and understandable financial information, international accounting standards will be needed. Progress is being made in this direction. The IASC and the International Organization of Securities Markets (IOSM) have reached agreement on 1999 as a target date for IOSM members to require financial disclosure based on IAS.

RESEARCH NOTE: DEVELOPING COUNTRIES' INVOLVEMENT IN THE IASC'S STANDARD-SETTING PROCESS

Robert K. Larson and Sara York Kenny

INTRODUCTION

International Accounting Standards (IAS), as developed by the International Accounting Standards Committee (IASC), are often touted as appropriate and beneficial for adoption and use by developing countries (Cairns 1990). Reasons supporting this contention include the views that adoption of IASs will increase developing countries' competitiveness in global equity markets, improve their accounting, reduce their accounting standard-setting costs, and facilitate further foreign investment (Wyatt 1991; IASC 1990; Peavey and Webster 1990; Samuels and Piper 1985). Therefore, if IAS are deemed appropriate for developing countries, then it should be considered desirable, if not absolutely necessary, for those from developing countries to participate in the process of determining IAS.

Advances in International Accounting, Supplement 1, pages 17-41.

ISBN: 0-7623-0461-8

But are those from developing countries actually participating in the establishment of IAS? The level of involvement in the standard-setting process by developing countries is not well documented. Wallace (1993), the only study to directly examine this issue, analyzed the period from 1973 to 1989. Wallace found low levels of participation by those in developing countries.

In late 1988 and early 1989, the IASC embarked on an initiative to review the accounting and financial reporting needs in developing and newly industrialized countries and to ultimately recommend any needed improvements to the IASC Board (Cairns 1990; Wallace 1993). The IASC formed a steering committee to guide the initiative.

At about the same time (1989), the IASC instituted a new, more open due process, designed to enhance the visibility and acceptability of the IASC's activities. Increased participation in the IASC's activities was encouraged. In the new process, comment letters are routinely released to the general public.

These changes provide the motivation for this study. We believe that these changes warrant reexamination of the participation of developing countries in the IASC's accounting standard-setting process. In this research note, we analyze the combined impacts of these factors to see whether there has been a change in the level of participation by those from developing countries.

This paper examines the participation of developing countries from 1989 to 1995 in several ways. We analyze IASC Board membership, membership on IASC steering committees, writers and their comment letters regarding IASC Exposure Drafts (EDs), and donations to the IASC. The comment letters examined were submitted in response to 16 different IASC EDs issued during the study period.

The rest of the paper is organized as follows. First, the prior literature is examined. The next section outlines the research questions, followed by a description of the research design. The results are then described, followed by a concluding discussion, which includes future research questions.

LITERATURE REVIEW

While six major studies have analyzed lobbying activities directed toward the IASC, few have focused on the participation by developing countries. This section briefly discusses the five general IASC lobbying papers before examining the one paper that focused on the participation of developing countries in the IASC's due process.

Wallace (1990) studied the IASC and outlined his view of the IASC's survival strategy. This conceptual paper outlined many of the issues and challenges facing the IASC. In part, Wallace notes the importance of constituent participation. While Wallace provides some information that relates to developing country participation (such as steering committee membership), his emphasis is on broader issues and constituents.

Kenny and Larson (1993) used content and other analysis to examine responses and respondents to ED 35 (accounting for joint ventures). Developing countries are only incidentally discussed by Kenny and Larson (1993). For example, their paper notes that IASC member bodies from Cyprus, Singapore, and Zimbabwe comprise their own cluster of comment letters that either are neutral or do not comment on ED 35 in general, proportionate consolidation, and ED 35 disclosures.

Guenther and Hussein (1995) empirically analyzed the IASC's LIFO controversy. Developing countries were included with all respondents on whether or not they supported LIFO in comment letters related to ED 32 and ED 38. Also, South Africa is included as an example of a country where LIFO is allowed for financial reporting purposes but not for tax purposes. Interestingly, Guenther and Hussein (1995) twice misstated that the South African Institute of Chartered Accountants (SAICA) supported the elimination of LIFO in ED 38, although the SAICA's letter clearly states "no comment" regarding ED 38 (IASC 1992, 33). Also, for some unknown reason, the IASC did not include the Bahamas' letter regarding ED 38 with the other comment letters. Overall, developing countries are only briefly mentioned by Guenther and Hussein.

Kenny and Larson (1995) provided a study of who responded through comment letters to 14 separate IASC EDs. Of the 14 EDs examined, both the SAICA and the Institute of Chartered Accountants of Zimbabwe responded to 11 EDs. In addition, it was noted that corporations from Hong Kong (2), India (3), Jamaica (1), and South Africa (1) had written a total of 12 comment letters. Though the level of response from developing and newly industrialized countries is noted in the study, no specific analysis of the responses is included.

Recently, MacArthur (1996) closely examined the content of corporate responses to ED 32 in a test of the role of culture in comment letters. However, only one South African corporation is included in MacArthur's study.

Although MacArthur (1996), Kenny and Larson (1993, 1995) and Guenther and Hussein (1995) included developing countries in their sample and analysis, they did not specifically focus on the participation of those from developing countries in the IASC's standard-setting process in any systematic manner. Wallace (1993) is the only study devoted to the analysis of developing countries.

Wallace (1993) specifically addressed lobbying activities by those in developing countries. Wallace uses a primarily descriptive analysis to detail his belief and finding that the level of participation by those from developing and newly industrialized countries is low. However, Wallace's discussion of comment letters does not extend beyond comment letters submitted about ED 32 (the comparability project) by September 1, 1989. Wallace does specifically cite concerns expressed by Zimbabwe that the IASC, and therefore the IASs, are dominated by U.S. and U.K. accounting thought, which may not serve the needs of developing countries.

RESEARCH QUESTIONS

Wallace's (1993) study provides a foundation for this research note in that it reveals issues to analyze in our study. First, Wallace noted that between 1973 and 1989, few developing countries were represented on either the IASC Board or IASC steering committees. Given the stated desire to increase the participation of developing countries, we wondered if their representation has changed since 1989:

Question 1. Do the IASC Board and the IASC steering committees still have few members from developing countries?

Wallace (1993) presented a few examples of the number of comment letters submitted to the IASC under the old due process, when the contents of the letters were kept confidential. We wondered whether the number of letters would increase under the new due process.

Question 2. Did either the absolute number or the relative percentage of letters submitted to the IASC in response to EDs from developing countries increase?

Kenny and Larson (1995) found that while IASC member bodies and accounting interests in general dominate comment letter responses to IASC EDs, corporations, business associations, banking interests, and security analysts, among others, also responded. We wondered if this was also true of those from developing countries.

Question 3. Do respondents to IASC EDs from developing countries mirror all respondents or are certain types of respondents from developing countries more heavily represented?

Limited finances and/or lack of expertise have been cited as possible reasons for the low level of participation by those from developing countries. Therefore, developing countries with higher levels of income might be expected to supply more participatants than developing countries with lower levels of income. Also, those from wealthier developing countries might be expected to have higher levels of expertise on certain accounting matters. Kaplan and Pany (1992) suggest that the number of words contained in comment letters may be considered a surrogate for the relative thoroughness of a reply when attempting to measure a respondent's relative expertise.

Question 4. Do respondents to IASC EDs tend to be from developing countries with higher levels of GNP per capita?

Question 5. Do respondents to IASC EDs from developing countries with higher levels of GNP per capita submit longer comment letters?

A new way of participating in the IASC due process is to donate money to the IASC. Since 1990, the IASC has solicited money from corporations and other organizations. The IASC has stated that "each contributor is regularly contacted in order to provide input on the issues and principles being considered in current projects" (IASC 1994b). We were curious to see if any money came from developing countries, given the assumption of limited resources in those countries.

Question 6. Do any organizations in developing countries, besides IASC Board members, donate money to the IASC?

RESEARCH DESIGN

To address the research questions, this study examines the participation of developing countries from 1989 to 1995 in several ways. This paper analyzes IASC Board membership, membership on IASC steering committees, writers and their comment letters regarding IASC EDs, and donations to the IASC. While the primary data came from the IASC, other data sources included Lexis/Nexis, Dow Jones Retrieval, Worldscope, Fry (1994), Hardy (1995), and the World Bank (1995). All data used are publicly available.

Comment Letters

Between 1989, the inception of the new due process, and January 1994, when the IASC again began to change its form of due process, the IASC issued 17 EDs. This study analyzes comment letters to 16 of those EDs (the comment letters for ED 33, accounting for income taxes, were not publicly available at the time of the study).[1]

Respondents were categorized in various ways in order to address the research questions. The categorization of respondents was done in a manner consistent with Kenny and Larson (1995), with a few exceptions as noted in this paper. In general, Kenny and Larson (1995) followed the procedures outlined by Tandy and Wilburn (1992) and Briloff (1986).

Wallace and Cravens (1994) found there to be an extremely high correlation between word counts and pages submitted (97%). Therefore, because pages are easier to understand, for discussion purposes we used pages submitted as a surrogate for relative expertise in order to address Question 5. Accordingly, addresses, salutations, and so on were excluded from analysis.

Definition of Developing Countries

While there are several different definitions of developing countries, we used a broad definition that incorporates both developing and newly industrialized countries as noted by the World Bank (1995). This broad definition increases the comparability of our study with Wallace (1993), who also appears to use a broad definition. Therefore, only European countries, Canada, the United States, Japan, Australia, and New Zealand were excluded.

Table 1. Developing Countries Represented on IASC Board, 1990 to 1995

India	-	term began early 1993
Jordan	-	term ended July 1995 [individuals from Saudi Arabia have served on Jordan's delegation]
Korea	-	term 1988 to early 1993
Malaysia	-	term began July 1995
Mexico	-	term began July 1995
Sri Lanka	-	joined Indian delegation July 1995
South Africa	-	on board entire period
Zimbabwe	-	joined South African delegation July 1995

RESULTS OF ANALYSIS

IASC Board Membership

Of the several ways in which developing countries can participate in the IASC's standard-setting process, probably the most direct and important way is to serve on the IASC's Board. Traditionally, Board membership has been limited to 13 member countries and up to four other organizations. Most countries represented on the IASC Board have been developed countries, while developing countries have been a small minority (Wallace 1993).

Table 1 lists developing countries that have been represented on the IASC Board since Wallace's earlier study. Before 1995, few developing countries served on the Board. However, in 1995, the IASC made a concerted effort to expand the number of representatives from developing countries serving on the Board. In the second half of 1995, representatives from India, Malaysia, Mexico, South Africa, Sri Lanka, and Zimbabwe served on the IASC Board (IASC 1995c). On the surface, this represents a major change. However, the reality is that in some cases two developing countries are now sharing one seat (IASC 1996).

Steering Committees

Another way to participate in the deliberations of the IASC is to serve as a member of one of its steering committees. Wallace (1993) has noted the limited representation by developing countries on IASC steering committees from 1973 to 1989. Table 2 lists the 11 most recent IASC steering committees and identifies any developing country members.

Table 2. Recent IASC Steering Committees and Membership from Developing Countries

Accounting Topic	*Developing Countries Represented on Steering Committee*
Interim Reporting*	Hong Kong, South Africa
Discontinued Operations*	Peru, Singapore
Intangible Assets**	none
Income Taxes**	Brazil
Earnings Per Share**	South Africa
Financial Instruments**	none
Presentation of Financial Statements**	Malaysia, South Africa
Financial Information by Segment**	India
Agriculture**#	India, Thailand, Zimbabwe
Retirement Benefit and Other Employee Benefit Costs***	Sri Lanka
Improvements to International Accounting Standards****	Jordan

Note: # Project funded by the World Bank and specifically geared for the needs of developing countries.
Sources: * IASC (1995f, 3).
** IASC (1995a, 10).
*** IASC (1995b, 6).
**** IASC (1994a, 10).

Representation of developing countries ranged from none to three members on these recent IASC steering committees. Two committees (Financial Instruments and Intangible Assets) had no members from developing countries. The only steering committee with as many as three members from developing countries was on Agriculture. This should be expected given that the project was funded by the World Bank and geared specifically toward developing countries. A total of 11 developing countries held a total of 14 seats on these 11 steering committees. These included Brazil, Hong Kong, India (2), Jordan, Malaysia, Peru, Singapore, Sri Lanka, South Africa (3), Thailand, and Zimbabwe.

Of these 11, all but three—Jordan, Peru, and Thailand—had previously served on at least one steering committee at some time between 1973 to 1989 (Wallace 1993). Thus, Wallace's list of 40 developing countries with IASC membership that had never served on a steering committee remains largely intact.

Wallace (1993) also found that most developing countries that had served on steering committees were or had been IASC Board members. This trend appears to be continuing. Of the 11 developing countries on the recent steering committees, only Peru and Thailand have never served on the IASC Board.

Comment Letters

Number of Responses

To determine the number of comment letters written from developing countries, all of the comment letters were surveyed. Initial numbers were revised as content analysis revealed that the IASC and some previous studies had undercounted the number of letters from developing countries. This occurred in several ways. For example, the African Development Bank actually sent two letters about ED 36, containing some conflicting advice. Similarly, the Institute of Chartered Accountants of Zimbabwe sent two separate letters about ED 32. Also, KPMG Peat Marwick's office in Hong Kong sent two separate letters about ED 48.

A related problem was how to count a letter that contained responses to several different EDs. For example, a letter from the Bahamas Institute of Chartered Accountants that the IASC included only in the ED 36 comment letter packet also contains responses for ED 37, 38 and 39. Similarly, the Institute of CPAs of Kenya's letter about EDs 41 and 42 was included by the IASC only under ED 41. In several other cases, however, letters such as the Mexican Institute of Financial Executives' letter discussing EDs 36, 37, 38, and 39 were included in each ED comment letter packet and counted as separate responses. For purposes of this study, we were consistent and counted as a response to an ED any letter that discussed a particular ED, even if the letter combined several responses.

Table 3 lists the number of comment letters both from developing countries and in total for the 16 EDs examined. One hundred, or 11%, of the 911 comment letters were determined to be from developing countries.

In terms of absolute numbers, the greatest number of letters received were for ED 32 (comparability project), which got 13 responses. ED 48 (financial instruments) received 11 responses; ED 36 (cash flow statement) had 10 responses; and ED 38 (inventories) had nine responses. The highest number of responses for ED 32 matches the fact that ED 32 received the largest number of letters for any ED analyzed in the study. ED 32, being the comparability project's first major ED, had the broadest ramifications of any ED in the history of the IASC and created significant interest. ED 32 also accounted for the greatest number of pages

Table 3. Number of Comment Letters By Exposure Drafts (EDs)

ED Number	*ED Issue Date*	*Number of Letters from Developing Countries*	*Percent of Letters from Developing Countries*	*Total Number of Letters*	*Once Part of ED 32?*	*Title*
32	1/1989	13	9%	140	—	Comparability of Financial Statements
34	7/1989	7	22%	32	No	Disclosures in the Financial Statements of Banks & Similar Financial Institutions
35	12/1989	6	13%	48	No	Financial Reporting of Interests in Joint Ventures
36	7/1991	10	20%	51	No	Cash Flow Statements
37	8/1991	8	15%	55	Yes	Research and Development Activities
38	8/1991	9	16%	57	Yes	Inventories
39	8/1991	7	13%	55	Yes	Capitalisation of Borrowing Costs
40	9/1991	4	5%	74	No	Financial Instruments
41	5/1992	4	8%	49	Yes	Revenue Recognition
42	5/1992	3	7%	41	Yes	Construction Contracts
43	5/1992	5	11%	46	Yes	Property, Plant and Equipment
44	5/1992	4	8%	52	Yes	The Effects of Changes in Foreign Exchange Rates
45	6/1992	3	6%	51	Yes	Business Combinations
46	7/1992	3	7%	43	Yes	Extraordinary Items, Fundamental Errors & Changes in Accounting Policies
47	12/1992	3	9%	35	Yes	Retirement Benefit Costs
48	9/1994	11	13%	82	No	Financial Instruments
	Total	100*	11%	911*		

Note: * Some totals are different from IASC or other studies due to methodological differences.

of comments with 56½ pages out of the 186 pages generated by developing countries.

The lowest number of responses, with three each, were for ED 42 (construction contracts), ED 45 (business combinations), ED 46 (extraordinary items, fundamental errors and changes in accounting policies), and ED 47 (retirement benefit costs). The EDs with the fewest total pages of comments were ED 42 (1½ pages), ED 47 (2½ pages), ED 41 (3 pages), and EDs 43, 45, and 46 (4½ pages each).

One assumption has been that the number of responses to EDs should increase over time as the work and significance of the IASC has become more well known. However, Kenny and Larson (1995) did not find much support for that thought. Previously, Wallace (1993) reported the following number and percentage of letters from developing countries for a few earlier EDs: ED 28 (4 letters, respresenting 12.5% of the responses); ED 31 (8 letters, or 33%); IASC framework (5 letters, or 14%). So in terms of developing countries, when more recent data is also analyzed, the trend does not appear to reflect either a general growth or a flat trajectory. Rather, overall, the number of responses actually appears to have decreased from 1989 to 1992, with only ED 48 eleiciting a higher response rate.

This same pattern was observed in the number of comment pages generated per ED. For example, for every respondent that responded to ED 32 and at least one other ED, the longest responses were always to ED 32. In addition, ED 32 had the highest average length of text. ED 32 also generated the longest response—18½ pages from the Institute of CPAs of Singapore.

In relative terms, responses from developing countries provide a somewhat different picture. The highest relative responses were for ED 34 , disclosures in the financial statements of banks and similar financial institutions (22%); ED 36, cash flow statements (20%); ED 38, inventories (16%); and ED 37, research and development (15%). Banking interests seemed quite interested in ED 34 and many were concerned about the proposed disclosures. For example, Bankorp (South Africa) supported the right to maintain secret reserves. But again, the percentage of responses from developing countries appears to decrease from 1989 to 1992, with only ED 48 providing an upward shot in 1994.

Who Responded and How Often

Letters were categorized by type of organization in a manner similar to Kenny and Larson (1995). Table 4 lists the number of comment letters received and the number of different respondents by type of organization by developing country. Letters from developing countries came primarily from IASC members. Of the 100 letters, 66 were from member bodies of the IASC. The remainder of the letters were from accounting firms (6), corporations and industry (15), banks and bank regulators (7), stock exchanges (2), and the Mexican Financial Executives Institute (4). While Kenny and Larson (1995) found that 31% of the letters in their sample came from IASC members, this study found that number to be

Table 4. Number of Comment Letters (Number of Different Respondents*) Categorized by Organization Type from Developing/Newly Industrialized Countries

Country	*IASC Members*	*Accounting Firms*	*Corporations and Industry*	*Banks and Bank Regulators*	*Stock Exchanges*	*Financial Executives Institute*	*Total*
Bahamas	5 (1)	—	—	—	—	—	5 (1)
Bermuda	—	1 (1)	—	1 (1)	—	—	2 (2)
Botswana	1 (1)	—	—	—	—	—	1 (1)
Brazil	1 (1)	—	—	—	—	—	1 (1)
Cyprus	3 (1)	—	—	—	—	—	3 (1)
Hong Kong	1 (1)	2 (1)	5 (2)	—	—	—	8 (4)
India	1 (1)	—	4 (4)	—	—	—	5 (5)
Israel	—	—	—	—	1 (1)	—	1 (1)
Ivory Coast (Cote d'Ivoire)	—	—	—	3 (1)	—	—	3 (1)
Jamaica	1 (1)	—	1 (1)	—	—	—	2 (2)
Jordan—see Saudi Arabia							
Kenya	7 (1)	—	—	—	—	—	7 (1)
Malawi	1 (1)	—	—	—	—	—	1 (1)
Malaysia	3 (2)	—	—	1 (1)	—	—	4 (3)
Mexico	1 (1)	—	—	—	—	4 (1)	5 (2)
Nigeria	1 (1)	—	—	—	—	—	1 (1)
Pakistan	4 (2)	—	—	—	—	—	4 (2)
Saudi Arabia	2 (1)	—	—	—	—	—	2 (1)
Singapore	6 (1)	—	—	—	—	—	6 (1)
South Africa	13 (1)	3 (1)	5 (1)	2 (2)	1 (1)	—	24 (6)
Trinidad and Tobago	2 (1)	—	—	—	—	—	2 (1)
Zimbabwe	13 (1)	—	—	—	—	—	13 (1)
Total	66 (20)	6 (3)	15 (8)	7 (5)	2 (2)	4 (1)	100 (39)
Percent of Total	66% (51%)	6% (8%)	15% (20%)	7% (13%)	2% (5%)	4% (3%)	100% (100%)

Note: * Does not consider the number of letters or EDs commented on.

66%. Thus, in developing countries, IASC members are the major source of ED comment letters. Few letters come from other sources.

Letters were also categorized to determine the number of different letter writers (regardless of the number of letters they might have written). This analysis presented a somewhat different picture (see Table 4 for details). The 100 letters were found to be written by only 39 different organizations. Twenty, or 51%, of the writers were IASC members. The remainder of the letter writers were accounting firms (3), corporations and industry (8), banks and bank regulators (5), stock exchanges (2), and the Mexican Financial Executives Institute. While Kenny and Larson (1995) found that 15% of the letters writers were IASC members, here that number is 51%. Again, in developing countries, IASC members are the largest group of writers.

Kenny and Larson (1995) found that only a few writers accounted for a fairly large percentage of the letters written to the IASC. After analyzing this study's data, a similar situation was found (see Table 5 for a detailed breakdown of respondents). Five of the 39 respondents generated 44 of the 100 comment letters. IASC members from the Bahamas, Kenya, Singapore, South Africa, and Zimbabwe accounted for 44% of all letters from developing countries.

Country Patterns

The letters were also analyzed for country patterns. First, letters were received from only 21 developing countries. Five countries generated 58 of the 100 letters: South Africa (24), Zimbabwe (13), Hong Kong (8), Kenya (7), and Singapore (6). A slightly different pattern emerged when examining the number of letter writers. Four countries provided 18 of the 39 letter writers: South Africa (6), India (5), Hong Kong (4), and Malaysia (3).

This portion of the analysis repeatedly found that comment letters, however analyzed, came predominately from countries that either had been or still were British colonies or protectorates. The only respondents not fitting this general description were Brazil, Ivory Coast, and Mexico. This small group accounted for only four of the 39 letter writers and nine of the 100 letters.

This pattern led to an examination of the current membership list of the IASC (IASC 1995d). Table 6 lists the 34 developing countries that have IASC members but from which no comment letters were received

Table 5. Comment Letters Written from Developing Countries by Exposure Draft

Country/Organization	*32*	*34*	*35*	*36*	*37*	*38*	*39*	*40*	*41*	*42*	*43*	*44*	*45*	*46*	*47*	*48*	*Total*	
Bahamas																		
The Bahamas Institute of Chartered Accountants#			X	X	X	X	X										5	5
Bermuda																		
Bermuda Monetary Authority		X															1	
Moore Stephens (CAs)					X												1	2
Botswana																		
The Botswana Institute of Accountants#																X	1	1
Brazil																		
Instituto Brasileiro de Contadores—IBRACON#	X																1	1
Cyprus																		
The Institute of Certified Public Accountants of Cyprus#	X		X			X											3	3
Hong Kong																		
Hong Kong Society of Accountants#	X																1	
Jardine Matheson Limited											X	X	X				3	
• 220th on Forbes' 1995 Foreign 500																		
• Sponsored ADR traded in United States																		
• Listed on Hong Kong, London, Sydney, and other stock exchanges																		
Cathay Pacific Airways												X				X	2	
• Listed on Hong Kong Stock Exchange																		
• 52% owned by Swire Pacific; which is 329th on Forbes' 1995 Foreign 500																		
• Each has unsponsored ADRs traded in United States																		
KPMG Peat Marwick																2	2	8
India																		
NLC Limited		X															1	
Anand Regional Cooperative Oilseeds Growers' Union Ltd.				X													1	

Hindustan Aeronautics Ltd.					X												1	
Ahmedabad Textile Industry's Research Association						X											1	
Institute of Cost and Works Accountants of India#								X									1	5
Israel																		
Tel Aviv Stock Exchange	X																1	1
Ivory Coast (Cote d'Ivoire)																		
African Development Bank				2			X										3	3
Jamaica																		
The Gleaner Company Ltd. (Publishes Newspapers)						X											1	
The Institute of Chartered Accountants of Jamaica#							X										1	2
Jordan—see Saudi Arabia																		
Kenya																		
Institute of Certified Public Accountants of Kenya#	X			X	X	X	X		X	X							7	7
Malawi																		
The Society of Accountants in Malawi#															X		1	1
Malaysia																		
Public Bank of Berhad Group (Malaysia's third largest banking group)		X															1	
• Listed on Kuala Lumpur Stock Exchange																		
Malaysian Institute of Accountants#				X												X	2	
The Malaysian Association of Certified Public Accountants#				X													1	4
Mexico																		
IMEF—Mexican Institute of Financial Executives				X	X	X	X										4	
Instituto Mexicano De Contadores Publicos, A.C.#																X	1	5
Nigeria																		
The Institute of Chartered Accountants of Nigeria#	X																1	1
Pakistan																		
The Institute of Chartered Accountants of Pakistan#									X	X	X						3	
Institute of Cost and Management Accountants of Pakistan#																X	1	4

(continued)

Table 5. (Continued)

Country/Organization	*32*	*34*	*35*	*36*	*37*	*38*	*39*	*40*	*41*	*42*	*43*	*44*	*45*	*46*	*47*	*48*	*Total*	
Saudi Arabia																		
Arab Society of Certified Accountants (ASCA)#		X						X									2	2
• While IASC lists under Jordan, letters written from Rijadh																		
Singapore																		
Institute of Certified Public Accountants of Singapore#	X		X	X				X	X		X						6	6
South Africa																		
The South African Institute of Chartered Accountants#	X	X	X	X	X	X	X	X			X	X		X	X	X	13	
Bankorp—Bank Holding Corporation of South Africa Ltd.		X															1	
• Listed on Johannesburg Stock Exchange																		
The Johannesburg Stock Exchange			X														1	
Price Waterhouse Meyernel					X	X	X										3	
The South African Breweries Ltd.	2												X	X		X	5	
• Listed on Johannesburg Stock Exchange																		
• 287th on Forbes' 1995 Foreign 500																		
• Had IASC Board Representation																		
UAL Merchant Bank Ltd. (part of Nedcor Bank Ltd. Group)																X	1	24
Trinidad and Tobago																		
The Institute of Chartered Accountants of Trinidad and Tobago#	X	X															2	2
Zimbabwe																		
The Institute of Chartered Accountants of Zimbabwe#	2		X		X	X			X	X	X	X	X	X	X	X	13	13
Total	13	7	6	10	8	9	7	4	4	3	5	4	3	3	3	11		100

Note: #Denotes IASC member.

Table 6. Developing Countries with Accounting Organizations That Have IASC Membership from which No Comment Letters Were Received for Any of the 16 Exposure Drafts Examined

Africa	*Latin America*
Egypt	Barbados
Ghana	Bolivia
Lesotho	Chile
Liberia	Colombia
Libya	Dominican Republic
Sudan	Ecuador
Swaziland	Panama
Tanzania	Paraguay
Tunisia	Peru
Zambia	Uruguay
Asia and Pacific Islands	*Middle East*
Bangladesh	Bahrain
Fiji	Iraq
Indonesia	Kuwait
Korea	Lebanon
The Philippines	Syria
Sri Lanka	Turkey
Thailand	
Taiwan	

Source: IASC (1995d).

for any of the 16 EDs examined. While some former U.K. colonies are listed, many are former colonies of either France, Spain, or the Netherlands.

In order to determine if there was a significant difference in responses depending upon whether a developing country was or had been a British colony or protectorate, a *t*-test was performed that included all developing countries with IASC members. The results (with their level of significance) found that former U.K. colonies sent more letters (.027), sent letters from a larger number of writers (.009), and sent more pages of comments (.082).

In a larger context, the vast majority of developing countries are not involved in the standard-setting process. While the 1995 IASC membership represents 86 countries (IASC 1995c) and includes a large number of developing countries, several dozen other developing countries are not members of the IASC. Included among non-members of the IASC are China and the countries of the former Soviet Union. It is also interesting to note that non-members include some former IASC members, such as Argentina and Venezuela. So in a larger context, the responses from 21 developing countries represent a very small response given the large number of developing countries both within and outside the IASC.

One possibility for the predominance of comment letters from developing countries with a strong past connection to the United Kingdom may simply be the fact of the English language. The approved text of IAS, EDs, and other IASC publications are those published in English by the IASC.[2] While the IASC has a list of the languages into which IAS and so on are translated and where to obtain them (IASC 1995e), the IASC does not maintain a list of which IASs and/or EDs are available in other languages. Therefore, part of the problem may be that EDs are not readily available in a number of languages commonly used in developing countries. Or, when they do become available, the comment period may have expired due to the time taken to make the translations. Also, in some countries translation expenses may be deemed too expensive to spend on an ED, which is only a draft.

Content Analysis

The comment letters were examined for both content and length. While the focus of this paper is not a detailed content analysis, several observations can be made. Consistent with the lobbying literature, letters tended to be at least somewhat negative and to suggest changes. Some letters proposed changes that were the direct opposite of the IASC's proposals. However, even those letters suggesting changes usually contained one or more statements of support for the IASC's efforts. This might be predictable, as most letter writers were themselves IASC members. But several of the letters, including some from IASC members, were actually quite negative.

In terms of numbers, about 10% of the letters were quite positive; another 15% or so were overall positive despite suggesting a few changes. Conversely, almost 25% of the letters had a somewhat or decidedly negative or critical tone. The largest group of letters, slightly over 40%, were either a mixture of positive and negative comments or tended to ask for clarification on various issues. This group was fairly large in part because of the broad range of issues discussed in ED 32 and the complex issues relating to some topics, such as financial instruments (ED 40 and 48). One interesting point is that 5% of the letters came from IASC members and, basically, just said stated "no comment."

Countries that submitted the most pages of comments were South Africa (60, or 32%), Singapore (27, or 15%), Zimbabwe (19.5, or 10%), Hong Kong (14.5, or 8%), Mexico (9.5, or 5%), Kenya (9, or 5%) and Malaysia (8.5, or 5%). Collectively, these seven countries provided 80% of the comment text.

Responses and Country Wealth

Tests were done to determine if there was any relationship between a country's wealth (as measured by Gross National Product per capita (GNPpc) and comment letter responses. In order to run *t*-tests based on GNPpc, countries were divided into two groups based on World Bank (1995) categorizations. Low-income and lower/middle-income countries were put into one group and upper/middle-income and high-income countries were put into a second group.

All tests were done in two parts. The first part looked only at actual respondents from developing countries while the second part included all developing countries that had IASC members.

For actual respondents, the *t*-test between the two GNPpc groups yielded one significant result. Wealthier countries submitted longer letters (at .098 level of significance).

When all developing countries that have IASC members were included, additional relationships emerged. The *t*-test (with their level of significance) found that countries with higher GNPpc provided more letters (.081), produced more writers who sent letters (.031), and contributed more total pages of text (.046).

Donations

A relatively new way to participate in the IASC standard-setting process is to make financial contributions. Board members have always given financial support to the IASC, but since 1990 the group has been soliciting funds from other sources, including accounting firms, corporations, and banks. Of the developing countries included in this study, five corporate donors were identified (see Table 7).[3] Interestingly, none of these corporations wrote to the IASC about any of the 16 EDs examined.

What characteristics do these five corporations have? South Africa has provided additional funds via three corporations: Anglo-Alpha,

Table 7. Corporations from Developing Countries Providing Donations to IASC since 1990 (Not including direct IASC Board Member Donations)

Hong Kong and Shanghai Bank (Hong Kong, now also London)
- Parent is HSBC Holdings PLC
- SIC 6020—Commercial Banks
  - HSBC is 72nd on Forbes' 1995 Foreign 500.
- HSBC is listed on multiple stock exchanges, including Hong Kong, London, Frankfurt and Singapore Stock Exchanges
- Sponsored ADR traded in United States

Minorco SA (South Africa, via legal domicile in Luxembourg)
- SIC 2873—Nitrogenous fertilizers
- Listed on Johannesburg, London and Luxembourg Stock Exchanges
- Unsponsored ADR traded in United States
- Ultimate parent per Directory of Corporate Affiliations: Anglo American Corporation of South Africa Limited via 39% direct ownership and the 20% owned by Anglo's affiliate De Beers Centenary AG (Switzerland).
  - Anglo American is 446th on Forbes' 1995 Foreign 500

Anglo-Alpha Limited (South Africa)
- SIC 3241—Cement, Hydraulic
- Listed on Johannesburg Stock Exchange
- Unsponsored ADR traded in United States
- Ultimate parent per Directory of Corporate Affiliations: Holderbank (Switzerland) via 30% ownership

Gencor Limited (South Africa)
- SIC 6719—Holding Companies (mining, forest products, finance)
- Listed on multiple stock exchanges, including Johannesburg, London, Frankfurt, and Geneva Stock Exchanges
- Unsponsored ADR traded in United States
- Parent corporation as defined by Directory of Corporate Affiliations.
- 31% owned by Sankorp (South Africa)

Samancor Limited (South Africa)
- SIC 1061—Ferroalloy ores, except vanadium
- Listed on Johannesburg Stock Exchange
- Unsponsored ADR traded in United States
- 36% owned by African Metals Ltd. (South Africa, which is owned by Gencor)

Sources: IASC (1995a, 1996), Fry (1994), Hardy (1995), Worldscope, Directory of Corporate Affiliations.

Gencor, and Samancor. All three are engaged primarily in mining and related activities, are listed on the Johannesburg Stock Exchange, and have unsponsored American Depositary Receipts (ADRs) traded in the United States. In addition, Minorco, while officially incorporated in Luxembourg, is ultimately controlled by Anglo American Corporation of South Africa. Again, this is primarily a mining and natural resources company with an unsponsored ADR traded in the United States. However, Anglo American is quite large and was listed as the 446th largest foreign corporation on Forbes' 1995 *Foreign 500* (Hardy 1995). Finally, the Hong Kong and Shanghai Bank gave money to the IASC, apparently through its U.K. offices. Its parent, HSBC Holdings, is one of the world's largest bank groups and ranked 72nd on Forbes' 1995 *Foreign 500*.

But how do these contributions compare with others? First, these five are only 4% of the approximately 125 organizations (primarily corporations) that have donated money to the IASC. Second, their contributions are relatively small, representing between 1.8% and 2% of all donations in 1993 and 1994 (not including the HSBC donation, which was included in the U.K. totals). Overall, the level of donations was not unexpected given the differences of wealth between developed and developing countries.

DISCUSSION

In this research note, we have addressed six questions. With prior literature as our guide, we explored the levels of participation on the part of the IASC's developing country constituency.

The first question asked if the role of developing countries, as expressed by participation on the IASC Board and steering committees, has changed since 1989. The results of the analysis are mixed. On the positive side, we note a dramatic increase in the level of participation by developing countries on the IASC Board, particularly since July 1, 1995. However, some developing countries are now sharing seats, so the actual voting balance between developed and developing countries has not dramatically changed. Also, membership on steering committees (except the one on agriculture) tends to continue its 1989 level of minimal participation by developing countries.

Given the goals of the IASC's developing country initiative, it would seem paramount to have more developing country participation on both the Board and most steering committees. However, participation in organizations is a gradual process, and it may be that as representatives become more comfortable in their roles on the Board, participation on committees will follow. Because the terms of Board members from four developing countries began only in mid-1995, it may be too early to expect higher levels of participation on steering committees.

The second research question asked whether either the absolute number or the percentage of letters from developing countries had increased under the new due process. In terms of absolute numbers, the average response went from slightly under six letters per ED to slightly over six letters per ED. In other words, no real change. In terms of percentage, the responses dwindled, down from almost 19% to 11%. While developing countries did not increase their letters after the new due process began, more letters were received from developed countries. Therefore, the relative voice of developing countries might be considered to have diminished. One final comment is that while Wallace reported that Argentina, Indonesia, the Philippines, Taiwan, and Turkey had written letters previously, we found none from those countries in the current analysis.

The third research question considered the specifics of which organizations from developing countries respond to IASC EDs. We noted that prior literature indicates that IASC member bodies and public accounting firms tend to be the organizations that respond to IASC EDs. We asked whether responses from developing countries also followed that trend. Of all responses from developing countries, 66% were from IASC members. The 66% is more than double the figure of 31% from IASC members found in prior research that examined all member countries.

The fourth and fifth research questions found relationships between a developing country's relative wealth and responses. In terms of actual respondents from developing countries, wealthier countries sent longer letters. When comparing all developing countries with IASC members, the wealthier countries provided more letters, more writers, and a greater number of total pages. The final question found, as expected, that few donations to the IASC came from developing countries.

In summary, we found low levels of participation from developing countries in all areas analyzed, including IASC Board membership, membership on IASC steering committees, comment letters, and donations. Further, we did not note any marked increase in the level of participation since 1989, in spite of the IASC's developing countries initiative and the new due process.

While we are not sure why this occurred, we suggest four possibilities: relevance, cost, inclusion, and language. Even with a concerted effort on the part of the IASC, its mandates may still seem irrelevant to many countries. If, as Zimbabwe's 1988 letter indicates, developing countries perceive that the IASC is U.S./U.K. and capital markets based,

IAS may seem irrelevant to the needs of developing countries at this time. While many developing countries are adopting IAS in various forms, this may still be an obstacle that needs to be addressed.

In addition, participation is costly. Where wealth is meager, it is unlikely to be spent on items that are perceived to be less relevant or vital; hence, IASC participation may well not occur.

Also, people often need to believe that their participation is valued. If participation is costly and if people do not believe that their views are considered, then participation is even less likely to occur. Research would be useful to determine if this view exists in developing countries.

Finally, participation may be discouraged simply because the cost and hassle of translating EDs into local languages outweigh any perceived benefits. The time allowed for comments may be insufficient, given the time taken to obtain translations. Of the comment letters sent, several noted that they were late in responding.

While this study extends the literature by analyzing the involvement of developing countries in the IASC's standard-setting process since 1989, the study also raises questions for future research. For example, we noted more responses from former British colonies than from other developing countries. The relationships between colonization, social development, culture, and participatory activities could be studied to better understand participation. Assuming that the IASC wishes to increase participation by developing countries, such a study may provide guidance for such policy issues. In addition, such a study may address other more pragmatic questions raised by this research note: Is the low level of participation on IASC steering committees related to the limited finances of those from developing countries? Does the need for EDs to be translated into local languages act as a major roadblock to writing comment? Why have some developing countries stopped writing comment letters regarding EDs? Are the views of developing countries impacting the shape of IAS? Finally, are those from developing countries satisfied or dissatisfied with the current content of IAS? If the ultimate purpose of IAS is decision usefulness, then studies of these questions may be valuable in shaping the direction the IASC takes in its quest for harmonization.

ACKNOWLEDGMENT

The authors thank the Center for International Business Education and Research at the University of Utah for its support of this project.

NOTES

1. The IASC did not make all comment letters public for a few EDs when it started its new due process. For example, ED 35 was issued early in the new due process and certain respondents, such as the IASC member in the Bahamas, did not release their comment letters for public review.

2. G. Bertol, personal communication, March 4, 1996.

3. While the IASC regularly provides lists of donating organizations, it has also agreed to keep contributions from a few organizations confidential.

REFERENCES

Briloff, A. J. 1986. Standards without standards/principles without principles/fairness without fairness. In *Advances in Accounting*, Vol. 3, ed. P.M.J. Reckers, 25–50. Stamford, CT: JAI Press.

Cairns, D. 1990. Financial reporting needs of developing and newly industrialized countries. *IASC News* (April): 12–14.

Fry, E. J. 1994. *International Investing with ADRs: Your Passport to Profits Worldwide*. Chicago, IL: International Publishing Corporation.

Guenther, D.A., and M.E.A. Hussein. 1995. Accounting standards and national tax laws: The IASC and the ban on LIFO. *Journal of Accounting and Public Policy* 14: 115–141.

Hardy, E.S. 1995. *Forbes* foreign rankings: Is there life in the laggards? *Forbes* (July 17): 226–266.

International Accounting Standards Committee (IASC). 1990. IASC's five year plan. *IASC News* (October): 6–8.

International Accounting Standards Committee (IASC). 1992. *Comment Letters on Exposure Draft E38: Inventories*. London: IASC.

International Accounting Standards Committee (IASC). 1994a. *IASC Annual Report, 1993*. London: IASC.

International Accounting Standards Committee (IASC). 1994b. IASC funding. *IASC Insight* (March): 2.

International Accounting Standards Committee (IASC). 1995a. *IASC Annual Report, 1994*. London: IASC.

International Accounting Standards Committee (IASC). 1995b. A question of discounting. *IASC Insight* (March): 5-6.

International Accounting Standards Committee (IASC). 1995c. IASC board restructured to widen representation. *IASC Insight* (June): 4.

International Accounting Standards Committee (IASC). 1995d. *Members of the International Accounting Standard Committee*. London: IASC, November 9.

International Accounting Standards Committee (IASC). 1995e . *Translations of International Accounting Standards and Their Sources*. London: IASC, November 11.

International Accounting Standards Committee (IASC). 1995f. New IASC projects: Interim reporting and discontinued operations. *IASC Insight* (December): 3.

International Accounting Standards Committee (IASC). 1996. *IASC Annual Report, 1995*. London: IASC.

Kaplan, S., and K. Pany. 1992. A study of public comment letters on the auditor's consideration of the going concern issue (SAS 59). In *Research in Accounting Regulation*, Vol. 6, ed. G.J. Previts, 3–23. Stamford, CT: JAI Press.

Kenny, S.Y., and R.K. Larson.1993. Lobbying behavior and the development of international accounting standards: The case of the IASC's joint venture project. *European Accounting Review* 2(3)(December): 531–554.

Kenny, S.Y., and R.K. Larson. 1995. The development of international accounting standards: An analysis of constituent participation in standard-setting. *The International Journal of Accounting* 30(4): 283–301.

MacArthur, J.B. 1996. An investigation into the influence of cultural factors in the international lobbying of the International Accounting Standards Committee: The case of E32, comparability of financial statements. *The International Journal of Accounting* 31(2): 213–237.

Peavey, D.E., and S. K. Webster. 1990. Is GAAP the gap to international markets? *Management Accounting* (August): 31–35.

Samuels, J.M., and A.G. Piper. 1985. *International Accounting: A Survey*. New York: St. Martin's Press.

Tandy, P.R., and N.L. Wilburn. 1992. Constituent participation in standard-setting: The FASB's first 100 statements. *Accounting Horizons* 6(June): 47–58.

Wallace, R.S.O. 1990. Survival strategies of a global organization: The case of the International Accounting Standards Committee. *Accounting Horizons* 4(June): 1–22.

Wallace, R.S.O. 1993. Development of accounting standards for developing and newly industrialized countries. In *Research in Third World Accounting*, Vol. 2, ed. R.S.O. Wallace, 121–165. Stamford, CT: JAI Press.

Wallace, W.A., and K.S. Cravens. 1994. An exploratory content analysis of terminology in public accounting firms' responses to AICPA peer reviews. In *Research in Accounting Regulation*, Vol. 8, ed. G.J. Previts, 3–32. Stamford, CT: JAI Press.

World Bank. 1995. *World Development Report 1995*. New York: Oxford University Press.

Wyatt, A.R. 1991. International accounting standards and organizations: Quo vadis? In *Handbook of International Accounting*, ed. F.D.S. Choi, 13.1–13.20. New York: Wiley.

THE IMPACT OF SOCIOECONOMIC AND POLITICAL ENVIRONMENT ON ACCOUNTING SYSTEM PREFERENCES IN DEVELOPING ECONOMIES

Naim A. Hassan

INTRODUCTION

At present, accounting standards, systems, and policies in many less-developed countries (LDCs) are in complete disarray. The socioeconomic, cultural, and political environments in these countries should have considerable influence on accounting systems/standards as well as the bodies that should have the authority to enforce them. The examination of accounting systems/standards in LDCs in the light of the prevailing environmental factors shows serious contradictions. These contradictions appear in many ways: (1) the adoption of a particular advanced industrialized country's accounting policies/standards (e.g.,

Advances in International Accounting, Supplement 1, pages 43-88.

ISBN: 0-7623-0461-8

Indonesia adopting those of the United States); (2) the continuation of following the precolonial country's accounting policies and practices (e.g., the acopting of British accounting standards and practices by India, Kenya, and Nigeria) (see Hove 1986); (3) the adoption, without any modification, of the international accounting standards (IAS) issued by the International Accounting Standards Committee (e.g., Jordan, Arab Gulf States); and (4) the nonexistence of any clear accounting policies, standards, and/or systems at all in many LDCs.

On the other hand, different groups in society have different interests, and this may result in different views and preferences regarding accounting systems/standards and accounting policies in general, especially as they might affect the sensitive issue of wealth distribution. Accounting policies, therefore, may be considered favorable or unfavorable by various groups in a country, including the government, depending on these groups' expectations. The government, which is a user of accounting information for economic planning purposes in many LDCs, may judge the accounting system and/or standards in regard to socioeconomic consequences and to how these standards will or will not facilitate economic planning and the implementation of these plans. If the government is an influential user and participant in setting accounting standards and policies (e.g., France), macroaccounting (national accounting) may dominate and influence accounting policies at the company level (i.e., microaccounting). In contrast, if the emphasis in a country is on investors' accounting information needs, including shareholders and stock markets, accounting standards and/or systems and policies may emphasize these groups' information needs, mainly stock market indicators, without regard to the information needs of the government or its agencies, and with minimal government intervention in accounting policies (see Hassan 1985).

EXPERTS' PREFERENCES FOR A DEMOCRATIC CHOICE OF THE MOST SOCIALLY DESIRABLE ACCOUNTING SYSTEM AND/OR STANDARDS ALTERNATIVES

May and Sundem (1976) have argued that accounting policymaking should be seen as a social choice process, one that is political by nature. To decide which accounting measurement and reporting alternatives are acceptable, an attempt should be made "to select the most socially desirable accounting alternative" (p. 751). They have also pointed out that, in a democratic fashion, it is important to ensure, in principle, that social policy is made sensitive to individual preferences, especially those of individuals affected by the use of accounting information. They called this choice process a collective choice rule (that is, accounting choice must be acceptable to the majority of persons, institutions, and other players who will be affected by the choice). Underlying the collective choice rule, there are two to be made: (1) the collective choice has a goal, which is to maximize the social welfare, and (2) policymakers must identify the set of accounting alternatives available. The essence of May and Sundem's argument is that the most desirable and acceptable accounting alternative should pass an acid test (i.e., the choice should rely on the consensus[1] of the groups affected by the choice, including business firms, governmental agencies, markets, individuals, and auditors). It is important to realize that members of these bodies and organizations may be represented in more than one capacity; they may be represented in various distinguishable roles.

Therefore, the choice of accounting systems/standards in a developing economy should be decided by the individuals, groups, organizations, and other bodies that will be affected by the choice. We see the selection process as a political one, and—again, in a democratic fashion—the choice must be made by them to obtain a general agreement/acceptance on which of the available accounting systems/standards should be adopted. Hence, we have developed a comprehensive questionnaire to identify the preferences of accounting experts in LDCs. Our task of establishing this collective choice rule is admittedly a difficult and a complicated task. Some even may argue that it would be difficult if not impossible to construct a completely satisfactory one. However, this process should provide a superior approach to that of any other method. May and Sundem (1976) stated that "no satisfactory resolution of the issues (to construct a social decision-making system) will abandon completely the ethical judgment that individuals' preferences are to account in accounting policy decisions" (p. 751).

OBJECTIVE AND METHODOLOGY

This study is the result of a major survey of the perceptions by accounting experts in LDCs of the main characteristics of the accounting system and/or standards relevant to these countries' needs. A questionnaire was developed and sent to 250 experts in accounting in 35 LDCs. The conclusions drawn from this study are therefore reflections of experts' views of the environment and requirements of these countries.

The situations of developing countries that were emphasized and put forward to the experts included a country's economic system, its stage of economic development, its political system, its public sector's size of its total economy, and the main users of its financial reporting. In addition, the characteristics of accounting system and/or standards in this study comprise: (1) the present system and/or standards currently in use in the country, and (2) another seven alternative systems and/or standards for the experts to choose among, ranging from a self-regulated accounting profession with a minimal set of standards and reporting requirements, to the adoption of IAS, to a comprehensive integrated micro- macroaccounting system (see Appendix A, part 10).

Part of the questionnaire (see Appendix A) was based on the American Accounting Association Report on International Accounting and its morphological structuring classification (AAA 1977). First, we identify the underlying properties[2] of a system (P_i) and then a choice of different elements (j) is made to describe each property. A morphology thus consists of P_i (properties) of a system; P_{ij} are the system's (P_i) elements (j). A choice of different elements for a particular property P_i should describe that system (observation). Thus, the process of composing morphologies includes: (1) the choice of the properties (differentiating factor); (2) the choice of elements for each property; and (3) finally, the composition of a morphology that lists the properties and elements on that morphology. An examination of a set of data (an empirical observation) should suggest the properties of that particular observation. Under this kind of structuring of properties and elements, a system can be described in morphological terms.

In this study, the two classifications (properties) applied to an LDC's macro-social systems, political and economic, are similar to the ones used in the AAA report (Edward Shils' classification of political systems, and Neuberger and Duffy's classifications of economic systems; see AAA 1977, pp. 93-96). In addition, we have introduced a refined classification of accounting systems based on our examinations of all models practiced worldwide (see Appendix A, parts 9 and 10). These accounting systems, as mentioned above, range from an accounting system with minimal set of standards and reporting requirements to the adoption of the IASs issued by the International Accounting Standards Committee to a comprehensive integrated micro-macroaccounting system.

The Sample: Country and Respondents

Thirty-seven LDCs are covered in this study, 10 from Africa, 13 from Asia, nine from the Middle-East, two from the South Pacific, and two from East Europe and a Caribbean country (see Appendix B). The backgrounds (expertise/experience) of the respondents cover a wide range of accounting experiences in terms of responsibilities, economic sector, and hierarchical level in different organizations (see Appendix B). Every effort was made to identify people involved in the accounting profession in the private sector, in the public sector, in government departments (local and federal), and in economic planning such as UN development programs or economic development budgeting. A number of economists (economic planners who use accounting information) are also included. At least 10 questionnaires were sent to each country's experts in different fields, except China (6) because it was considered a straightforward case. In total, 366 questionnaires were sent to experts. The total number returned was 129, or 35.3%. However, six questionnaires were eliminated for various reasons, such as a lack of awareness of the significance of questions or bias. Therefore, the total number of usable questionnaires was 123.

The detailed responses provided by many respondents indicate their full awareness of the socioeconomic and political parameters in their countries, other players (domestic as well as international), and their close involvement in the use and/or development of accounting system and/or standards. In addition, many respondents are directly responsible/involved in the economic development process in their countries (e.g., examining, formulating, and finalizing project budgets; or monitoring and reviewing the allocation and the implementation for changes of activities, for example, head of a state planning division). Many are public accountants in the private sector, and some have their own accounting practices with close relationships with the Big Six international accounting firms. Others have spent years with a UN development program. Still others have varied experiences such as senior accountant in the public and the private sectors for more than 25 years; one is currently is a financial manager of a joint stock company in Saudi Arabia (see Appendix B).

The Accounting Alternatives, from a Laissez-Faire Approach to Micro-Macro-integrated Systems

For a proper implementation of the collective choice rule, accounting policymakers must identify the set of accounting alternatives available. We have done exactly that. The number of accounting system and/or standards alternatives specified for experts to choose from are included in part 10 of the questionnaire. Something should be said here about uniform accounting systems whose company accounts (microaccounting[3]) are linked with a national accounting system (macroaccounting). Many macroeconomic models emphasize fiscal and monetary policies. Economists should require information at the national level not only to examine the impact of taxation policies on personal and corporation incomes, output, productivity, and employment in different industries and regions but also to recognize a wide range of repercussions on business investment, consumer credit, housing, and so on. The examination of changes in these interrelated variables as a result of a taxation policy, for instance, requires an integration of macroaccounting with other related economic and social data; the published accounts of firms should constitute a very important part of such data. Under such an environment, business accounting is perceived as a major and important source of the data required for the compilation of aggregates at the national level. Actually, if the financial accounting data (corporate reports) are not channeled adequately by a well-structured system, the compilation of national accounts can be a very difficult task indeed. In this case, references have to be made to other sources—for example, tax records, national insurance contributions, import duties, other statistics on production, and so on. These statistics may have been collected in different forms for different purposes. Macroaccounting statisticians, therefore, have to work out their calculations from quite a mess of different statistics; this always involves a large element of estimation, guesswork, and, of course, a certain margin of error. In addition, censuses, surveys, questionnaires, and the like are heavily used in such situations (see Weetman 1983). Economists, national income accountants, tax authorities, or decision makers at the national level may therefore lobby for a high degree of uniformity, which would influence business accounting policies to make them more compatible with macroaccounting requirements (see Mirghani 1982; Perera 1989).

In France, for example, the politico-economic environment is quite different from that of other European countries or the United States. The

French economy is not a typical laissez-faire economy because most economic activities are planned according to successive five-year plans. The National Economic Council and the General Secretariat prepare these plans and evaluate the economic performance of the country on a half-yearly basis and on the basis of the targets. In such an environment, there must be a heavy use of national economic accounting systems. In addition, the accounting policymaking bodies always find it necessary to influence microaccounting in such a way as to make the compilation of economic data at the national level easier. This would, in turn, facilitate the decision-making process at the national level by making the relevant data for different decisions available all the time.

Germany follows, to a degree, an approach similar to the French system, where macroaccounting is considered a framework of the national accounting system and microaccounting as a subset of that system. Business accounting policies in these countries (France and Germany) therefore are different from prevailing policies in Anglo-Saxon countries such as the United Kingdom and the United States, and, in general, are greatly influenced by macroaccounting concepts, structures, classifications, valuation, and measurements and are characterized by greater uniformity and detail (see Hassan 1985). Under the Anglo-Saxon type of accounting, the development of accounting policies and regulations is largely left to the accounting profession, normally a private-sector body, and is characterized by self-reliance, pragmatism, and conservatism. In addition, the system heavily emphasizes the external reporting and information requirements of shareholders and investors, and great flexibility in compliance with standards to give a "true and fair" view of the company's performance. Further, the strong influences of large organizations, including accounting firms, on the policymaking process are paramount. This contrasts with accounting policies in uniform systems enforced by law and detailed legal requirements.

SURVEY RESULTS

Economic System

Only four of the countries surveyed are considered to have traditional economies (Bhutan, Solomon Islands, Uganda, and Kiribati). Two are market economies (Thailand and Jamaica); 15 are planned economies (China, India, Egypt, Libya, Bangladesh, Botswana, Tanzania, Zambia,

Sudan, and the Gulf States),[4] and the rest are planned market economies. The types of economic system of surveyed countries are as follows:

Traditional economies	11%
Market economy	6%
Planned market economy	40%
Planned economy	43%

Most LDC economies are mixed economies, with intense government control. Five-year economic plans are common and are used for economic planning in most LDCs. A central planning agency or a ministry of economic planning is normally created as an important government body, along with other bodies such as national development banks, central banks, customs and excise, immigration, and so on.

Long-term planning may cover 25 years, divided into five-year plans decomposed into annual plans.[5] Plans are reviewed annually. Strict planning as well as measures of a market-planned economy exist side-by-side, applied to different sectors of the economy (e.g., Botswana). In addition, a "traditional way of life" whereby most people are still engaged in "subsistence farming" also prevails (e.g., Uganda):

> India, a vast country of 800m people, has great diversity. The agricultural sector contributes 30% to GNP and is largely traditional. However, India has a very good infrastructural base and a vast reserve of technically trained manpower. The public sector constitutes 25% of GNP but covers the core industries and the key service sectors such as banking, insurance. Agricultural is entirely in the private hands but government influences production by fixing prices for procurement of wheat, rice, and so on. Small-scale industries are governed by market economy conditions. However, there has been an acute shortage of capital. On the other hand, India has also been unable to effectively control its growth of population, there is great poverty—almost half the population lives below poverty line. All in all, it is a planned economy aiming at equitable distribution of income among population (India).

In planned market economies, governments control the economy in many ways:

1. Price controls by which the government dictates the price of various commodities, industrial and consumers (e.g., sugar, fertilizers, cement, oil products, rice, and other essentials[6] such as transportation—e.g., Indonesia, Kenya, Botswana).

2. A strong and sizable public sector: "The country's economic system is mainly led by the public sector, it is still dominating, very little (a minor) role is played by the private sector." State-owned enterprises are also price setters in their industries (e.g., Indonesia, Sudan).
3. "Investment licensing" sets priorities and prohibits investment in certain sectors (e.g., Egypt, Indonesia).
4. Taxation, differential treatment of enterprises, packages of regulations, and minimum wages are also among other methods in use by LDC governments.

Unfortunately, a number of economies of LDCs are in a chaotic situation: "They're assumed to follow a planned market philosophy, but this seems to be in theory not in practice" (Nigeria).

In a number of LDCs, socioeconomic reforms have been taking place since 1980s. Eastern European countries, in particular, have moved toward free market economies due to the deficiencies of centrally planned economies (e.g., Poland). The situation in LDCs in Africa and Asia may be quite different. Many respondents expressed their doubts regarding the relevance of market economic systems (including economic structural adjustments, privatization, liberalization, etc.) to their countries and their people:

> Our economic system has been dictated to a degree by international organizations which provide us with our borrowing needs. These dictated certain economic structures by which market forces will influence all economic activities in our country. They asked us to sell state-owned enterprises to make them more efficient (it is believed!), to let profits determine the allocation of resources, to have a stock market, etc. (Jamaica).[7]

Stage of Economic Development

The majority of LDCs are in a pre-take-off stage of economic development; some preferred the phrase economy of shortages to describe their economies. In addition, a number of LDCs that selected the take-off stage indicated that parts of the economy nonetheless should be considered as traditional at the pre-take-off stage, as a Chinese respondent indicated:

> China is a large country. The rural areas are very traditional, in a pretake-off stage. Other parts of the country, in some of the major cities, take-off would describe the economic environment (China).

However, many LDCs indicated that their countries were undergoing dynamic industrialization and encouraging foreign investments (Mauritius, Kenya). On the other hand, other countries expressed very pessimistic views as regards their potential economic development, even in cases where a country is not short of natural resources, such as Sudan:

> The economy has been in a stagnated situation for the last 15 years, still at the pretake-off stage, and I don't think it will go beyond that stage because of draught occurring every year (Sudan).

> I hesitantly ticked take-off because the country should have conveniently been in the take-off stage because of the impact of the oil sector in the economy but the funds realized were mismanaged to the extent that there was improper take-off (Nigeria).

Stages of economic development of countries surveyed are as follows:

Traditional society	6%
Pre-take-off	60
Take-off	34
Drive to maturity	0
Mass consumption	0

Country's Political System

The question related to political systems was a sensitive one, and either a detailed response was given to explain the country's real system or very little was said. The majority of respondents revealed that their political system were authoritarian one, a one-party democracy with a centralized politico-economic system (e.g., Tanzania). Some systems are labeled one-party democracies but are actually authoritarian systems (e.g., Malawi, Kenya, Zambia). If not a one-party system, often there is a one-man system, where the country is ruled by a dynasty (monarch) system, a king, a prince, or one family.

Multiple political parties may exist in other countries, but again, there is always one that is dominant. In addition, opposition parties are small, fragmented, and ineffective to the extent that it is unrealistic to describe these countries as democracies. Typical responses revealed the following:

> Our system is a one-party system with a democratically elected parliament pursuing a socialist path (Kenya).

> One-party participatory democracy which has brought about unity in the nation. Tribes now are working together as one. The change to multi-party system from one party will be introduced gradually (Zambia).

Surprisingly, some of the respondents expressed the view that democracy is not an appropriate choice for LDCs for these reasons:

> Government has to be in complete control to effect the pace of economic development given the limited available resources (Kenya).

> One party state build around a presidential personality; multi-party democracy is not encouraged, though parties have not been banned (Uganda).

> We have a democracy based on the U.K. Westminster model. With the Speaker, whips, etc., it is a complete democracy. Sometimes, I do think that democracy is a luxury which the Third World cannot afford! (Mauritius).

Military regimes are common in LDCs; some labeled their systems as military totalitarian systems and attributed many of the country's hindrances to consistent military intervention (e.g., Nigeria). Very few LDCs, however, enjoy full democracy (e.g., India, Pakistan, Mauritius, Botswana—the last with five political parties). In these few democracies, however, uncertainties about how long the country might enjoy political democracy prevail:

> A type of full democracy exists in the country, but the army is an apparent player in politics being a pressure group. Parliament has not a strong footing and as such it is difficult to predict when the system is going back to be an authoritarian one (Pakistan).

> The country has a multi-party system and effective opposition role is appreciated (Botswana).

In many LDCs, it is clear that the political systems, whatever labels they bear, are not democracies and that it is not incorrect to describe them as authoritarian systems. However, cultural as well as other societal factors, such as the level of literacy and complexity of the LDC, may have something to do with this. The need for a tribal chief or a leader of the community coupled with a popularistic culture may explain this dominating political system.

The type of political systems of the countries surveyed are as follows:

Complete democracy	11%
Personalism (guardianship democracy)	20
Modernizing led by elites	34
Totalitarian authoritarian	12
Traditional tribal/dynastic (monarch)	23

Public-Sector Size of Total Economy (State Ownership/Relative Contribution to GDP)

Many LDCs nationalized almost all economic activities after gaining their independence in the 1960s and the 1970s, which resulted in a huge public sector and the need to pursue a planned (or a planned market) economic system. For example, in Tanzania, "all commanding heights of the economy, i.e., banks, insurances, agriculture, and so on, were nationalized by the government in 1967" (Tanzanian respondent). The public sector in the Gulf states, consisting mainly of revenues from oil sales, is estimated to be over 90% of the total economy.

The classification into public/private sector and the corresponding size of each was not a straightforward calculation in some cases. For example, the percentage of sector varies between the industrial and the agriculture sectors. In a number of LDCs, the size of the public sector in industry may reach 50%–90%, whereas it is only 30% or less in agriculture (e.g., India, Nepal, Jordan, Poland). Furthermore, part of the economy could be described as informal:

> Formal sector forms 60% and informal sector 40%. In the formal sector, 40% is owned by the public sector and 20% by the private sector (India).

> It is difficult to say precisely the size of the public sector because of the Structural Adjustment Program which is bringing about privatization and commercialization of public enterprises (Nigeria).

Nevertheless, it is clear that the public sector is dominant in almost all LDC economies. About 80% of the countries in the sample have a sizable public sector accounting for 50% or more of total GDP, and in about 49% of LDCs, the public sector accounts for 70% or more of total GDP.

The types of public sector size of total economy in the countries surveyed are as follows:

90% and above	26%
70%–90%	23
50%–70%	31
40 %–50%	9
30 %–40%	11
Less than 30%	0

As regards economic shifts in strength between the public and private sectors, respondents had much to say, especially on the issue of privatization. The impression was that LDCs have recently adopted more than one policy to attract investments to their countries:

> Government is to keep the current relative size of public/private sectors in the economy (Botswana).
>
> Trend is toward privatization and commercialization (Nepal).
>
> Trend is toward encouraging new private investment, both foreign and domestic (Tanzania).
>
> Trend is toward encouraging mixed capital companies (Bangladesh).[8]
>
> Trend is also toward raising the efficiency of public sector industries without selling them off (Kenya).[9]
>
> Only talking about privatization, but nothing in practice yet (Egypt)!

A number of LDCs have actually been active in privatization (e.g., Botswana has privatized the country's railways and post office). Other countries have undertaken limited reforms. China has decided that the main industrial base is to remain nationalized; privatization is to apply only to small business activities and enterprises established as joint ventures in the Free Economic Zones.

Noticeably, it seems that many LDCs are not convinced that the move toward privatization (selling off state-owned enterprises) and liberalization of their economies is positive. Actually, over 70% of the respondents indicated that their countries had not had any choice as pressure from international organizations was forcing them to pursue privatization.[10] Many reasons against privatization were given, including its unpopularity, potential cause of political unrest (active trade unions are against it), and threats to national stability, described by some respondents as follows:

> Recent trends are toward privatization because of the pressure from the donor agencies like the World Bank, IMF, U.S. AID, etc. (Nepal).
>
> Trend is toward privatization, but this is going slow because the government is reluctant to release the many state-owned industries (India).
>
> Privatization is taken place because of outside influence, from international agencies/donors and overseas quarters who dictate policy (Indonesia).
>
> The public sector remains the dominant force in the Egyptian economy, in spite of five years of reforms—backed by the IMF and the World Bank—and an official commitment to privatization! (Egypt).
>
> Not clear-cut direction, paying lip-service to privatization in a bid to copying the West. But is the good for the West is good for us (Nigeria).
>
> The country has swallowed the IMF/World Bank dose toward divestiture and privatization of public-owned businesses, but nothing has improved, it is getting worse! (Uganda).

In addition, some believe that in an LDC, government involvement is inevitable.

> We need both, publicly established and privately established business (Botswana).
>
> Public sector is still needed in order to avoid the ownership by non-indigenous traders. Privatization might not be suitable for Indonesia because most of the economic activities are in the hands of the Chinese community, and so the privatization will disturb the national stability if they [the Chinese] increase their control of the economy (Indonesia).

It may be that it is too early to take for granted the views expressed by a Sudanese respondent as to potential changes that privatization might bring to LDCs' economic systems—which, in turn, might have a substantial influence on the type of accounting systems/standards relevant to the needs of these countries:

> Trend is unpredictable because it is subject to the political system of the day; which by turn is always changing (Sudan).[11]

Main Users of Accounting Information

The main users of accounting information in surveyed countries are as follows:

Mainly shareholders and investors	6%
Mainly government	26
Both government and investors but emphasis on government	48
Both investors and government but emphasis on investors	20

These figures demonstrate the well-known fact that in LDCs, the main user of accounting information is the government and its departments, including the tax authorities. The high percentage of 74% (26% + 48%) of countries where company financial statements are mainly produced for government use (26%, including China, Poland, Uganda, Sudan, and Tanzania) and for various users that put emphasis on government needs (48%, including Indonesia, Nigeria, Sudan, Turkey, and Egypt).

> There is no stock exchange or modern investment vehicles, hence, government is the main user (Uganda).

Company annual reports and published financial statements are produced mainly for the shareholders and investors in only two countries in the sample: Mauritius and Botswana. However, only 26% (6% + 20%) of the sample indicated that the main users, or those whose needs are emphasized, are investors. In addition, in the few LDCs where shareholder/investor information needs were a priority, these investors were mainly institutions and included very few individuals.

> The listed companies are mainly MNCs with few citizens owing shares except for institutions, and there is lack of interest in accounting information by the public (Botswana).

> There is no stock market in the country. Shareholders and investors, however, are the main users of accounting information. The government is interested only for tax purposes and the performance of its portfolio companies (Solomon Islands).

It is interesting to note that the accounting systems/standards of many LDCs were inherited from their colonizers; many of these countries actually use the U.K. system and/or standards. The U.K. system, which was introduced and taught for generations in these LDCs, is not actually compatible with their politicoeconomic systems, and it can be argued that a different type of system would be more appropriate. However, because the U.K. system prevailed for such a long time, many LDCs continued to use it even after gaining independence. For example, India continues to follow the U.K. system, even though that system emphasizes shareholders' and investors' needs.

Current Accounting Systems and/or Standards in LDCs

The fact that many LDCs follow their colonial systems, principles, and regulations, or even maintain similar professional organizations and bodies, was not unexpected. However, the number of LDCs adopting the inherited colonial accounting system, especially the U.K. one, came as a surprise. Eighteen out of 37 LDCs surveyed use an accounting system and/or standards based on that of the U.K., the former colonial government (e.g., Kenya, Nigeria, Uganda, Ghana, Sudan, India, Pakistan, Malaysia). Experts in these countries are fully aware that the U.K.-based system was designed mainly to serve investors, not the economic development process.

> The government continues to use the colonial system of published financial accounts. No changes have been made to the inherited colonial Companies Act and Tax Laws which regulate the accounts of the private sector which was designed mainly for investors use (Kenya).

> India was a British colony and, thus, its accounting system was quite similar to the one in Britain. However, the Indian Institute of Chartered Accountants has done tremendous work in the area of standardization of accounting practice and the evolving standards. There is no uniform accounting system as far as enterprises (both public and private) and government are concerned (India).

> Accounting system or standards have not yet developed into unique accounting standards. Mainly influence by ACCA (Scotland) and ACA (England and Wales); hence, U.K. standards are emulated (Uganda).

> Accounting system and practices modeled on the British system. The system was inherited from the British colonial government and most of the professional accountants are trained in Britain (Nigeria).[12]

In countries where the government is active in economic planning, the adoption of a uniform accounting system is the norm. The uniform system is always backed up by laws and rules to enforce compliance (e.g., Commercial Code, Company Act):

> Law and rules flowing from central authorities to companies make the system operational (Poland).

In addition, LDCs that adopt a uniform system have relatively effective and advanced accounting bodies and teaching institutions to support the system:

> There is a National Board of Accountants and Auditors plus the Tanzanian Audit Corporation in addition to various national institutions of higher learning that support the uniform system (Tanzania).

In a typical fully planned economy/totalitarian politicoeconomic system, the uniform system is a very comprehensive one, covering almost every aspect of the economy. In some cases, it may comprise a number of subsystems covering different industries and provinces/regions:

> In China, different industries have different charts of accounts recommended by the regulations. Accounting law governs duties, responsibilities, and procedures to follow (China).[13]

In still other LDCs, accounting is in turmoil because there is a lack of any kind of accounting standards (e.g., Nepal)[14] or professional organization—private or government—to advise on accounting. However, these countries are in the process of setting up GAAP (or adopting IAS) and stock exchange commissions (e.g., Bangladesh).

A few LDCs have recently decided to follow the international accounting standards prescribed by the International Accounting Standards Committee (IASC). However, few enterprises could be found in these countries that were opting to prepare their financial statements on the basis of the IAS. The major reason given by the respondents for the adoption of the IASs was simply international pressure from donor countries or MNCs. In other LDCs, the absence of national accounting standards or an accounting organization was due to the fact that the country could not afford them. It is also interesting to note that adherence to the IAS has not been made mandatory in these LDCs (see also Abu-Nassar and Rutherford 1996, 74):[15]

> There is no act in the country which requires adherence to IAS. Auditors, when they go out to audit, always stress these standards (their adoption) despite their omission in the act. Most of our accountants are educated in national universities, where the U.S. education system is adopted, including accounting (Indonesia).

According to this, we could argue that the accounting systems/standards of many LDCs originated in colonial conditions, mainly under the United Kingdom. The U.K. system, however, is a pragmatic one developed primarily to provide information for shareholders, investors, and business needs. In addition, the accounting programs taught in these LDCs are based on the U.K. system, where accounting is about company accounts, with the profit-and-loss statement, balance sheet, profitability, and stock market/financial markets accounting ratios. These programs do not cover the role of accounting in the economic development process and its requirements. Furthermore, many accountants in LDC actually were taught in the United Kingdom and qualified as Chartered Accountants.

According to this discussion, various reasons—many historical—may explain the diversity of accounting systems/standards currently followed or adopted in LDCs. Most important, these systems/standards were not simply designed for the economic and political environments of postcolonial LDCs or to serve the development process.[16]

The current accounting system or standard of the surveyed countries is as follows:

a.	Precolonial system/standards	30%
b.	Nonexistent system/standards	2
c.	Limited standards for external reporting, mainly to serve intestors	0
d.	Limited standards for external reporting, prescribed by tax laws, mainly serve investors and government taxations	21
e.	Uniform accounting system (micro/macro integration)	19
f.	Adoption of IAS	21
g.	Choice of (d) or (f) for private sector and (e) for public sector	7

Preferences for Accounting Systems/Standards Appropriate to a Country's Politicoeconomic Environment

The conclusion to be drawn from the data is that uniform systems are preferred by LDC experts. A uniform system with a prescribed chart of accounts (with its definitions, classifications, and measurements) must be adhered to by all units in the economy. However, of the total who preferred a uniform system (80% of the sample), 55% of these opted for choice (d), a kind of a simple uniform system,[17] and 45% chose (e), the most elaborate uniform system.[18] In addition, a number of respondents are aware of the potential difficulties of changing their current system, mainly a precolonial one, to a uniform system as they requested an adequate period to be provided for a smooth transition:

a.	Laissez-faire approach, limited standards, emphasis on external reporting to investors	2%
b.	Comprehensive detailed set of standards, emphasis on external reporting to investors	4
c.	Set of standards, less comprehensive compared to (b), emphasis on external reporting mainly to investors and, to a lesser degree, for government needs	7
d.	Uniform system (micro-macro integration), emphasis on external reporting to serve government's and investors—compulsory for all	44
e.	Comprehensive detailed uniform system (micro-aacro integration), tailored mainly to serve government's needs covering all branches of accounting and budgeting	36
f.	Preference for a particular country's system and/or standards	3
g.	Preference for international accounting standards	4

The choice of a uniform system aimed at serving both government and investors but with an emphasis on government needs was preferred by many experts. The same is also preferred, to our surprise, by the Arab Gulf States. In these countries, it might have been necessary to follow the IAS in the short run because of the lack of a national accounting system and/or standards (see Hassan 1984). But the pressure from the prevailing politicoeconomic environment has made the experts from these countries to opt for a uniform system. Experts from countries in the Gulf States and Kenya described their preferences as follows:

> The [uniform] system (d) is a compatible system to Qatar's needs. I believe that the government, as it is the case in all the Gulf States, would like to be always in control of the economy, even with a new but slow move toward privatizing very few state-owned enterprises. The reasons include (1) the desire of the government to keep the welfare system as a means of distributing the oil wealth (2) the government monopoly of the oil and gas resources, and (3) the government desire to ensure the stability of the traditional political structure (Qatar).

> Most of our accounting standards in Saudi Arabia (SA) come from the U.S. standards which emphasize shareholders' and investors' needs, and ignore the government's needs for accounting information. I would like to see the system and/or standards in SA much more relevant to the government information needs—after all, corporations in SA may be seen as an extension of the government effort to serve the welfare society (Saudi Arabia).

> As the essence of any accounting system is to provide appropriate information to the users, any system appropriate to my country should be able to portray accurately the needs not only of investors, but also achieve government accounting objectives necessary for economic development. The system should also simplify reporting for purposes of ascertaining government tax liability (Kenya).

On the other hand, experts who opted for the comprehensive detailed uniform system (see Appendix A, part 10, all economists surveyed opted for this system) commented as follows:

> I recommend system (e) to be adopted by my country; our current system is precolonial British. This system (e) would bring rapid development as well as the privilege of masses to have an overview of the nation's national economic and social advancement at a glance (Nigeria).

> In a country like Pakistan where the public sector has a dominating share in GNP, and where private sector is mainly held by 22 big families, the accounting system should be per (e) (Pakistan).

> We have had a comprehensive uniform system since early 1960s; it has been working very well. We must keep using this system as the public sector is still dominant and playing a crucial role in the economy particularly in banking, industry and agricultural (Egypt).

> I think it is necessary to adopt a system different from that of the colonial days in order to further enhance our economic and political anticipations (Zimbabwe).

> We need a system which enables the government to evaluate the performance of both sectors (private and public) toward economic development programs and to discover areas of weaknesses in the economy. We need accounting tools which are correctly appropriate to the economy (Sudan).

> Preference is for (e), the comprehensive detailed system in order to include the private enterprise accounts with the overall country's accounting system. This would also show the contribution of the private sector made toward economic development through macro-conomic indicators (India).

A number of LDCs have had a uniform system for years (e.g., China, Egypt, Turkey). In China, the system currently being followed is the type described in Appendix A, part 10(e), because private sector companies of substantial size do not exist. However, joint ventures in Free Economic Zones may use systems similar to those in the West, which seems appropriate because of the profit motive.

> The system in China is suitable for its economic system. However, the major problem is implementing the system efficiently and accurately throughout the country. Education and training of skilled accountants and auditors are still greatly needed to upgrade the profession (China).

Many respondents indicated that a uniform system of the type described in Appendix A, part 10(d) or (e) was essential. Some respondents strongly expressed a preferences for a comprehensive detailed uniform system:

> A uniform system is essential for government to control all major industries (let alone small factories) through government agencies and ministries, and the management of those industries. A uniform system would ensure total compliance not only by the public sector but also by private enterprises (Indonesia).

> This is the only system which can help the government to posses a good accounting system which incorporates all the sectors of the economy, with its rules and regulations that apply to the public or the private sector (India).

It is interesting that there was a difference of opinion regarding the implications of recent trends toward privatization and the endeavors of LDCs to attract foreign private investments and to deal with international organizations such as donors, the World Bank, and the International Monetary Fund. The difference in opinion was not about the choice of the uniform system but about its applicability to the private sector, especially foreign companies. For example, a respondent who chose (d), a uniform system, commented:

> I prefer (10-d) but not to be compulsory to private sector companies as the government is trying to encourage foreign investors to invest in the country (Nepal).

In contrast to these comments, while recognizing the need to accommodate foreign companies and investors, a respondent from Mauritius indicated that the uniform system should apply to the private as well as the public sector:

> In my opinion, and as more and more production sector units are privatized and the number of companies increases, there should be more regulations to the accounting function. In addition, all companies (private and public), being the production sector in the economy, should submit reliable, standardized returns to the Central Statistical Office (CSO) to make up the figures for GNP and other macroeconomic indicators required for economic planning. Therefore, the integration of micro- and-macro-accounting is suggested (Mauritius).

In small economies such as that of the Solomon Islands, understandably, a simple accounting model was requested, perhaps a simple version of choice (e), a uniform system. The respondent stated few criteria for his country's ideal accounting uniform system, which would be simply a system that:

- Operates well, is easy to operate (given that a sufficient number of skilled accountants is not available);
- Is simple, not complicated;
- Is able to produce a lot of economic accounts, not just the profit-and-loss statement and balance sheet;
- Would be helpful in dealing with the IMF, Asia Development Bank, and other international organizations, especially when applying for loans;
- Is able to produce accounts which show our ability to pay back these loans; and
- Can produce accounts to their (international organizations') standards.

Rejection of International Accounting Standards

Many comments were provided voluntarily regarding the adoption of either the IAS or a particular country's system/standards. In addition, participants rejected the IAS on different grounds as inappropriate to their environment's economy, size of companies, and scale of economic activity in general:

> I reject any standards from any country or the IAS because the local conditions—social, economic and political—will have to be considered (e.g., India).

> We all know that the IAS are impractical for LDCs. Even in developed countries, which have experts in accounting and their accounting techniques are developed, they still have difficulties in applying the IAS. Our economies are simple and we do not have a strong private sector as such compared with the developed world. In addition, all economic sectors in my country must report to the central government for planning purposes, etc. National income accounts and a uniform system are needed to know the wealth of the country and to allocate this efficiently and equitably (Libya).

Only 4% of the respondents chose the IAS. They all stated that their choice was due either to MNCs' pressures or the lack of any kind of national accounting standards or the lack of resources and skills to develop them. Many also expressed concern that not all the standards issued by the IASC were suitable for a particular country and requested the establishment of a national accounting committee to decide on these matters (Botswana is an example).

> We have adopted the IASs as we do not have the capacity and resources to have our own. Also, investors come from different countries and they are the main users of their accounts! IAS will maintain our links with foreign countries. We have reached the conclusion that there is no need to enforce restrictive practices on them (foreign investors) or to be inflexible (Botswana).

Therefore, we conclude that the countries that have adopted IAS are very concerned about foreign investors and the need to attract them. These countries also depend heavily on foreign investment as well as "cross-border trading" relative to other LDCs. In addition, they are aware that the IAS would not directly serve their information needs or provide relevant information required for the formulation of economic development plans.

Reasons for Differences between Experts' Preferences and Countries' Current Systems

The questionnaire (Appendex A, part 11) sought to determine the reasons behind the differences between a country's current system and the choice made by the expert of the most appropriate system and/or standards for his or her country. These should explain the many factors that contributed to these differences, which may include historical, societal, cultural, psychological, economical, and political (including foreign pressures) factors, or even ignorance!

Needs of Economic Planning

The need for a uniform system for economic planning purposes was made clear by all respondents. The many advantages of such a system were also mentioned when the reasons of such preference was asked. The main theme underlying support for a uniform system was that government in LDCs is still dominant in every aspect in the economy and its accounting information needs should be given priority.

The state will continue to play an increasingly vital and leading role in economic, production, resource policy and utilization, investment patterns, income distribution and consumption, creating and developing infrastructure necessary for growth and economic development in the foreseeable future through annual plans, five-year plans, monetary and fiscal policies (India).

We have a five-year planning economy; and most companies are owned by government (there are now new few private companies) so we need to move from precolonial (U.K.) to a uniform system to suit our economic system and structure (Solomon Islands).

I have chosen (d) from the precolonial U.K.; the reasons are (a) the current accounting system is geared more toward the private sector and external reporting (b) the necessary information for economic development planning is not always available. Government has to be realized as the main user, so emphasis in the current system which is mostly on private sector is undesirable, and my choice is that information should be available to both private sector and the government (Nigeria).

The present system (U.K.) does not cater for accounting information needs at national level, that is, does not provide accounting information which is relevant to enable the preparation of national income accounting (Tanzania).

Emphasis should be on government-controlled accounting system (e) to ensure a unified and effective national development plans and for an effective grasp of all institutional machinery within the Nigerian economy (Nigeria).

Lack of reliable data at the national level is a hindrance in LDCs, these are necessary for decision making and development programs. So gradual movement to that direction (to a uniform system) is preferred (Zimbabwe).

A Remedy for Deficient Macroaccounting Systems

LDCs with experience of preparing national income accounts are well aware of the problems of such a task in the absence of accounting uniformity. A number of respondents touched on this issue, identifying the advantages of having a uniform accounting system in preparing national income accounts. This is clearly linked to the previous factor of the need for a system and/or standards that should facilitate the economic planning process.

In Egypt, the public sector is dominant. The choice of (e) will secure the information requirements of national accountants. It is well-known that the systems of national accounts in most LDCs, if they exist, are unreliable and deficient. So the compilation of the data on the production sector of the economy (public and pri-

> vate) based on a comprehensive accounting uniform system should help reducing that deficiencies (Egypt).[19]

> I strongly recommend a uniform system of the (10-e) type, and apart from the need for economic planning, I am aware that the national income accounts follow different accounting principles (e.g., cash basis rather than accrual) so a uniform system would help in this respect (India).

The Precolonial Accounting System

Many LDC experts appear to have rejected the precolonial system (mainly British) as being incompatible with their countries' needs. Some even have expressed their rejection in strong words because they believed that the precolonial system was designed in a way to help foreign investors and foreign companies and, if it is continued in their countries, will do the same thing (that is, help the MNCs at the expense of national interests, socioeconomic development, and so forth).

> This precolonial system (U.K.) ... [does not provide a link between micro- and macrosystems with emphasis on shareholders' and investors needs' and external reporting only] ... being used in my country at the moment, does create many loop-holes for the multinational companies to cash in, to exploit LDCs resulting in the detriment of the scarce local resources (Nigeria).

> The reason [behind the difference between the present system and preference] is that accounting standards or system had been left to private sector. Probably it was not thought that it was a system a government should worry about because their master (colonial) also left accounting systems to private sector. Even our advisors provided by our colonial masters made us believe that accounting systems are only for firms by teaching systems suitable for private sector accounting only (Botswana).

> We are using the British system—but more emphasis should be put on government needs because the private sector is small and therefore there is not much demand for U.K. type of accounting information and reporting methods. There should be a system of National Accounting whereby all information from various units, sectors and regions is linked to national level. It should be easier in this way to find out information on the performance of various sectors of the economy (Uganda)

> The present system is a formerly colonial legacy, while I think the French system of accounting would be appropriate for my country because as a developing country, it will reduce energy and effort while trying to plan, control and coordinate economic activities in the country. The system will make things easier for national economic planners in terms of getting quick data all over the country and make the best of the few available professional accountants in the country (Nigeria).

Although they realize that the current accounting precolonial system and/or standards are not relevant to their politicoeconomic environment, many LDCs still use them. Among the reasons given for this are: (1) political instability (e.g., Sudan—leaders are occupied with other urgent matters), (2) costs of adopting a new system, and (3) the influence of international agencies, see below for more on that reason (e.g., Nigeria). In the case of India, another example, it seems that a combination of historical and psychological reasons were behind the continuation with the precolonial system and the resistance to change in favor of continuity:

> In India, the accounting profession evolved on the lines of the U.K. as the latter had introduced it as colonizers. The system has served well because the Company Law and the Income Tax Laws had also been fashioned on the British system. The die is now cast and it is impossible to move out of the grave—nor does there appear any compelling need to modify the present system. The accounting model should be well evolved, rather stable but not rigid. The abundant English case law and practice bring stability and at the same time do not restrain us from making any changes we deem necessary (India).

Precommunist Accounting Systems

It seems that former communist countries would not like to abandon altogether the uniform system approach because they recognize that it offers advantages over separating macroaccounting from microaccounting altogether. However, they realize that any uniform system under their new politicoeconomic systems should accommodate private-sector needs for accounting information (i.e., commercial accounts should be provided by the system, along with government information needed for planning and monitoring the economy).

> I'd prefer to move from a comprehensive uniform system of the (9-e) type which serves mainly the government to a simple uniform system of the type (10-d) which accommodates for both private sector and government as well. My reasons are (a) changes of political system: toward democratization, (b) to serve the capital market, and (c) for more financial accountability and deregulation (Poland).

> Historically, our system and/or standards were developed from the Soviet Union. Professional organizations of accountants and financial experts had not in the past enough influence on the development in the respective fields (Slovania).

> The old comprehensive system was inefficient and unuseful for the central authorities as well as inconvenient for the business units. It created bureaucracy which was expensive and slow (Poland).

Dominance of the Private Sector, Capital Markets, and Multinationals

In a few LDCs (such as Malaysia, Jamaica, Thailand, and Mauritius), the private sector is strong and dominates many aspects of the economy, including accounting. This environment may be assimilated in other countries where pressures from MNCs and precolonial practices are prevailing.

The preferences of these countries' experts, however, was for a simple uniform system, which would enable them to prepare a set of national income accounts because the countries had not prepared such accounts before.

> The country doesn't prepare national income accounts, but we should have them (Malaysia).

They also indicated that such a change might be opposed by the private sector and MNCs, or that complying with the new system might create problems for the private sector. The experts believed that the private sector is against regulations, including a comprehensive system and/or standards of accounting, because the private sector generally attempts to evade taxes, or at least pay less in taxes. Furthermore, few respondents expressed concern about the role of the private sector in promoting a kind of a culture where corruption flourishes, including collusion with the people in power and subsequently choice of accounting policies which serve the private sector:

> There might be obstacles owing to the conflicting views of various thinkers or pressure groups. It appears that the private sector in the Sudan is controlled by a few millionaires who from time to time make collusion with those in power and authority be they military or bureaucratic elites (Sudan).

> The emphasis is currently directed to be of more benefits to the shareholders and investors as users. However, the government requires the national accounts to the country's development, so I have a preference to a uniform system (Jamaica).

> In Thailand, the current system (9-d, limited number of standards) does not help at all. The disclosure is not enough, inadequate and unreliable, especially in the private sector. Some companies (as well as some ministers) hide their figures. The limited and unreliable disclosure by the private sector aim mainly to evade taxes or pay less taxes (Thailand).

In addition, respondents indicated that capital markets do not play the same role as in LDCs as they do in the developed world. They are new phenomenon in LDCs; they do not operate properly and are inefficient and still in their development stage. Furthermore, many respondents expressed concern about the importation of MNCs' foreign accounting principles and standards, including IASs, which are incompatible with LDCs' needs.

> The adoption of the inherited British (colonial) Companies Act, which is entirely biased to private accounting and procedures and the fact that major companies in Kenya are foreign multinationals. These foreign multinational follow the line of IASs. The IASs may not necessarily conform with government regulations (e.g., treatment of certain items for ascertainment of government taxes) or needs for economic development activities (Kenya).

Pressures from Donors

The pressures from international donors to opt for a particular accounting system and/or standards were mentioned by some experts as the reason for their preferences and for the current system and/or standards in their countries.

> Influence from International donor agencies can not be ignored, when 70% of the total plan outlay is being financed by foreign aid (Nepal).

Combined or Multiple Reasons

As indicated above, the reasons behind the difference of an expert's choice and the country's present system and/or standards could be attributed to many factors. It should also be noted that these attributes do not operate separately; they are actually in force at the same time, in the same country. For example, a precolonial accounting system may still be in use, at the same time as MNCs and donor agencies are enforcing the adoption of IAS, while the dominance of the private sector and other factors are still in effect.

> The reasons are (a) importation and use of developed country (U.K.) accounting practices, the impact of colonialism (b) pressures from MNCs (c) pressures from economic aid agencies, and (d) domination by developed countries' professional accounting bodies (e.g., by awarding professional qualifications based on their countries accounting practices) (Zimbabwe).

> There are many reasons behind my choice of 10-e as an appropriate system and our current practice at the moment of IAS and U.S. standards. Among these are

> (1) the influence from international accounting firms; they all influence the current accounting practice in Indonesia, (2) educating accountants in our national universities following the U.S. system, (3) our graduates from overseas bring about the adoption of U.S./IAS models, (4) the wrong perception of the accounting profession of their role in the country! (Indonesia).

> It is not clear what accounting system is being used in my country at the moment and whether the emphasis is on government or private sector needs. In many cases, a company may have to prepare two sets of external reports, one for the government and another for investors. There is no law to enforce one set of standards. The use of different standards in the country makes it extremely difficult for the government to assess the companies' performances. In addition, company accounting reports has never been used to prepare the national accounts; economists had to struggle to prepare them. Further, MNCs use their own accounting standards (Indonesia).

Other Reasons

Additional reasons cited by respondents included the following:

- The wrong perception of the role of accounting and the accounting profession in the country;
- The education of accountants (and teachers) in our national universities is based on Western type (Anglo-Saxon) of accounting (mainly to report profit and loss and balance sheet of companies);
- Accounting graduates from overseas bring about the adoption of Western type of accounting (e.g., U.S./IAS models);
- The influence of international accounting firms;
- The need to impose more control on the private sector because of corruption, which is increasing and becoming a serious problem;
- Accounting is not an organized profession; there are no codes for directing it;
- Accounting is left to individuals who are not learned in the field;
- Lack of accounting advice.
- Lack of government control, or little government direction of accounting system and/or standards;
- The country has never prepared a set of national income accounts (macroaccounting); even, that there is a national lack of awareness of the importance of such accounts;
- Poor accounting standards;
- Not enough technology, no money, no training facilities;

- No proper markets exist; black markets and inflation have led to improper accounting system;
- Industry is not developed and, naturally, accounting is also in its early developing stage;
- As accounting is developing, it has to develop with emphasis on gradual movement to national accounting (i.e., to a uniform system); and
- Company laws are outmoded and nobody follows the prescribed laws.

A SUMMARY OF THE QUESTIONNAIRE RESULTS

The results presented in Table 1 could be summarized further to emphasize the most indicative figures: those describing the overall system (environment in LDCs); and the choice of accounting system and/or standards, which is perceived by experts as the most relevant for LDCs (see Table 2).

Table 1. Summary of the Questionnaire Results

Parameters	*Systems/Choices and Percentages*					
Economic system	Traditional economies 11%	Planned economies 43%	Planned market economies 40%	Market economies 6%		
Political system	Traditional/ tribal 23%	Totalitarian/ authoritarian 12%	Modernizing by elites 34%	Personalism democracy 20%	Complete democracy 11%	
Public sector size	90% + 26%	70-90% 23%	50-70% 31%	40-50% 9%	30-40% 11%	< 30% 0%
Users of accounting statements	Merely government 26%	Emphasis on government 48%	Emphasis on investors 20%	Merely investors 6%		
Experts' preference	Elaborate uniform system 36%	Simple uniform system 44%	External reporting to government and investors 7%	External reporting to investors (and IAS or U.K./ U.S. system) 11%	Laissez faire 2%	

Table 2. Most Indicative Figures of LDCs:
Typical Systems and Preference of Accounting Alternative

Parameter	*System/Choice*	*Percentage*
Economic system	Planned/Mixed market-Planned	83
Political system	Absence of democracy*	69†
Public-sector size	Sizable (50%+)	80
Users of accounting statements	Merely (or emphasis on) government	74
Experts' preferences	Uniform system (elaborate/simple)	80††

Notes: * These include traditional, totalitarian/authoritarian, and elite systems.
† If personalism democracies are included, the total would be 89%. (Many analysts believe that these should be included and, therefore, 89% accurately represents the political systems which are not democracies according to Western understanding.)
†† 36% for elaborate and 44% for simple uniform system.

Conclusions

It has been argued that business accounting policies may or may not be influenced by macroaccounting concepts, methods, and requirements, leaving other systems and policies between them. LDCs may, therefore, choose a laissez-faire approach with a limited number of standards regulated by a private-sector body with minimal intervention from government and emphasis on external reporting, mainly to investors. Alternatively, they may choose a coherent, multidimensional system that integrates microaccounting with national economic accounting based on a uniform chart of accounts with financial reporting emphasising government information needs. Various systems, as indicated in part 10 of the questionnaire, can be established on the continuum between these two extremes.

The results of the questionnaire (Table 1) indicate a preference by LDC experts for uniform accounting systems. The attraction and the justification given for this preference[20] include:

1. The accounting uniform system would be compatible with the politicoeconomic systems of most LDCs:

   > My choice of (10-d), different from our current precolonial (British), is due to the differences in the economic and political environment prevailing now in my country, my country is that uses the accounting system (Pakistan).

2. The system would facilitate the compilation of national income accounts, which are necessary for economic planning, a necessity in almost all LDCs;

3. The system would enable the government to control and direct major industries (public and private) toward the desired developmental targets and plans. In LDC environments, many believe that the emphasis should be on government accounting information needs—that is, macroaccounting emphasis—for the sake of national economic planning;
4. The chart of accounts in uniform systems (e.g., French type) would specify clearly the definitions of the accounts (normally, economically meaningful and relevant accounts for economic planning);
5. The uniform system would also prescribe the financial statements and other economic reports (including different kinds of budgets), their layout, classifications, measurement, and so on;
6. The uniform system would enable governments of LDCs to deal with international agencies, such as the World Bank, Intenational Monetary Fund, donors, and so on, by swiftly producing reliable macroeconomic and other economic reports and ratios required by these agencies;
7. The system would produce more reliable information and reports, which would render comparability a much easier or a straightforward task; and
8. The system would require fewer highly skilled and expensive accountants (of whom there is a scarcity in LDCs), and accounting technicians can be relied on to operate the system once established and known.

We may conclude that in the majority of LDCs, accounting systems/standards need an overhaul or change because many are irrelevant, inconsistent, or incompatible with their environment or the country's accounting information needs. In addition, the majority of experts believe that the adoption of the IAS is not the right answer to these countries accounting problems. IAS, they believe, have been derived to suit the advanced industrialized countries, and they doubt the applicability and relevance of these standards to their needs. Many have stated, in effect, that what is best for the advanced industrialized countries is not necessarily best for developing countries. That is to say, LDCs require a simpler accounting system and reporting methods than the highly sophisticated systems of advanced countries and this must serve the macroeconomic purposes and information needs of economic planners as well as the needs of private-sector investors. This can be achieved only through the adoption of a simple uniform accounting system, linking company accounts with the national accounting system, with well-defined concepts, classifications, measurement, and valuation basis in a well-defined chart of accounts.

Regarding the fast-changing scene in LDCs, the results of this study reflect both the environment and accounting system and/or standards preferences in late 1995 and early 1996. One may ask whether these results and preferences will be any different in the coming five or 10 years. The author believes that an updating of these research results should be made in the future to ascertain whether they are applicable to future environments, if the environment of the LDCs does ever change. We sincerely hope it will change to one that benefits the people of LDCs.

APPENDIX A

A QUESTIONNAIRE

To examine the impact of politico-economic systems on accounting in LDCs and the perception of **the characteristics of the most relevant accounting system and practices for LDCs** from experts-eyes who are well aware of the requirements of these countries.

1. Name ....

2. Country ....

3. Expertise background

   ....
   ....
   ....

4. Country's economic system:

   (a) Traditional economy; (a primitive tribal with traditional rules and customs; mainly prevails in primitive societies) . . . .

   (b) Market economy; (profit-oriented economy, where allocation of resources and determination of final bill of goods are left to market forces) . . . . .

   (c) Planned market economy; (manipulation of the market takes place by a central agent through directing actions) . . . .

   (d) Planned economy; (centralised economy where a comprehensive plan, to be adhered to, is worked out by a central agent) . . . .

Comments:

....
....
....
....
....
....
....
....
....

5. **Stage of economic development**:

(a) Traditional society . . . .

(b) Pre-take-off . . . .

(c) Take-off . . . .

(d) Drive to maturity . . . .

(e) Mass consumption . . . .

Comments:

....
....
....
....
....

6. **Country's political system:**

(a) Complete democracy; (parliament is effective and dominant, with effective opposition and various parties - economically developed western type) . .

(b) Personalism (guardianship) democracy; power is concentrated in hand of individuals rather than parties (e.g. personality-oriented) . . . .

(c) Modernising system held by elites, military in most cases - recently independent states trying to bring rapid change in face of culture . . . . . .

(d) Totalitarian/authoritarian system held by elites of party (one party); a centralised politico-economic system . . . .

(e) Traditional tribal and dynastic (monarch) system . . . .

Comments:

....
....
....
....
....
....
....

7. **<u>Public sector size of total economy</u>: (state/private ownership): (mixed ownership to be divided between both, if possible)**

(a) **<u>Percentage</u>:**

90% and above . . . .

70-90% . . . .

50-70% . . . .

40-50% . . . .

30-40% . . . .

less than 30% . . . .

(b) **<u>Recent trend</u>**

(i) Towards more nationalisation . . . .

(ii) Towards denationalization (privatisation) . . . .

(iii) Other ....
....

<u>Comments</u>:..
....
....

8. **<u>Main users of accounting information</u>**

(a) Shareholders, investors, and private financial market, (stock Markets).

(b) Government as the main user (this includes management of the public sector at units, sector, ministerial levels).

(c) Government, shareholders and investors, but emphasis on government.

(d) Government, shareholders and investors, but emphasis on shareholders and investors.

<u>Comments</u>:
....
....
....

9. **Characteristics of current accounting system and practices adopted in your country at present:**

(a) Pre-colonial system; principles, standards and professional organisation etc . . . .

(b) Non-existence of accounting standards, regulations or professional bodies . . . .

(c) Existence of limited accounting standards and regulations, with emphasis on external reporting, mainly to owners/shareholders . . . .

(d) A **limited** number of accounting principles and standards prescribed by tax or company laws, to serve government (mainly taxation) and investors accounting information needs . . . .

(e) An adoption of a **uniform accounting system**, with integration of firms' accounts with national economic accounting based on a uniform chart of accounts . . . .

(f) Adoption of the **International Accounting Standards** issued by the International Accounting Standards Committee . . . .

Comments:

....
....
....
....
....
....
....
....
....
....
....
....
....

10. Characteristics of accounting system you believe to be most appropriate to your country's politico-economic system:

(a) A self-regulated (private) profession with minimal interference from government, **(a Laissez-Faire approach)** and with limited number of accounting standards (with wide discretion in choosing among accounting methods), emphasising external reporting and aiming at serving mainly the shareholders and investors (Stock Markets) interests. **(eg. UK)**

(b) A detailed accounting regulations and standards, emphasising **external reporting serving mainly shareholders/investors and stock market)**; **law (or semi-private body) would determine these reporting requirements. (eg. USA)**

(c) A system which emphasises the private sector companies and to some extent the government's information needs, and using economic and commercial (eg profitability) performance indicators, **but published financial statements are NOT linked with national income accounts** in an integrated micro-macro-accounting system.

(d) A system which emphasises the private sector companies as well as the government's information needs, and using economic and commercial performance indicators, **but linked with national income accounting with a simple chart of accounts;** the system would be compulsory to private sector companies. **(eg. France)**

Cont/...

(e) A system which emphasises the government (all levels) and its production units information needs, using mainly economic performance indicators, and **linked with national income accounting in a comprehensive integrated micro-macro system.** The system would comprise also budgets (fiscal, monetary and cash budgets) and cost/management accounting tools. The system is to be compulsory to private sector companies. **(eg. socialist economies)**

(f) A preference for a **particular country's** accounting model - specify country, model and say why.

....
....
....
....
....
....
....
....
....
....

(g) A preference for the **International Accounting Standards** (Issued by the International Accounting Standards Committee), **say Why?**

....
....
....
....
....
....
....
....
....
....

11. **Reasons for differences between 9 and 10 above (specifically between current system and your preference as most appropriate**, (see number 12 before trying this question).

....

....

....

....

....

....

....

....

....

....

....

....

....

....

....

....

....

....

....

12. **The obstacles and problems which contribute to differences between 9 and 10 above.**

....

....

....

....

....

....

....

....

....

....

....

....

....

....

....

....

....

....

....

....

13. <u>Any other comments:</u> (for example: other preferences for accounting system/standards not mentioned in this questionnaire):

Dr. Naim A Hassan
University of Birmingham
UK
Jan.,1996
Fax: 44 121 414 6678
Email: N.A.Hassan@bham.ac.uk

APPENDIX B

Table B.1. Third World Countries Represented (37 countries)

Bangladesh	Bhutan
Botswana	China
Cyprus (North)	Egypt
Ghana	Gulf States*
India	Indonesia
Jamaica	Jordan
Kenya	Kiribati
Libya	Malawi
Malaysia	Mauritius
Nepal	Nigeria
Pakistan	Poland
Slovania	Solomon Islands
Sri Lanka	Sudan
Tanzania	Thailand
Turkey	Uganda
Zambia	Zimbabwe

Notes: * These include: Saudi Arabia, Qatar, Bahrain, Kuwait, United Arab Emirates, and Oman.

Table B.2. Professional Expertise of Respondents*

Under-Secretary, Ministry of Finance	5
Chief Executive Officers, Budget & Finance	11
Finance Officers, Local Government	8
UN Development Programme	1
Economic Development Budgeting	8
Auditor, General Office (Senior Positions)	10
Public Accountant, Private Sector	25
Accountant, Research Dept, Treasury	3
Accountant, Public Sector (e.g., Utilities)	9
Accountant, in both Private & Public Sectors	6
Academics**	19
Senior Banking Officer	3
Business Consultant	1
Economists	7
Division Head, Central Bank	1
IT specialist, Accounting systems & Programming	3
Cost Accountant	4
Internal Auditor	2
Not mentioned	3

Notes: * A respondent may be represented in more than one capacity, in various dinstinguishable roles, and therefore may be included in more than one group.

** Many of the academics practice accounting and consultancy in different capacities.

APPENDIX C

Covering Letter to Questionnaire

Date

Dear Sir

Enclosed please find a questionnaire examining and identifying the most relevant accounting system and standards for developing nations. The objective of my study is to find out that accounting system and/or standards which are compatible to the needs of developing economies, considering their socioeconomic, political and cultural environment.

I would be most grateful if you could spend few minutes to answer these few questions. Your cooperation is very much appreciated. You have been chosen as being knowledgable and very acquainted with accounting problems and system and/or standards needs of the developing world.

Thank you again, and your early response will be very much appreciated.

Yours sincerely
Dr. Naim A Hassan

NOTES

1. For example, this process is performed in the United States by the Financial Accounting Standards Board and the Securities and Exchange Commission and in the United Kingdom by the Accounting Standards Board.

2. Because we deal with a complex system, a tiering structure is established (i.e., more than one property is used in the morphology; see AAA 1977, 99, and Appendix A).

3. The term *macroaccounting* is currently understood to embrace a number of techniques arranged in a systematic way; each technique reports on different aspects of the economy. The set of National Income and Product Accounts is concerned with production, consumption, and investment flows. These flows measure and report in monetary values on the nation's gross national product (GNP) and income and its distribution by factors of production, private and public consumption, and capital formation aggregates. The Funds Flow Statement demonstrates how production, consumption, and

investment activities are financed as it explains the changes in the assets and liabilities of different sectors in the economy. Balance-of-Payments Accounts comprise the information on the international trade figures, as well as foreign financial transactions. Input-Output Tables present the interrelationships between the various parts of the economy, especially the technical relationships between all industries. While these tools portray the flowing aspects of economic and financial activities, the National Balance Sheets provide information on the stock of national wealth (see UN 1968).

4. Respondents from the Gulf have stated that these economies are better described as planned economies. The governments are in full control of every aspect (and decision) of the economy. The private sector is too small, and about 90% of the budget revenues comes from oil sales. Recently, however, a handful of state-owned companies has been privatized. Future trends, however, are very difficult to predict.

5. In Indonesia, the current plan is the second five-year plan, which the government calls the "pre-take-off plan."

6. Although some LDC governments have recently attempted to liberalize their economies, it is noted that the prices of essential commodities are still under government control in almost all countries: "If prices aren't controlled, the black markets will thrive!" (a comment provided by many respondents).

7. Others believe that multinational corporations dominate their economies apart from the influences of other international organizations, such as the World Band, International Monetary Fund (e.g., Botswana).

8. In Bangladesh, the government is encouraging private investment, including foreign investment, either as joint ventures or independent industry.

9. Instead of privatization, some LDCs have opted to enhance the efficiency of state-owned enterprises, following different policies to do so (e.g., hiring professional managerial expertise, locally or internationally; reducing government involvement in their management; and inviting international companies as partners).

10. "Too many African governments continue to drag their heels over privatization, reluctant to lose the patronage that helps keep them in office. Throughout much of Africa, reform is too slow, international monitoring is too lax.... African leaders have learnt how to do enough to keep the threat of aid sanctions at bay" ("Editorial Comment" 1996). In effect, the *Financial Times* editorial quoted here was commenting on the election of President Robert Mugabe, pointing out that the president had "step[ped] up his harsh criticisms of business and farming communities dominated by 80,000--100,000 whites still living in the country ... during the campaign the president repeatedly criticized foreign companies, and lashed out at the World Bank and IMF-supported privatization programs."

11. Sudan, as an example of many LDCs, has been through a number of socio-economic and political changes during the last two decades. Sudan had attempted first a Western type of market economy and then shifted to a rather socialist economic system. When these two attempts failed, the country settled on a kind of compromise and developed a planned market economy. Further, in the last few years, Sudan has introduced a complete Islamic economic system, a system uniquely different from all previously attempted ones.

12. Few LDCs that still follow the U.K. standards have indicated that minor elements were added to accommodate for tax purposes (Uganda). Others (Solomon Islands) have decided to move to another advanced countries standards and are now

moving toward the Australian standards. Another LDC, Ghana, is using a combination of U.S./U.K. standards, but limited numbers have been adopted.

13. In other LDCs where a uniform system is in use, the system is adhered to only by state-owned enterprises. In addition, banks and insurance companies may keep a different type of accounts from the one used in industrial or commercial enterprises (Turkey).

14. To solve the problem, a respondent reported, "A Western consultancy firm is developing a model under the auspicious of NNDP and Asian Development Bank." [He adds: "A U.S. system probably!"] (Nepal).

15. The accounting profession in Jordan has been recently formally established and has yet to issue local statements of accounting practice. It has recommended adoption of International Accounting Standards, effective January 1990, but in the absence of any legal power or effective disciplinary mechanism, the use of these standards is likely to come about slowly and a limited way. The Amman Financial Market has so far issued no requirements relating to the content of company annual accounts.

16. Many of the experts surveyed in LDCs preferred different accounting system/standards from those currently prevailing in their countries.

17. LDC experts who opted for this system are from India, Zimbabwe, Poland, Indonesia, Kenya, Egypt, Malaysia, Uganda, Thailand, Sudan, Bangladesh, and Qatar.

18. Among the LDC experts who chose this system are those from Pakistan, Libya, Bangladesh, Egypt, Nigeria, Tanzania, Ghana, Uganda, China (already there), Zambia, Botswana, Sudan, India, and Indonesia.

19. The influence on Egypt to abandon its uniform accounting system in favor of the IAS has been going on for years. In effect, the private-sector professional body, which is ineffective and does not have statutory recognition, declared in a theatrical meeting in 1987 the adoption of IAS. However, no support was given to that direction by the government, which still uses the uniform system for the state-owned companies. The pressure from international agencies and donors has been intense, and it may not be long before the government declares its support or outright adoption of the IAS. A number of writers have openly rejected such a change in accounting policy in Egypt after years of successful application of its uniform system, (see, e.g., Briston and El-Ashker 1984).

20. A couple of responses were excluded because of clear personal biases for a particular country's system regardless of any objective considerations: "I would prefer (10-b); being near or close the British Model of accounting. It is the model I understand and in which I have been trained in since my Secondary School days to higher Institutes and University" (Nigeria, Sudan).

REFERENCES

Abu-Nassar, M., and B. Rutherford. 1996. External users of financial reports in less developed countries: The case of Jordan. *British Accounting Review* (March).

American Accounting Association (AAA). 1976. Report of the committee on accounting in developing countries. *Accounting Review* 51(Supplement): 189-212.

American Accounting Association (AAA). 1977. Report of the committee on international accounting. *Accounting Review* 52(Supplement): 65–132.

Briston, R., and A. El-Ashkar. 1984. The Egyptian accounting system: A case study in western influence. *International Journal of Accounting Education and Research* 19(2): 129–155.

Editorial comment. 1996. *Financial Times* (March 18): 15.

Hassan, N.A. 1984. International accounting standards: A short-term solution in the case of the arab gulf states. In *The Recent Accounting and Economic Development in the Middle-East*, ed. V.K. Zimmerman. Urbana-Champaign, IL: University of Illinois.

Hassan, N.A. 1985. Different business accounting policies as a function of macro-accounting policies: A comparative study in selected european countries. In *The Recent Accounting and Economic Development in the Middle-East*, ed. V.K. Zimmerman Urbana-Champaign, IL: University of Illinois.

Hove, M.R. 1986. Accounting practices in developing countries: Colonialism's legacy of inappropriate technologies. *International Journal of Accounting Education and Research* (Fall) 22(1): 81–100.

May, R.G., and G.L. Sundem. 1976. Research for accounting policy: An overview. *Accounting Review* (October): 747–763.

Mirghani, M.A. 1982. A framework for a linkage between microaccounting and macro-accounting for purposes of development planning in developing countries. *International Journal of Accounting Education and Research* (May) 18(1): 57–68.

Perera, M.H.B. 1989. Accounting in developing countries: A case for a localised uniformity. *British Accounting Review* (June) 21(2): 141–158.

United Nations. 1968. *Systems of National Accounts (SNA)*. United Nations Publications, Series F, No 2. New York: United Nations.

Weetman, P. 1983. Why U.K. company accounts are useless for national planning? *Certified Accountant* (June): 24–25.

CLIENT FINANCIAL REPORTING CHALLENGES TO BANKERS AT THE EBRD

William H. Sholem

INTRODUCTION

Since I am a banker, not an accounting professional well versed in accounting standards evolution, I accepted with extreme trepidation the invitation to speak in a forum on a topic on which I readily admit ignorance: the Development of Accounting Standards in Transitional and Developing Economies.

Whether for better or for worse, my work as a lending executive—and more recently as a practitioner of so-called limited recourse project financing—has not dictated my remaining abreast of the myriad of changes in accounting standards in the United States or elsewhere—let alone the proliferation of competing groups of accounting standards, each vying for recognition in developed nation economies and in the

Advances in International Accounting, Supplement 1, pages 89-100.

ISBN: 0-7623-0461-8

countries of operations of the European Bank for Reconstruction and Development (EBRD).

Instead, my objective is to provide an off-the-record perspective of one lending officer in describing (albeit on a basis devoid of any attempt at formal research) the challenges faced by the European Bank for Reconstruction and Development with regard to the quality of the financial reports it receives from prospective and existing clients in the course of its loan and/or equity investment appraisal and monitoring.

I will say little about the substance of accounting standards in specific terms, but I will (through a few intentionally "sanitized" illustrations) indicate how the absence of or deficiencies in accounting standards, at least as you know them in the West, and lack of familiarity of chief accountants with internationally acceptable practice constitute a major obstacle to efficient conduct of the business of the EBRD and of other financial intermediaries attempting alongside us to carry out prudent business in Central and Eastern Europe and the former Soviet Union.

CATALYTIC ROLE OF THE EUROPEAN BANK FOR RECONSTRUCTION AND DEVELOPMENT

Since 1944, a number of international financial institutions (IFIs) have been established by treaty under international law for the somewhat similar purposes of promoting economic progress and the reconstruction and development of national economies through direct financing or by promoting the flow of financial resources from others. A few of you may vaguely recall the era of the Marshall Plan of the United States and the formation of the International Bank for Reconstruction and Development. That entity later assumed the label "World Bank" when the focus of its activities shifted from war-torn Europe to the less-developed countries elsewhere.

After the fall of state Communism in the early 1990s, a new need arose on our side of the Atlantic for massive amounts of capital in former "command economies" which functioned for decades as foils to various forms of Western capitalism. Several IFIs, including the World Bank (and its sister entity for the private sector, the International Finance Corporation), the European Investment Bank, the Asian Development Bank, and the Islamic Development Bank, started to provide financing for some or all of the countries of Central and Eastern Europe and the former Soviet Union. The EBRD (the newest of the IFIs) was established to provide financing only to that region.

The EBRD was formed under an agreement signed in May 1990 by 39 countries and two European organizations: the then European Economic Community (EEC) and the European Investment Bank (EIB). The EBRD commenced operations in April 1991, and, as a result of the fragmentation of some of its original shareholders, now has 59 members: 57 countries, as well as the EC and EIB. I will not list the bank's countries of operations. Just visualize Churchill's "From Stettin in the Baltic to Trieste in the Adriatic..." and think of a band of 25 independent states stretching eastward to Russia's Pacific coastline, to Mongolia, and to Iran. That varied lot is the EBRD's unique clientele. Bosnia-Herzgovina has applied for membership, and the EBRD is are hopeful it can assist there.

The EBRD was not established for the broad purpose of financing "reconstruction and development" or to be a clone of the IMF, the World Bank, or any other IFI. The EBRD's purpose is specific and more focused: "to foster the transition to market-oriented economies and to promote private and entrepreneurial initiative in its member countries in Central and Eastern Europe and the former Soviet Union committed to and applying the principles of multiparty democracy, pluralism and market economics." Moreover, the EBRD's activities center on the financing of specific projects, not on the financing of balance of payments or policy-based macroeconomic reform packages.

Furthermore, the EBRD is particularly interested in the financing of private-sector projects. Although the bank may and indeed does finance "public sector" projects, a fundamental limitation on such financing is built into its founding agreement, which provides that not more than 40% of the amount of the bank's total commitments shall be provided to the state sector.

Criticism of the EBRD in the popular press during early 1993 may have given the impression that the bank has been slow in becoming operational. Such an impression is incorrect. In the five years since its founding, it signed over 300 projects worth over ECU 6 billion. Its commitments last year alone totaled ECU 2 billion. Over the past three years, its commitments on private-sector transactions have increased from around half to over three-quarters of its annual activities. Thus, the bank is exceeding its minimum target of 60% of operations in the private sector. The share of equity investments in the bank's total commitments has increased substantially over the past three years, so that it now constitutes 24% of the bank's portfolio on a flow basis. The EBRD is now beginning to exit from some matured equity investments. In addition, it has been the catalytic factor in mobilizing cofinanciers for its projects; for every ECU it committed in 1995, it mobilized an additional ECU 2.50 from commercial and official sources for its clients.

Bank staff must observe three special criteria in project selection: all projects must meet sound banking principles; the EBRD must not displace finance for investment that would have been available (on reasonable terms) without its involvement (the bank calls that "additionality"); and it provides finance only for projects that advance transition or have what it calls a "transition impact." I would stress that, although the EBRD is owned by governments, it must operate as a bank.

The EBRD does this by applying certain precepts in its loan and equity investment operations.

1. *Sound Banking Principles.* All projects and investment programs to be financed by the EBRD must be carefully appraised, structured, and monitored in accordance with sound banking practices and the high standards set by the other IFIs. The EBRD wants to be repaid and to receive commensurate returns.

Moreover, as required by the EBRD agreement, the bank makes arrangements to ensure that the proceeds of its financing are used only for the purposes for which the financing is granted and with due attention to considerations of economy and efficiency. In public-sector projects, these arrangements are enforced primarily by: (1) requiring borrowers to procure goods and services through procedures, especially international competitive bidding, which the EBRD judges to be likely to result in cost-efficient procurement; and (2) by disbursing the proceeds of its loans only on submission of documentation that the expenditure involved is consistent with the lending agreements. In private-sector projects, the EBRD's concerns for economy and efficiency are normally met if the project entity follows established commercial practices that result in making capital investments in a cost-effective manner and on clear arm's-length terms of purchase.

During the construction of a project, the bank engages in a continuous monitoring and supervision process in recognition of the fact that inevitable changes in projects may occur, and the bank will want to be satisfied that such changes are contributing toward successful project completion.

2. *Financing for Projects.* The EBRD provides for both "financing for projects" and "project financing," the latter focusing primarily on the assets and cash flows of a specific project enterprise.

A typical example of the type of financing for projects that the EBRD provides is the following. In fulfilling its objective to foster the transition of its countries of operations to market economies, the bank has financed a number of "infrastructure" projects necessary for public services development by extending unsecured loans to, or guaranteed by, sovereign states. In these instances, while a careful study is made to assess that the project is technically sound and economically viable, the EBRD looks to the credit of the sovereign as the ultimate source for debt service of a loan. Lending in this way is, of course, identical to the traditional form of financing provided by the World Bank and by the regional development banks and the European Investment Bank in some of our countries of operations.

3. *Project Financing.* However, the EBRD specializes in providing "project financing," mostly in the form of asset-secured loans, where the EBRD has no recourse or limited recourse to the sponsors (including sovereigns) for the repayment or servicing of the loans. This is the typical structure for the EBRD's financing of private-sector owned and controlled projects. In these projects, the EBRD will consider capital structures that finance two-thirds to three-quarters of project costs with debt and will expect the sponsors to provide the balance as equity.

For its own account, the EBRD is normally prepared to finance up to 35% of the long-term capital of an obligor (that is, total equity plus reserves and long-term debt) estimated on a pro forma basis. For a new project with a special-purpose company established as the borrower, this would equate to 35% of project value.

Consistent with its "preferred creditor" status as an IFI, the bank's policy is not to reschedule its loans to private-sector borrowers where the borrower's inability to service its debt is due to a general foreign exchange shortage in the borrower's country. However, like any other lender, the EBRD takes the commercial risk of private-sector projects to which it lends or in which it invests.

4. *Flexible Financing Techniques.* The EBRD employs a wide variety of financing techniques in a flexible manner to meet the needs of projects and their sponsors. Financing from the bank, which is available on a market rather than a subsidized or concessionary basis, may take the form of loans (with a maximum final maturity of 10 years for commercial enterprises and 15 years for infrastructure projects). The bank may also provide technical advice and assistance on a grant or reimbursable basis and, upon request, mobilizes and deploys resources, providing that the deployment is consistent with the bank's objectives.

There are a few activities in which the EBRD is not permitted to engage. For example, the tobacco, hard liquor, arms manufacturing, and gambling industries are prohibited sectors. The agreement establishing the bank prohibits the EBRD from issuing guarantees for export credits and undertaking insurance activities.

5. *Environmental Considerations.* The EBRD is the first IFI whose founding agreement directs the bank to "promote in the full range of its activities environmentally sound and sustainable development." Accordingly, the EBRD rigorously assesses and monitors the environmental aspects of all of its projects both before and during implementation. The bank takes its mandate in this regard very seriously.

6. *Transaction Size.* As a rule of thumb, the standard minimum lending requirement for the bank is ECU 5 million, although this can be flexible if the project has fundamental benefits for the country. While the bank does not primarily provide direct funding to small and medium-sized enterprises (SMEs), its Financial Institutions Team does employ a number of techniques to reach private-sector SMEs through carefully selected local financial intermediaries (credit lines, medium-term loans, trade finance guarantees, equity funds, and early stage venture capital funds).

Project Preparation, Appraisal and Monitoring: Client Financial Statements

A great deal of preparatory work normally precedes any new project. Sponsors, the EBRD, and financial institutions that are cofinancing a project want to ensure, to the greatest extent possible, that the project will be technically sound and financially viable, that it will comply with local laws and regulations (especially environmental requirements), that it will be soundly managed, and that the financing plan will be realistic and adequate.

Specialized technical consultants normally are required to prepare and/or validate feasibility studies. The added requirement for arranging and packaging the financing of projects (involving the delineation of various political and commercial risks among sponsors, financiers, and project beneficiaries) often requires the sponsors to employ financial advisers as well as experienced legal counsel to perform these vital "financial engineering" tasks.

Affecting all of these activities—and especially those regarding a project for an existing, functioning corporate entity (whether it be state-owned or private-sector controlled, or "in transition" from the former to the latter, as is so often the case for the EBRD's clientele) is the necessity for the management of the company to provide the normal array of financial statements of a minimum quality on a timely basis.

As in the cases of the company management and of the investment, governmental, employee, and consumer communities, the EBRD and its cofinanciers in a client enterprise need meaningful financial statements. It is axiomatic that the EBRD needs these tools to determine that sound financial management techniques are being employed and to enable lenders and investors to both trace and project the financial performance and financial condition of the project enterprise through the application of well-recognized accounting standards and through the use of fair and transparent client-based accounting policies. The bank also insists that an outside auditor opine on financial statements so prepared.

It must come as no surprise to accounting professionals when I say that, without intelligible, consistent, reliable financial statements based on internationally accepted accounting standards and resulting from proper audit from a well-constructed system of company accounts and control, "diagnostic" work at the EBRD—both in project appraisal and in post-disbursement project monitoring—is severely hampered if not precluded outright.

I wish to illustrate some of the challenges that have already been experienced by the EBRD in terms of financial reports submitted by what is a unique clientele largely from a command-economy-based provenance. I need not dwell on problems that many accounting professionals have faced for years, if not decades, in improving the quality of financial reporting by companies in the so-called emerging nations or in nations that have "graduated" from that appellation to the status of newly industrialized countries. The EBRD faces those "traditional" challenges—and more.

Let me give you a potpourri of omissions, deficiencies, and practices in accountancy borne of almost 40 years of a peculiar variety of highly centralized decision making under a political/economic system in which the words *market* or *borrowing* became almost of no significance to the company accountant or, for that matter, the nomenklatura of the state. Generally, accountancy was (and still is, in some of EBRD countries of operation) focused on units of output—rather than on prices and costs, on differentiation between capital and operating expenditure, and on timing of accruals and cash flows. Rather than being commercially oriented in what it receives from skilled entrepreneurs, the EBRD is dealing with the remnants of an approach to accountancy that was governmental oligarchy driven and taxation dominated in its orientation.

For the most part, the entities providing the "challenging" financial reports are, predictably, companies that are either state-owned enterprises (often recently transformed from government agencies into limited liability corporations), which are continuing to operate in the public sector, or are former SOEs that have been wholly or partially privatized and that may or may not have international or foreign companies among their shareholders. As to this latter group, to the degree that there is a "foreign strategic investor" in the company, the task of any needed transformation of accounting activity is usually completed before the EBRD is given a proposition for appraisal. But where the heavy hand of command economy management is still in evidence (and this is still the case in many areas), the bank is often faced with something which is, to paraphrase a Star Trek character, "Yes, it's accounting—but not as we know it."

Let me refer to a typical starting point, namely, the "model" Quarterly and Annual Accounts Form No. 1 approved by the Ministry of Finance and Central Statistical Office of the USSR in 1987. It consists of the asset elements of a balance sheet, makes cursory mention of liabilities, contains no reference to shareholders' equity, and gives no calculation of profit and loss. Of course, most enterprises with which the EBRD deals now work on the basis of a more "international" version of Form 1 of 1995 vintage, or its equivalent outside Russia. But the important point to remember is that there is a huge accounting standards establishment and a huge training gulf between 1987 norms and 1993 norms which is only now starting to be filled. Copies of these forms are available from the Center for International Education and Research in Accounting at the University of Illinois.

Another example of something along the lines of Form 1 is from a hypothetical, newly "corporatized" state-owned enterprise that is slated for at least 51% privatization, mainly to a foreign strategic investor in the same line of business.

Put yourself in the shoes of that foreign strategic investor, in the shoes of a banker trying to make a loan to the company, in the shoes of an institutional investor thinking of taking a small position in the shares of the company, or in the shoes of a local citizen being urged to part with a bit of scarce cash or some privatization vouchers for a tiny share of the ownership of the company. Those few pages, without any notes, any accounting standards in published form, or any exposition of accounting policies for the company are what the chief executive officer and the chief accountant hand to you. The two of them are genuine in their efforts and become somewhat quizzical (if not annoyed) in their demeanor if you ask, "Is that all there is?" They are honestly bewildered and manifestly despairing when, after several weeks on their own, crossing on foot unaided the difficult 1987-1993 bridge, the banker from the EBRD (or anyone else needing complete financial statements) asks, "Is that all there is?" One computer-literate wag is quoted to have responded to a colleague, in mockery of the likes of Steve Jobs and Bill Gates, "I guess this is a case, as you in America say, of 'What You See Is What You Get!'"

This is what we often get at the EBRD. At best, we are still in an era when there is a lot of "restatement" needed by a skilled Western-oriented accountant (notice, please, that I did not say Western accountant) of company-prepared accounts to a work product that follows internationally acceptable accounting standards and practices. At worst, we have found ourselves in a situation where the best course of action is to draw a pair of lines on the past and start afresh by means of providing costly, time-consuming technical assistance (funded by some Western donor government or by the European Union) to establish an entirely new accounting system for the company in question. These are attractive consultancy jobs, and they are often essential to the EBRD in moving forward with a prospective client. Unfortunately, they are highly expensive, single-client exercises, and they are not an effective way, in my view, of dealing with a generalized problem in a country.

Now, let me describe the flavor of some of the differences between "accounting out there..." and "accounting, as we know it." Here is what the EBRD has been encountering:

- Cash-basis approach rather than universal use of the accrual basis in transaction recordation;
- Fixed asset revaluation indices bearing no relation to differentials in purchasing power;
- Fund accounting in which certain types of costs or expenses are charged directly to specific types of reserves rather than to the profit-and-loss account;
- Barter dealings involving a multitude of intermediate transactions;
- Absence of any systematic determination of the realizable value of accounts receivable;
- Ceilings on advertising, entertainment, bank interest, and travel expenses—driven by government taxation policy taking precedence over accounting norms;
- Absence of management accounting tools in a number of customary applications, including the absence of: analysis by job, activity, or cost center; cash flow statements/variance analysis; performance indicators/variance analysis; recordation of purchasing commitments; and investment appraisal techniques;
- Use of general overheads in production costs (i.e., no absorption accounting);
- Anticipated future losses being recognized only when they are actually incurred; and
- Last but not least, an auditing profession in its infancy and occasionally confronted with criminality in some areas.

CONCLUSIONS

Except when a strong foreign sponsor is in evidence, generally the EBRD is finding that many of its prospective and existing clients are presenting fundamental deficiencies in terms of accounting systems, control, and talent within company management. In the last analysis, despite the laudable progress that has been made in many countries in the establishment of internationally recognized international accounting standards and in the creation of an accounting profession containing practitioners catering to the needs of a corporate and financial intermediary clientele, we perceive grave inattention to the professional needs of the worker at the coalface—the chief accountant.

I suggest that there is a manifest, urgent need to develop an institute for continuing education of company accountants, to be placed in at least one of the countries of operations of the EBRD, to serve as a training center offering one- and two-week "short courses" on a series of core and advanced accounting and audit topics. Its object would be, very simply, to reorient chief accountants so that they gain a clear and concise understanding and expertise in handling international concepts in both accounting and auditing from the perspective of enterprise managers. Such an institute should offer its short courses on a repeating basis in such a manner that chief accountants could, over time, build up a formal or informal "portfolio" of focused expertise, possibly resulting in some form of internationally recognized accreditation. English might be the "base" language for the conduct of the short courses, but students should not suffer because of a lack of fluency in English. That is, courses should be presented so that linguistic barriers are surmounted through the use of multilingual communication techniques based on the latest advances in computer-based technology for audiovisual language translation devices focused on teaching needs.

The notion of such institutes for continuing education is not new. Years ago, before the widespread advent in the United States of the MBA degree, such an institute functioned annually during the summer in New Jersey for American bank executives and lending officers. A continuing education institute along the lines of what I have just described already exists in Budapest for bankers from the EBRD's countries of operation.

I note with great pride that my alma mater at Urbana-Champaign has been instrumental (with the aid of the Mellon and Ford Foundations) in the creation and establishment of an MBA program at the University of Warsaw in Poland.

The upside potential for improving the capabilities of company accountants in the EBRD's "territory" is immense. I am confident that such an initiative will have a substantial, immediate, positive impact, enabling the EBRD and others to function much more effectively in fostering private investment and private entrepreneurship in the countries of Central and Eastern Europe and the former Soviet Union. The Center for International Education and Research in Accounting could contribute its leadership, possibly in concert with other professional bodies and development institutions, to help bankers at the EBRD work with those accountants in overcoming challenges in the field—challenges that are holding back these new market-based economies and that you in the profession can eradicate.

PART II

INTERNATIONAL ACCOUNTING STANDARDS AND THE PROBLEMS OF PRIVATIZATION IN TRANSITIONAL ECONOMIES

PRIVATIZATION:
ISSUES AND PROBLEMS

Marc F. Massoud

INTRODUCTION

Privatization is a policy process whereby a government reduces its role as an owner and manager of business enterprises in the interest of other actors, such as individuals or corporations. This process consists of a complex interlocking set of operations that depends on the state of the economy. In a developed market economy such as that of the United States or the United Kingdom, the emphasis is on the transfer of state assets into private hands to remove politics from business decisions, thereby making a more efficient use of assets. In developing market economics such as that of Chile, this objective of privatization is still present, but the need to develop capital markets is also an important objective, as well as a constraint on the process. Although there are substantial differences in the privatization experiences of developed and

Advances in International Accounting, Supplement 1, pages 103-111.

ISBN: 0-7623-0461-8

developing countries, the private sector has typically been at least a modest component of the economy.

In contrast, the privatization process in postcommunist countries takes a different definition. In this case, privatization plays an integral role in the transformation of the entire current economy into one that is market-driven. Privatization, therefore, as used to describe the process elsewhere, does not adequately describe the enormity of the restructuring of an economy into an entirely different form, with new institutions and management skills. It requires the processing of a large stock of enterprises from state-owned to privately owned and the development of the necessary elements and institutions of a market economy.

FORMS OF PRIVATIZATION

It is not easy to give a simple list of the forms of privatization. However, there are four major forms:

- *Classic centralized privatization.* Preparation by government experts or consultants of an individual company or a small group of related companies, possibly including restructuring, for sale by tender, auction, or through a stock market.
- *Self-privatization or decentralized privatization*, by liquidation or conversion and sale upon petition of employees or investors. Government experts limit themselves to establishing general guidelines and general approval of projects that are proposed and detailed by the enterprise insiders or other investors.
- *Mass privatization.* The simultaneous or near-simultaneous obligatory preparation (including possible conversion) of a large number of enterprises for auction, sale, or give away, accompanied by mass distribution of the means of acquisition (vouchers or subsidized credits).
- *Covert privatization.* From the general public's point of view, the unintended or hidden transfer of assets through distorted pricing arrangements—in the simplest cases, as sales of assets from state-owned enterprises (SOEs) to private companies and individuals, or through more subtle forms such as wage payments in excess of productivity, underpricing of sales through a front company, or overpricing of supplies from a front company.

The resulting ownership can take any form permitted in the country's commercial code, and ownership configurations can be highly concentrated in a single investor or widely distributed among more or less equal owners, as in an employee-owned cooperative company. Minority shareholding by the state or other public agencies also occurs.

DIFFICULTIES OF PRIVATIZATION

Substantial difficulties inhibit the rapid implementation of privatization programs. Some of these are:

- A shortage of market-oriented professional managers;
- An inadequate financial structure;
- Undeveloped capital markets;
- Inappropriate corporate governance practices;
- An insubstantial private sector;
- A monopolistic market structure; and
- The large number of enterprises to be privatized.

Moreover, the banking system does not have experience in operating under market discipline, nor does it have experience in developing or exercising market discipline on its borrowers. These institutions, therefore, cannot be relied upon for governance, monitoring, and capital allocation. Furthermore, most private individuals have very limited accumulated wealth and, therefore, face severely limited capital constraints due to the poor state of the capital market and banking sectors.

In addition, almost all participants have almost no information. The government does not know the underlying value of the assets, and the citizens have even less knowledge, having never seen an income statement or a balance sheet. While managers may have more information regarding the assets they control, even their information is not of very high quality because they have not been operating under market conditions.

The underlying assumption behind privatization is that the citizens will start to trade corporate shares on the market in such a way that prices are established and the value of such firms may be revealed. Also implicit is the assumption that the market on its own will engage in information gathering and attempt to price the securities on a semi-informed basis.

STOCK MARKETS, TRADING, AND COSTS

Organized security exchanges are said to provide important benefits to businesses and individuals in at least three ways:

1. Security exchanges facilitate the investment process by providing a marketplace in which to conduct transactions efficiently and relatively inexpensively;
2. By providing a market, exchanges create an institution in which continuous transactions test the values of securities; and
3. Security prices are relatively more stable. Organized markets improve liquidity by providing continuous markets that make for more frequent, but smaller, price changes.

The most basic form of privatization is to distribute actual shares in each company to each citizen as a form of an initial endowment. The value of the endowment that a person receives in any one firm is small; however, it may be a large proportion of that person's overall wealth. This level of smallness may result in a no-trade situation and, therefore, inhibit price discovery and/or changes in control.

Trading would involve incurring brokerage and transaction costs. These costs are likely to be large compared to the underlying value of the shares to be traded. In fact, depending on the eventual market structure that evolves, it is likely that the brokerage and transaction costs would exceed the value of the shares themselves. As a result, it can be expected that no trading will occur. Transacting has some minimum fixed costs that must be met, regardless of volume. These costs are large, relatively speaking, even on modernized U.S. exchanges. Presumably, they would be prohibitively expensive in underdeveloped exchanges. Therefore, it is likely that no trading in individual securities would occur, due to high brokerage costs. This would inhibit the development of a secondary market and result in thin capital markets.

One might argue that exchange could occur if transaction costs were reduced. One way this could occur is by informal, noncentralized trading. However, this would lead to the result of wide and dispersed trading, which would result in noneffective price discovery. Without centralized reporting of transactions, prices would vary from location to location and participants would be unable to learn each other's trades. Centralized, liquid capital markets would not occur, preventing price discovery and thus proper resource allocation. Therefore, informal, noncentralized trading would develop to reduce transaction costs, resulting in ineffective price discovery.

It follows that if no trading occurred due to excessive brokerage costs, there would not be any incentive to accumulate information, because the cost of acting on that information would exceed the value of that information itself due to brokerage costs alone. Therefore, another implication is that information accumulation would not occur if high brokerage costs prevented trading or cause noncentralized trading. Such uninformed disperse trading might lead to speculative behavior, resulting in high uncertainty and volatility, and ultimately undermining investors' confidence in the system itself.

THE ECONOMIC VALUE OF INFORMATION

The number of informed traders is determined based on the cost of acquiring such information. The information could have a very high cost but low quality. Therefore, with the possible exception of management, it is likely that there would be few, if any, informed traders in the market. More accurately, the relative asymmetry in information between market participants would be low since the quality of information would be so poor, and the cost of accumulating information so high. Thus, there would be little information accumulation; the price system would not be informative; and the markets would be very thin due to high information costs.

A key assumption in the privatization process is that the market, on its own, will accumulate information and value the securities, thereby relieving the government of its responsibility to do so during the privatization process. As noted above, such a reliance on the market could hinder the development of capital markets and the process itself.

Information is, in many ways, a public good. As such, economic theory predicts that it will be underproduced in a competitive economy. Therefore, reliance on the market for the production of information seems short-sighted. In addition, if one assumes risk-averse investors, firms would be valued below their true value if there is an underproduction of information. Many schemes purport to "solve" the privatization problem by leaving information accumulation to the private sector. As shown, this is more likely to complicate the problem.

MANAGEMENT CONTROL

An investor would also want to increase the value of his or her holdings by increasing the value of the underlying assets. In this case, sometimes it would be necessary to remove or change management, or at least management controls and incentives. But changing management requires the collective action of individual investors, who must be united and organized. If organizational costs are so large that they exceed the expected return that the investor will receive, then no one will undertake such an organization because the costs outweigh the benefits. With a diverse shareholder base, it is likely that the costs of organization will be very large. Wide dispersion of shareholders results in no organizational activity or control.

It would not be in any individual's interest to initiate or complete any organizational activity unless he or she could accumulate enough shares to overcome organizational costs. If, due to capital constraints or brokerage costs, the individual could not accumulate sufficient shares or if a market did not exist for trading, no such action would take place. However, this in turn would prevent the accumulation of shares and, thereby, external change in control. If so, there neither be trading nor an increase in efficiency in the use of the underlying assets would take place, and thus the aims of privatization will have been thwarted.

IMPLICATIONS

Transaction costs will prevent trading, information accumulation, and control changes. Organizational costs are always high with an atomized shareholder base. Information accumulation costs will also take on new importance because they will be quite high due to the poor quality of information available. Lack of liquidity in the marketplace will hurt many investors looking for intertemporal transfers and hurt the economy in preventing price discovery and control changes.

VOUCHER SYSTEMS

Under voucher systems, vouchers instead of shares are distributed and are used in auctions for shares of state-owned enterprises to determine the initial distribution of shares. Every citizen receives the same initial endowment of vouchers and, therefore, everyone starts off equally. Prior to auction, vouchers can be traded for money. After the auction, a secondary market for shares will develop.

Many believe that the use of vouchers results in superior and different competitive equilibria than the free distribution of shares. While it is true that the voucher system will likely result in a different initial endowment of shares immediately after the auction takes place, it is not necessarily true that the resulting competitive equilibria will be any different than the one that results from the free distribution of shares. While voucher auctions may be intuitively appealing because the process seems competitive, the emerging results are not necessarily relative prices. Establishing relative prices still requires an investment in information. Unless there is substantial investment in information, auctions do not solve the problem of valuation.

PRIVATIZATION AND ACCOUNTING

The existence of state-owned enterprises has been rationalized on economic grounds, on the prospect of open market failure, on monopolistic arguments justifying government ownership, and so-called strategic national security requirements. However, these public enterprises never presented any feedback about the use of public funds. Appropriate accounting standards to provide opinions that would satisfy the citizens (the owners of public enterprise) were almost nonexistent.

The track record of accountability, sound accounting, and effective auditing of public enterprises in most countries is generally one of weakness and inefficiency by public-sector accountants, often compounded by: (1) weak, uninformative, and nonconstructive auditing, and (2) direct and indirect political interference to obscure the true financial status and performance of the organizations.

As we shift to private ownership, accounting is vital for an effective allocation of economic resources and for a rewarding relationship among business, capital markets, and society. To enhance a capital market and its institutions, an accounting system must be developed. The system must be used to continuously record the financial progress of the enterprise through the privatization process and to assist it in operating effectively in the private sector following the sale.

The accounting system must produce reports in accordance with (preferably) international accounting standards or other recognizable, acceptable standards to determine the current status and performance of the enterprise. In addition, the accounting system must ensure that all necessary controls are in place to guarantee the efficient use of the enterprise's resources. So, developments in both financial and managerial accounting are needed.

PRIVATIZATION AND EMPLOYMENT

Does there necessarily exist a close correlation between the privatization of state-owned enterprises and an increase of unemployment? In theory, this question will be answered yes. It is common knowledge that in socialist state enterprises, as well as in Egypt, excess employment is normal, and every private owner will first try to diminish those costs that can be reduced without any capital infusion. In general, the unquestioned excess employment in large, formerly socialist industries will have to be reduced to improve productivity and competitiveness, but the core questions seem to be how well prepared the respective countries are to face mass privatization and what kind of structural deficiencies have to be overcome. Of course, there are substantial differences, because the relative weight of problematic heavy industry enterprises varies from country to country. It is obvious that privatization of these companies threatens employment much more than does privatization of industries that are closer to consumer's needs. Consumer industries have a better chance of restructuring their production patterns according to international competition and acquiring foreign capital than do heavy industries, because the latter have been overproducing in all these countries. This means that in countries with already high (open or hidden) unemployment, the threat of a possible increase of unemployment as a result of privatization is a highly sensitive political issue, which may, in turn, slow the privatization process.

SUMMARY

The successful transformation of a command economy into a market economy based on private enterprises cannot be forced. Such a transformation necessitates the following basic conditions:

- A stable political system;
- A common fundamental acceptance of the economic policy to be followed;

- A proven and uncomplicated legal system;
- An efficient and flexible social welfare system that, within a free market system, can absorb and moderate structural unemployment;
- A well-organized and trustworthy financial system and currency; and
- Above all, a market-oriented accounting and reporting system.

BIBLIOGRAPHY

Balley, R.W. 1987. Uses and misuses of privatization. In *Prospects for Privatization*, ed. S.H. Hanke. New York: Academy of Political Science.

Cook, P., and C. Kirkpatrick. 1988. *Privatization in Less Developed Countries*. Sussex, UK: Wheat-Sheaf.

Domberger, S., and J. Piggott. 1986. Privatization policies and public enterprises: A survey. *Economic Record* (June).

Donahue, J. 1989. *The Privatization Decision*. New York: Basic Books.

Finley, L.K., ed. 1989. *Public Sector Privatization: Alternative Approaches to Service Delivery*. Westport, CT: Quorum Books.

Gayle, D., and J. Goodrich, eds. 1990. *Privatization and Deregulation in Global Perspective*. Westport, CT: Quorum Books.

Heald, D. 1984. Privatization: Analyzing its appeal and limitation. *Fiscal Studies* (February).

Karp, R.C., ed. 1993. *Central and Eastern Europe: The Challenge of Transition*. Oxford, UK: Oxford University Press.

Kay, J.A., and D. Thompson. 1986. Privatization: A policy in search of a rationale. *Economic Journal* (March).

Letwin, O. 1988. *Privatizing the World*. London: Pinter.

Ohasi, T.M., and T.P. Roth. 1988. *Privatization: Theory and Practice*. Vancouver, Canada: Fraser Institute.

Vickers, J., and G. Yarrow. 1988. *Privatization: An Economic Analysis*. Cambridge, MA: MIT.

Walder, M., ed. *Privatization: Tactics and Techniques*. Vancouver, Canada: Fraser Institute.

ACCOUNTING AND PRIVATIZATION: SOME PROBLEMS AND CHALLENGES IN POLAND'S TRANSITIONAL ECONOMY

Maureen Berry

THE RESHAPING OF POLISH ACCOUNTING

The shock treatments introduced into the Polish economy after the political havoc of the late 1980s were, for various reasons, neither feasible nor desirable as a way of effecting accounting change. For one thing, some 130,000 bookkeepers needed to be retrained, but resources were virtually nonexistent and the accounting function commanded no priority. Also, introducing changes into a function so tied to regulations—one which which consumes vast quantities of formatted paper and is time-consuming and expensive—was strongly resisted by both the authorities and the accountants themselves.

Advances in International Accounting, Supplement 1, pages 113-128.

ISBN: 0-7623-0461-8

Solutions soon began to appear to the problems of scarcity of resources, when golden opportunities to provide technical assistance while furthering the interests of their domestic investors, were recognized by major players in the accounting technology field, particularly from the United Kingdom, continental Europe, and Scandinavia. The United States arrived on the scene relatively late, mainly because it was slower in marshaling financial support.

The general perceptions of the trainee groups—who were, initially at least, enthusiastic participants—were that some advance market studies would have been both necessary and useful. Few of the trainers seemed to know much, if anything, about accounting concepts or practices in a command economy, which would have informed them about the entry level of understanding of their trainees. Also, because trainers from different countries were in competition with each other, training was rarely, if ever, integrated or coordinated. As a consequence, training courses tended to be repetitive and at a very basic bookkeeping level with which the trainees were already familiar. What they needed was an understanding of the linkages between accounting under a command economy or a market economy, to assist them in bridging from the old system to the new.

THE RESTRUCTURING OF POLISH ACCOUNTING

The first major restructuring of Polish accounting in the transition period took effect with the Ministry of Finance Instructions of January 15, 1991 (*Dziennik Ustaw* 1991a). Under these provisions, the role of the accounting function shifted from a primary emphasis on uniform record keeping for macroeconomic purposes toward meeting the needs of a market economy, as expressed mainly in related directives of the European Union (EU). This orientation stemmed from the fact that professional accountants from EU member countries had a significant role in drafting the Instructions, which was due in some measure to Poland's interest in joining that body.

Some of the major changes introduced by the 1991 Instructions included:

- Doing away with mandatory charts of accounts for particular economic sectors and instead permitting individual enterprises to select their own;

- Abandoning fund accounting, where state-owned enterprises (SOEs) recorded transactions by activity cycles, and returning to the basic commercial accounting equation;
- Lifting controls over the availability of bank funds for settling transactions, as well as previous requirements to keep separate bank accounts for separate fund activities;
- Making enterprises responsible for maintaining their own records of receivables and payables, functions that had previously been performed by the banks as part of their payment clearing activities;
- Recognizing market cost-based balance sheet valuations through adoption of the conservatism/prudence rule; and
- Allowing certain provisions not previously permitted, such as allowances for doubtful accounts, as well as certain capital reserves, such as a legal reserve, provided for in some continental European countries.

It was generally recognized that these Instructions were a stop-gap that need revision when the Polish market economy matured. Accordingly, work continued on an accounting law project that reached fruition in September of 1994 (*Dziennik Ustaw* 1994a). This law comprehensively covers banking, insurance, government, and the remaining sectors of the economy, to the extent that each are individually affected by its provisions. Standard charts of accounts are only required for the public sector, and the financial statement formats are customized. Certain provisions have been retained from the 1991 Instructions, including:

- Retention of authority for accounting standard-setting by the Ministry of Finance, rather than an independent body, but in cooperation with other interested parties such as the National Bank of Poland and the Securities Commission;
- Required asset revaluations, usually as an inflation adjustment, as and when determined by the Ministry of Finance;
- Valuation of inventories at the lower of cost or market or net realizable value where "cost" may be calculated at FIFO, LIFO, average, or standard adjusted for variances. Because of recent Polish experiences with high rates of inflation, in practice, average cost is usually used;

- Valuation of property, plant, and equipment at acquisition cost; and
- Recording intangible fixed assets at historical acquisition cost with straight-line amortization and revaluation not permitted.

Certain modifications to the 1991 Instructions were introduced in the Accounting Act. These included:

- Allowing an enterprise more discretion in establishing its own depreciation schedules for property, plant, and equipment, as well as allowing it to provide for residual values, which was not previously permitted; items of small value may either be written off when put into service or may be depreciated using group methods;
- Removing the lower monetary limitation for determining whether an asset may be classified as property, plant, and equipment; lands taken over for perpetual use are to be reported off-balance sheet and no longer included in tangible fixed assets; and
- Permitting inclusion of the costs of successfully completed development products or technologies in the intangibles category; also, increasing the amortization period for certain intangible assets to five years and allowing enterprises to set up their own amortization schedules for certain other items;

Some new accounting provisions include the following:

- Restricting the classification of revenues and expenses as extraordinary to those not likely to recur in the usual course of events; examples of qualifying circumstances include events that occur by chance, relinquishing or suspending a certain type of activity, sale of part of an enterprise's organization, or the results of restructuring or renovation. Items that were previously classified as extraordinary because they fell outside an enterprise's ordinary (basic) operations, such as gains or losses on sales of assets, must now be reported as part of the operating result;
- Including subsidies for investment or development work in unearned income rather than, as previously, recording them as a state enterprise fund or immediately including them in income. This unearned income is transferred, proportionately, to earned

operating income as the related asset is depreciated or amortized; and

- Introducing, for the first time, the concept of deferred taxes. It is now theoretically possible for there to be a difference between income before taxes and taxable income. However, while deferred tax liabilities must be accrued in full, accrual of deferred tax assets is optional. This is presumably because, under Polish tax regulations, it is unlikely that deferred tax assets would be realized.

FINANCIAL REPORTING

The 1994 Accounting Act goes beyond the provisions of the European Union's Fourth Directive by requiring a cash flow statement. However, use of the indirect method is specified, even though International Accounting Standard 7 expresses a preference for the alternative, direct method, as does Financial Accounting Standard 95 in the United States. The difference between these two methods is that while both disclose the net change in cash generated by or used in operations, the direct method lists the major classes of gross operating receipts and expenditures in its calculations, while the indirect method adjusts the financial result from an accrual to a cash basis through a series of account balance adjustments. The direct method is favored by financial analysts and is easier to grasp than the indirect method, particularly for those who have little understanding of accounting. So, from the standpoint of providing accounting information useful for decision making by unsophisticated investors in a transitional economy, this requiring use of the indirect method over the direct approach is unfortunate.

A second new requirement of the 1994 Accounting Act is the provision of "additional information." This supplementary information is to consist of data that are not otherwise included in the balance sheet and the profit-and-loss account. It is essential for disclosing honestly and clearly ("*rzetelnie i jasno*") a business's financial status, financial result, and earning capacity. A number of the items specifically required to be reported as additional information (para. 48) had previously been submitted as information supplementary to the balance sheet. They are now specifically identified, as well as expanded, under a separate category of additional information. These include:

1. Explanation of the methods used to prepare the financial report, including reasons for any change from those followed in a prior period;
2. Supplementary data about the various line items and elements of the balance sheet and the profit and loss account;
3. Other significant information essential for understanding financial statement items;
4. The proposed distribution of profit or coverage of loss; and
5. Basic information about the workforce and enterprise components ("*organy*").

After the financial statements and the auditor's report have been accepted at the general meeting of shareholders, they are filed with a regional court and published in a government periodical, *Monitor Polski B*, which was created for this purpose in 1993.

ACCOUNTING AND THE CAPITAL MARKETS

The Polish capital market has benefitted from the early establishment of a legal framework, clearly aimed at investor protection, through both general and specific enactments. The Public Trading and Mutual Funds Act of March 22, 1991 (*Dziennik Ustaw* 1991b) contains basic and general, comprehensive provisions covering such market functions as the introduction of securities, secondary trading, takeovers, the Securities Commission, brokerage firms, and trust funds (Golembiowski 1994, 149).

The Warsaw Stock Exchange (WSE) was established as a single shareholder company of the State Treasury in April 1991. It began trading with listed shares of five formerly state-owned enterprises (SOEs), which had been privatized through stock offerings, using banking facilities, a few months earlier. Subsequent specific legislation includes, among others, Instructions of the Council of Ministers of July 29, 1991 (*Dziennik Ustaw* 1991c), replaced by the Instructions of the Council of Ministers of October 11, 1994 (*Dziennik Ustaw* 1994c), which followed on the heels of the Accounting Act, which had been passed less than a month earlier, and laid down prospectus requirements, including financial reporting, for publicly traded securities. The National Investment Funds (NFIs) law of April 30, 1993 (*Dziennik Ustaw* 1993) and the Ministry of Finance Instructions of December 22, 1995 (*Dziennik*

Ustaw 1996) govern NFI accounting. The NFIs are the vehicles for carrying out Poland's mass privatization program, which commenced with coupon sales to eligible Polish citizens at the end of 1995.

The prospectus requirements of the Polish Securities Commission are based on those of developed capital markets, an environment which the Polish market does not, however, yet match. It is arguable that putting stiff listing requirements into place ahead of their time has retarded the market's growth.

The stated objectives of the prospectus (*Dziennik Ustaw* 1991c, para. 2) are that it act as a source of information about the issuer, and other identified parties, in a true and fair ("*prawdziwy I rzetelny*") manner, disclose their economic and legal situation, and provide a comprehensive description of the proposed issue.

A prospectus is to include the following nine parts, and there are extensive additional provisions governing the required contents of each part:

- Introduction;
- Data about the issue;
- Data about the issuer;
- Data about the management personnel;
- Data about the activities of the issuer;
- Information about growth perspectives;
- Financial data;
- Additional information; and
- Enclosures.

The section on financial information (para. 11) is to include the following:

1. A financial audit report;
2. Selected financial data for the last three fiscal years, including an income statement, a balance sheet, and a statement of financial flows, as detailed in the Instructions, which varies depending on the nature of the issuer's operations. The Instructions identify in detail the line item contents of the three statements;
3. Financial data for the predecessor legal entity if the issuer has been in business for less than a year and its legal predecessor was a different legal person;

4. With reference to item 3, an integral part of the audit report should be information about relations between the legal predecessor and the issuer as well as the manner and extent of the taking over of the current and fixed assets and the long- and short-term receivables;
5. Should the issuer have branches or plants that issue financial reports independently, and should it conduct joint financial management with them, the information disclosed in the prospectus should be congruent with the consolidated balance sheet and income statement;
6. If the prospectus is issued more than 90 days after the end of the previous fiscal period, data about the issuer's financial situation should be supplemented by a balance sheet and income statement covering every full quarter of the current fiscal period;
7. If the last three years of the issuer's activities were marked by a high level of inflation—that is, higher than 20% annually—financial data, at least with respect to sales data, should be adjusted by an inflation index with disclosure of the source of the index and the methods by which it was used; and
8. The Other Information category should include significant items about the proposed issue, other than those otherwise identified.

LIMITATIONS OF DISCLOSURE USEFULLNESS

Various doubts may be raised about the usefulness of such disclosure requirements for investors in transitional economies, although the investor protection controls are undeniable. Such doubts may fall under two main headings: first, the quality of the data and its interpretation, and second its potential for use, whatever its quality, by investors.

Presenting comparative three-year statistics for earning capacity evaluation requires some degree of comparability in business conditions, accounting methods, and other major factors affecting financial reporting such as management continuity, over time. At least in the early years, listed companies were former state-owned enterprises (SOEs) and, as such, their past operating history had little, if any, bearing on their future business prospects. Further, including financial data from prior years with those of post-privatization periods, for comparative purposes, is inherently misleading because when these privatized companies were SOEs, they used different accounting systems. So, although their prior-year statements were reformatted to match their post-privatization reports, the underlying transactions could be quite disparate from year to year. Further, accepting financial data from a legal predecessor could exacerbate the potential lack of relevance, unless only a name change were involved.

Another negative feature of the prospectus regulations has to do with the required treatment of accounting for inflation. Poland, in common with other transitional economies, experienced severe inflation as it went through economic turbulence in its move away from centralized price setting. Restricting the inflation adjustment to one financial statement item only provides only a token recognition of the irrelevance of unadjusted comparative data, without recognizing the basic need of an investor for data that is useful.

The other major question is whether the investor in a transitional economy is likely to use the financial information disclosed in the prospectus. The five-year history of the WSE's operations suggests that the price/earnings ratio is probably one of the few, if not the only financial, indicator likely to stimulate interest. This is because it is relatively simple for the unsophisticated investor to understand and use and it is heavily emphasized by those offering securities. The Securities Commission is alert to the high potential for error in calculating the earnings per share amount, which is the price/earnings ratio denominator, and has taken action against companies that have used erroneous computations.

THE WARSAW STOCK EXCHANGE

Transitional economies need mature stock markets for at least two major reasons: to help finance private-sector growth and to help determine market prices for newly privatized enterprises ("Warsaw Stock Exchange" 1995, 38). For emerging capital markets to become strong and active, however, a number of institutions and institutional arrangements must be in place, supervised, controlled, and functioning properly. These mechanisms include, as in the Polish case, transparent markets with efficient clearing and settlement systems; supervisory authorities, such as a Securities Commission; market intermediaries, such as brokers and dealers; and supporting intermediaries, such as transfer agents and registrars (Lieberman et al. 1995, 36).

Poland, as well as Hungary, chose relatively slow, deliberate approaches to capital market development, marked by control measures such as price transparency and financial disclosure aimed at investor protection. That is, Poland and Hungary provided the infrastructure, but not maximum opportunities, for the large-scale investments needed for solid market growth. The Czech Republic and Russia, on the other hand, provided market opportunities by prioritizing mass privatization with vouchers. However, the lack of transparency with respect to financial information and shares did not foster either investor confidence or protection.

The path taken by Poland and Hungary—that is, to give a high priority to investor protection—is a long-term strategy that sacrifices market growth in the short term. This seems to be a lesson drawn from the short history of the WSE, which was initially marked by erratic swings but seems to be finally settling down. In 1993, when the WSE had been operating for two years, it constituted the world's leading growing market ("Warsaw Stock Exchange" 1995, 39). By the end of that year, the index had risen from a starting base of 1,000 to 12,439; two months later, it peaked at 20,196. It was driven by the fever of small, speculative investors, about half of them retailers, sparked by at least two phenomena—the drop in commercial bank deposit rates where savings were traditionally invested, and high trading profits, that is, capital gains, caused by too many speculative buyers competing for too few listed shares. This drove up the price/earnings ratio from an average of 3.2 in 1992 to about 33 in 1993, or roughly two to three times the ratio in mature markets, depending on the sector involved.

Such behavior seems to have been little, if at all, influenced by reported financial data: "Few troubled with mundane things like looking at traded firms' financial results; companies would report lower than expected earnings, yet their stock prices rose anyway" ("Warsaw Stock Exchange" 1995, 39).

The bull market ended in the first quarter of 1994 and trading proceeded more cautiously, although still irrationally: "By the end of 1994's third quarter, for example, listed companies' sales were up 43 percent; their profits up 83.9 percent; and the market down about 30 percent" ("Warsaw Stock Exchange" 1995, 39).

Stable, growing markets need capital from seasoned investors—in particular, institutional ones, such as investment and pension funds. A number of factors, however, have adversely affected the WSE's development prospects: its small size, its volatility, the continuing lack of legislation to allow closed funds, political turmoil, and the two-year delay in getting the mass privatization program off the ground ("Warsaw Stock Exchange" 1995, 39)

At the close of 1995, there were 63 listed companies, compared to 44 the year before, but little change in the market indicators and average price/earnings ratios of 6:8, including a low of 4:2 for the banking sector and 13:0 for the food industry (*Gazeta Bankowa* 1995). While it is still too soon to evaluate which stock market operating strategy, investor protection or market expansion, holds better promise for faster stock market maturity, the relative lack of stock market swindles in Poland and Hungary is likely to promote more investor confidence and build an improved investment climate.

RESTRUCTURING THE POLISH ACCOUNTING PROFESSION

This brief survey of problems facing the accounting function in Poland's transitional economy concludes with an overview of the restructuring of the accounting profession.

Poland is one of the few transitional economies whose profession, which originated in the early years of this century, was kept alive during the socialist period, although under altered circumstances. Briefly, most of the thousands of accounting and finance personnel were members of the Association of Accountants in Poland (AAP), with headquarters physically located within the Ministry of Finance, that carried out many Ministry-supported training programs. Among these training programs were the examination and accreditation of "expert accountants," a status that included a qualification to perform audits of state-owned enterprises, under contract with the Ministry, usually carried out by SOE chief accountants while on leave from their regular employment. Few of the expert accountants had any notion of auditing principles or practices in market economies, such as internal control evaluation, risk assessment, and sampling, but concentrated on legal compliance.

The new infrastructure for the accounting profession was laid down in the regulation of October 19, 1991, and subsequent amendments in 1992 and 1994 (*Dziennik Ustaw* 1991d, 1992, 1994d). These provided for a self-governing Chamber of Auditors, organized at the national and regional levels.

At the national level, the governing bodies consist of: the National Council of Expert Auditors (15 members), the National Review Council

(5 members), the National Disciplinary Court (11 members), the National Disciplinary Spokesperson (1 member), and the National Disciplinary Spokesperson's Deputies (4 members). The president of the National Council, who is elected by the general membership of the Chamber, as are all governing officials, is the long-standing president of the AAP, whose headquarters still occupy the same premises within the Ministry of Finance.

The initial strategy was to allow all those who met certain minimum requirements to register as expert auditors with the Ministry of Finance for a transitional period only. The restrictions provided for in the 1991 regulation were carried through to the 1994 Act (*Dziennik Ustaw* 1994b) that accompanied the Accounting Act.

Qualified expert auditors are now required to pass professional examinations and complete their higher education—that is, to have a university degree. Several innovations were introduced in the 1994 Act:

- Two registers of expert auditors will be maintained by the National Chamber: one for those who only have the diploma, and another for those also entitled to practice their profession. This is similar to arrangements in the United States where some states permit those who pass the examinations for Certified Public Accountant (CPA) to use the CPA title but do not issue them a license to practice until they have completed various other requirements, such as obtaining qualifying work experience;
- Those entitled to carry out the function of expert auditor include: expert auditors (EAs) practicing under their own name; civil partnerships, silent or otherwise, where all partners are EAs; and legal persons, including stock companies and cooperatives, for example, in which the majority of members of management, as well as the supervisory body, are EAs or are using EAs to perform professional duties. This rules out the setting up of professional firms by unqualified persons who subcontract out professional assignments. Expert auditors are not restricted to audit engagements but may carry out other professional activities, such as keeping books, providing tax and other consulting services, and lecturing or training;
- Professional qualifications usually require Polish citizenship. However, congruent with the Eighth Directive of the European Union (EU), foreign nationals with appropriate qualifications may

be registered to practice in Poland if they pass certain examinations in the Polish language;

- Membership in the National Chamber is not restricted to individuals but is open to auditing firms registered on the qualified roll; and
- Registered EAs can keep their current qualification only until the transition period ends in 1998. To renew it, they must, by that time, have obtained the necessary higher education degree, passed the professional examinations set by the Chamber, and acquired two years of qualifying experience. To be entitled to practice, however, they must be fully engaged in the profession and not, for example, be carrying out other duties in a nonprofessional capacity, such as employment as a chief accountant or finance director of an enterprise. This is similar to requirements in some continental European countries, although not in the United Kingdom or the United States.

The Chamber was officially organized in June of 1992. During the following 18 months, some 9,086 names were registered on the list of qualified EAs, and 588 professional firms (*kancelarii*), and 331 other auditing entities were established (Balinski 1994, 110). Meanwhile, the Chamber laid down the ground rules for qualifying its members and supervising its work.

Audit quality deficiencies were expected in the transition period and, in fact, encountered during reviews by the Chamber at the national and regional levels. Those most frequently uncovered included:

- Not informing the Chamber that an audit engagement had been entered into, constituting an ethical violation;
- Accepting an engagement without possessing the necessary specialist knowledge—for example, auditing computerized records without any knowledge of informatics;
- Issuing reports in an inappropriate format in violation of professional principles;
- Omitting from the report an evaluation of the activities of the entity's management as required by law and professional standards;
- Faulty accumulation and filing of audit documentation, particularly with respect to audit workpapers; and

- Not informing the Chamber, as legally required, of certain organizational changes, such as establishing branches or subsidiaries, or changes in the audit firm's management.

The main cause of substandard performance problems was attributed to the failure of about one-third of the registered EAs to make use of the available training materials and other rich resources of the Chamber and the AAP.

During the following year, the number of registered professionals started to thin out. As of June 1995, the following statistics were available (Ranchunkowosc 1995, 388):

Number of registered EAs:	8,857
EAs registered as engaged in their profession	2,312
EAs qualified to audit:	596
Stock companies	3
Limited liability companies	229
Civil law companies	16
Cooperatives	1
Practicing auditors in chambers (*kancelarii*)	347

It is evident from the above statistics that qualified auditors are in short supply as Poland's market-oriented economy expands. This is one of the main reasons why Poland was forced to change its requirements for certain reporting entities from annual to periodic audits and to exempt certain state-owned entities from independent audits altogether.

Further, attempts to upgrade professional qualifications had a rocky start. The professional examination process, designed and administered by the Chamber and consisting of seven written and three oral parts, began recently. In the first year, around 200 candidates sat the examinations, which were based on higher quality standards, and none passed (Rachunkowosc 1995, 389). This surprising outcome was contested by the candidates and others, who raised questions about the examination design, contents, advance publicity about the scope, and the adequacy of training programs. Some claimed, for example, that they were not prepared for questions on accounting for banks, insurance companies, and the public sector. Examiners, on the other hand, privately deplored the low level of preparation and responses in some of the papers submitted.

Another approach to the certification process is being tried by a number of international accounting firms, who encourage and support their employees to qualify through correspondence courses with a prominent chartered association headquartered in the United Kingdom.

SUMMARY AND PROSPECTS

Poland has achieved much over the six years or so that it has struggled through large-scale political, economic, and social change. In the financial field, it has established a new legal infrastructure, which included legislating a self-governing accounting profession, and passed a comprehensive Accounting Act that both meets the related European Union directives and exceeds them by requiring a cash-flow statement. The Securities Commission was both established early and acted early to impose regulations governing financial reporting for publicly listed companies. These institutional arrangements are, however, more mature than the environment in which they operate.

The general public has little experience with financial reporting, and even less with the accounting function, so published financial data seems to be largely ignored by small speculative investors. This situation is unlikely to change until the financial markets broaden and deepen so as to attract large, institutional investors. This may be imminent now that the mass privatization program, through national investment funds, is getting under way.

Accounting's potential for decision usefulness still has not been fully grasped by the local community, if the experiences of those in the information technology field is any guide. Accounting packages proliferate, from both domestic and international sources, but, as experts complain, "the financial and analytical skills needed to use these packages properly are still rare" ("Warsaw Stock Exchange" 1995, 45). Traditionally, enterprise managers viewed accounting records mainly as a source for preparing mandatory government reports. Now, the integrated, computerized financial systems being rapidly introduced throughout Eastern Europe may "require users to be more literate in international accounting standards" ("Warsaw Stock Exchange" 1995, 45).

Among the fastest and most effective ways to introduce this change in perceptions about accounting's potential usefulness for decision making is taking place in the many MBA programs that exist throughout the country. These programs attract many students who already have Masters degrees but are studying business for the first time. Another major influence may stem from the foreign investors—and, in particular, international accounting firms—that have established a commanding presence both in Poland and throughout the region.

REFERENCES

Accounting IT: Bean counters. 1996. *Business Central Europe* (March): 45.

Balinski, J. 1994. II Krajowy Zjazd Bieglych Rewidentow. *Rachunkowosc* (March): 09–112.

Dziennik Ustaw. 1991a. Nr 10, poz. 35 (January 15).

Dziennik Ustaw. 1991b. Nr 35, poz. 155 (April 25).

Dziennik Ustaw. 1991c. Nr 71, poz. 308 (August 12).

Dziennik Ustaw. 1991d. Nr 111, poz. 480.

Dziennik Ustaw. 1992. Nr 21, poz. 85.

Dziennik Ustaw. 1993. Nr 44, poz. 202 (May 31).

Dziennik Ustaw. 1994a. Nr 121, poz. 591 (November 19).

Dziennik Ustaw. 1994b. Nr 121, poz. 592 (November 19).

Dziennik Ustaw. 1994c. Nr 128, poz. 631.

Dziennik Ustaw. 1994d. Nr 4, poz. 17.

Dziennik Ustaw. 1996. Nr 2, poz. 13 (January 5).

Gazeta Bankowa. 1995. Nr 53, December 31.

Golembiowski, J.W., ed. 1994. *Transforming the Polish Economy.* Warsaw: Warsaw School of Economics.

Lieberman, I.W., et al. 1995. *Mass Privatization in Central and Eastern Europe and the Former Soviet Union: A Comparative Analysis.* Studies of Economies in Transition No. 16. Washington, DC: The World Bank.

Rachunkowosc. 1995. III Krajowy Zjazd Bieglych Rewidentow (August): 387–389.

Warsaw stock exchange: Wake-up call. 1995. *Business Central Europe* (February): 39–40.

THE FINANCIAL MANAGEMENT ASPECT OF PRIVATIZATION:

AN ASSESSMENT OF INTERNATIONAL EXPERIENCES

Adolf J.H. Enthoven

SCOPE OF RESEARCH STUDY

The International Consortium on Governmental Financial Management (ICGFM), an international grouping of organizations involved in governmental financial management that represents over 250,000 members, has carried out a global research study dealing with the financial management aspects of privatization (e.g., accounting and auditing).

This study was based on questionnaires mailed out to accountants, auditors, and Treasury officials around the world in accordance with the structural layout of the information sought by countries.

Advances in International Accounting, Supplement 1, pages 129-145.

ISBN: 0-7623-0461-8

Responses were received from a large number of countries, but not all feedback pertained to the financial management issues involved in privatization for these countries. However, the replies give a clear insight into some of the major aspects and problems involved in the financial management aspects of privatization. These findings are summarized in this paper.

The study focused on the ways that privatization, from a financial management point of view, has been pursued in many countries around the world. The specific lessons learned in these countries could be of benefit to other countries dealing with privatization issues or intending to pursue privatization, as well as to persons or organizations doing further research in this field. The following issues were assessed from a country and general point of view:

- The nature of privatization, capital formation, and accounting;
- The history and significance of privatization;
- Countries reporting on privatization efforts;
- The role of accounting systems and procedures;
- The role of auditing and the audit process;
- Legal issues in privatization;
- Finance and capital market issues;
- Performance evaluation in privatization; and
- Educational and training issues in financial management.

The remainder of this paper covers the essential aspects for each topic.

THE NATURE AND CONTENTS OF PRIVATIZATION AND CAPITAL FORMATION

This topic describes the structural nature and contents of privatization in the economic process.

Privatization encompasses the transfer of property rights from the state to enterprises and individuals, and contracting out the delivery of public services to the private sector or cutbacks in state activities to allow greater room for private initiative.

Capital formation can be described as goods and services produced for use in future productive processes. The availability and accumulation of capital is needed to increase domestic output (value added) to desired levels.

As for sources of capital, private sources can originate from the household or business enterprises sectors and may be subclassified as original or reinvested. The government might well be able to stimulate private capital formation from domestic and foreign sources by means of economic, fiscal, or monetary policies. Foreign sources can be a significant source of capital formation. Foreign funds—whether in the form of equity, loans, credits, or grants—generally will be required to help finance the importation of goods and services.

The capital formation process is highly dependent on the effectiveness of the institutions which channel the money/capital flows. Savings available for investment or reinvestment can be converted into investment directly or by means of financial institutions (intermediaries) and the "market" place. The functioning of the money and capital markets generally needs improvement in order to enhance productive investments. The development of soundly functioning capital markets is again largely a problem of creating a proper "environment" whereby economic, financial, and fiscal policies play a big part. Corporate and personal tax rules, for example, have a bearing on the degree to which the marketplace is used.

Security markets, where trading takes place in bonds and capital stock, are hampered in many countries by a lack of corporate business forms, distrust in financial reports, inadequate disclosure practices, and the unwillingness of companies to allow outside participation (i.e., borrowing may be preferred to sharing ownership and control). The principal advantage of an organized security market (stock exchange) is that shares and bonds traded are of fair, publicly known quality.

The privatization process can be in a variety of forms, such as public share offerings, trade sales, deregulation, joint ventures, management-employee buyouts, contracting out, and so forth. In all these forms, there are legal, financial, organizational, and accounting/auditing issues involved, and the critical accounting/auditing aspects especially pertain to:

1. Feasibility (project) studies and cost-benefit analysis. It needs to be determined, by means of sound cost accounting standards, whether the operations can be viable, preferably on a discounted basis;

2. Adoption of internationally accepted accounting and auditing standards;
3. The reliability and relevance of the information (data) reflected;
4. Financial reports, which need to be issued on a regular basis;
5. The ability of stakeholders to transact their shares or "coupons" issued for privatization purposes by the government;
6. Access by the board of directors to all the financial information;
7. The involvement of the accounting profession—in cooperation with the government—in developing accounting and auditing standards, setting criteria for issuing certificates to qualified accountants and auditors, registering and controling its members, offering training programs and continuing education courses, and so forth; and
8. Education at universities and institutions. The training for accountants/auditors at educational institutions should convey a broader insight into the variety of financial, accounting, organizational, and legal issues involved in "market-oriented" systems. The accounting/auditing roles in the overall process of capital formation and markets comprise the following two main features:
   a. Satisfactory financial reporting and meaningful full and fair disclosure—for internal and external purposes—supported by sound accounting legislation, standards, and practices, including the consolidation of financial statements and other accepted norms for reporting; and
   b. Ensuring that capital funds are distributed according to priority criteria—that is, from a national point of view, whereby the generation of surplus can help the required further capital accumulation (capital formation).

To be effective, the accounting and auditing profession must be an organized body, which is necessary for: developing a sound capital market; stimulating financial institutions; furthering capital formation; educational and training purposes; and regulatory requirements. The profession could be of a private or public institutional nature.

The availability, formation, and use of capital are important factors in the economic growth and development process. Reinvested and distributed profits in the business sector, and savings in the household and government sectors, constitute the principal sources of capital formation.

Corporate growth, and the corporate form of organization that enables smaller savings to be accumulated in the capital market, make heavy demands upon legal, fiscal, and accounting procedures. Accounting and auditing have to meet these important social and economic demands.

The role of accounting in privatization, investment, and capital formation is twofold; first, to generate sufficient investor confidence to stimulate the flow of capital, and second, to help ensure the continued efficient use of capital once this has been accumulated.

THE HISTORY AND SIGNIFICANCE OF PRIVATIZATION

Since the early 1980s, a massive wave of privatization of government enterprises and government activities (e.g., restructuring of the state sector) has occurred. This was enhanced by the clear belief that government operations were not as effectively and efficiently run as would be warranted. Further, the globalization of international production and service operations put great pressure on government-run entities to be able to compete in the global marketplace. These two forces lead governments in a number of countries around the world to cast off many enterprises. This, in turn, could generate the necessary funding for other government activities. The notion started to prevail that government-operated companies should either be sold to the private sector and/or be run more efficiently.

Governments recognized that privatization had major economic, social, and financial benefits, while also enhancing the motivational attitudes in their countries. Private initiative came to be seen as a major force for stimulating domestic economic growth and reducing foreign dependence. The need to encourage domestic savings—and a capital market—were major factors. However, many countries also recognized that privatization is a lengthy and elaborate process, and that a series of well-designed steps in carrying out the privatization process were warranted.

Communities everywhere were demanding that more efficient and effective services be provided by the government. Providing services at the lowest cost would mean that society benefits in that there would be a freeing up of resources, thus enabling more services to be provided.

Forms of Privatization

The six forms of privatization can be described as follows:

- A *management-employee buy-out* is a technique whereby managers and employees acquire a controlling interest in a company. If they have to obtain financing in connection with the purchase, it is referred to as a leveraged buy-out and the company's assets are used as security for the loans.
- In addition to management-employee buy-outs, another technique for large-scale privatization is the *joint venture*, a hybrid approach which reflects elements of other methods.
- A *public share offering*, used most frequently when large amounts of capital need to be raised and spread ownership is a major objective, is the technique that generally creates the most public awareness of the privatization process. It is also the most technically difficult approach.
- In major industrial countries, *contracting-out* has become a most popular method of providing such local government services as garbage collection, street cleaning, catering for the elderly, and government office cleaning. In the United States, urban public transport and various prison operations are notable additions to this list. One of the main reasons for choosing to contract out services rather than, say, sell franchises, is that these services are usually supplied free of charge. Contracting out is a strategy favored by various governments because they believe it is cost effective. *Cost effectiveness* means that services are provided at the lowest possible cost for a given level of service. If government departments are to provide cost effective services and the cost of contracting out a service is less than the cost of providing it inhouse, then ceteris paribus, the service should be provided by that external party.
- *Deregulation* is a process of removing obstacles which prevent private sector companies from competing with state-owned monopoly enterprises, as well as designing a new regulatory environment to protect the consumer while encouraging a competitive environment.
- *Trade sales* have been widely used to privatize relatively small or medium-sized state-owned enterprises, usually in poor financial

> condition; to downsize an enterprise by disposing of certain segregable parts, such as individual assets or groups of assets (e.g., units or plants); or to dispose of assets, with or without liabilities, after a company that could not be sold as a going concern has been wound up.

Various other methods of privatization include trying to sell the whole business or individual parts of the business, or selling the plant and equipment only. This may be done through competitive bidding, the public offering of shares, or employee-ownership plans.

The experience of a number of countries reflected in the study shows the various methods used by different countries in their privatization efforts. Countries undertaking privatization may take cognizance of the various approaches used.

THE ROLE OF ACCOUNTING SYSTEMS AND PROCEDURES

In assessing privatization, the accounting system and its data (information) play a critical role. Unfortunately, the accounting structures and processes in many government enterprises have been outdated, devoid of adequate structural and systematic set-up, and lacking in relevant data.

Valuation criteria are generally based on historical cost, and the value of existing services performed is generally not effectively measured. The question of valuation remains a haunting issue, as book value may have limited significance. Not only are financial statements void of sound financial accounting principles, but adequate cost-benefit analyses either have not been carried out or were deficient. The financial value of the enterprise may not be properly reflected, and better (international) criteria may be needed to reflect the real operational activities (income/expense and assets/liabilities).

In privatization, it is usual to prepare a comprehensive feasibility study setting forth the potential of the to-be-denationalized entity in a competitive context. A considerable amount of internal and external data must be reflected in such a feasibility study in order to incorporate the relevant costs and benefits. Without such comprehensive studies, both the government and other parties involved may be left in the dark, and privatization might be hampered. Therefore, it is critical that extensive financial and cost accounting measurements and reports be carried out, based on acceptable standards of measurement and reporting, including discounted cash flow analyses of the entity as a going concern. As part of the feasibility studies, a social (national) cost-benefit study also may have to be prepared, reflecting the value of the company to the country.

The quality of the accounting data assembled for past transactions, particularly in the transition from a planned to a market economy, has generally been considered inadequate for providing reliable information to investors, based on various experiences with privatization audits. This is due to such factors as: concentration of bookkeeping and fiscal regulations in the same standard-setting body; an emphasis on production rather than profitability; and a lack of external accountability (e.g., reporting standards).

High inflation, unless properly accounted for, can distort measures of enterprise performance. Thus, long-lived assets that appear in the financial statements may have been acquired in previous periods when the general purchasing power of money was higher. In keeping with the "matching principle," the costs of those assets, representing historical purchasing power, are typically deducted from revenues, which represent current purchasing power. The result is a performance measure expressed in money of mixed purchasing power—a figure that is difficult to interpret.

THE ROLE OF AUDITING AND THE AUDIT PROCESS IN PRIVATIZATION

The auditing activities carried out by most countries' State Audit Institutions (SAI) tend to go beyond the pure verification of data. They become involved in preliminary audits of information for privatization, while preparing extensive reports on the operational and economic aspects of entities to be investigated. They also assess the efficiency of the privatization entities and the impact of the development of the market economy, while evaluating organizational, legal, and financial aspects resulting from privatization. Beyond checking procedures, there is a focus on evaluating the efficiency and aims of the privatization aspects. The audit also reviews the methods used for accounting and valuation of assets in a number of countries.

In several countries, the SAI work closely with external auditors (i.e., certified or chartered accountants) in preparing their appraisals. The prime focus of a SAI is its accountability to government—either the parliament or government agencies—in assessing the legitimacy and procedures of the transactions carried out under privatization.

Essentially, the SAIs are independent institutions with their own mandate to check upon the economy, efficiency, and effectiveness with which government departments carry out tasks such as privatization. Privatization studies have become a distinct audit responsibility of SAI.

LEGAL ISSUES IN PRIVATIZATION

The legal issues pertaining to privatization must be seen within the general framework that privatization at the enterprise level takes place under a national legal framework and in accordance with national economic development policies. These vary, not only between market economies and centrally planned economies but also among countries within either category.

Of special importance to newly created private enterprises is the constitutional and basic legal structure of the country. That structure determines whether the state guarantees some fundamental rights to private individuals (and corporations) are guaranteed by the state, such as the rule of law, the right to seek redress, due process, nondiscrimination, and the right to hold private property. Another essential guarantee for private enterprises (usually granted by the constitution or basic laws of the country) is protection against arbitrary nationalization or expropriation, and an assurance that if the expropriation takes place, fair compensation will be paid (for example, under the International Center for Settlement of Disputes by the World Bank).

Reporting requirements of a financial, accounting, legal, and administrative nature preferably should be spelled out, including the law on the valuation of assets and liabilities. Tax responsibilities also need clarification; accordingly, tax laws are of critical importance. The right of sale of properties requires elaboration, while the forms of incorporation of privatized entities, which also involve property rights, have to be set forth. In many countries, divestiture has to be passed by the congress or parliament. In other countries, a separate privatization agency is created, usually subordinate to the Ministry of Finance or Economic Affairs.

FINANCE AND CAPITAL MARKET ISSUES

In conjunction with privatization, there is a need for a good functional capital market and sound securities trading mechanism (e.g., laws and regulations) in most countries. Some countries have made elaborate efforts to develop such securities markets, without which the needed domestic capital formation and capital flows could not materialize.

Merely establishing a stock market is not sufficient, as all sorts of legislative requirements are necessary regarding the issuance and trading of securities. The stock exchange should be a transparent institution. One critical issue is the need for a certified audit reports and generally (preferably, international) accepted accounting standards covering financial statements and disclosures. (The training of securities brokers and financial analysts also has to be developed.)

The government may use the revenues generated by privatization to retire debt or assist in further capital developments. Also, the government may find itself with increased tax revenues due to effective privatization activities.

PERFORMANCE EVALUATION IN PRIVATIZATION

Performance review of privatization activities should include a thorough appraisal, covering not only whether the original objectives were achieved but also the micro- and macroeconomic and financial impacts of an enterprises on the national economy. It should be determined whether the proper procedures were followed, and where the ultimate control of the privatized enterprise rests. This evaluation process may provide lessons for future privatization.

If privatization activities are to result in economic efficiencies and enhanced economic development, then the strategies used must be evaluated to guide similar future efforts. The impact of the privatized entities on the state budget warrants looking into, to ensure that it generates positive results.

A special agency or body should be charged with reviewing the performance of the privatized entities and producing a comprehensive cost-benefit model, covering the impact that privatization efforts has had on the economy, and whether it has resulted in a more open (market) economy.

Before privatization is undertaken, it might be necessary to review existing operations, reengineer some key areas, and develop a systematic approach toward the disposal of the company or assets. (The U.K. experience, described in Appendix A, offers an example of a good layout and approach.)

EDUCATIONAL AND TRAINING ISSUES

Accountants in privatizing countries, particularly those where significant changes are occurring such as in Central and Eastern Europe, may have to expand their conceptual and practical knowledge. They will have to learn internationally accepted accounting principles (standards) that rely on such concepts as going concern, economic entity, monetary unit, and periodicity; the principles of (historical) cost, revenue recognition, matching, and full disclosure; and the constraints of cost-benefit considerations, materiality, conservatism, and industry practice. Some of these concepts may not be new, but there may be significant differences in the ways in which they would be applied under new (international) approaches to accounting. The general adaptation of international accounting and auditing standards, and a wider dissemination of the existing body of accounting and auditing knowledge, are critical issues in privatization and economic development.

In addition, accountants and auditors will need to view themselves in new roles. In market economies, an accountant generally leaves the pure bookkeeping function to electronic equipment and is concerned with directing management's attention to areas which suggest the need for solutions in which the accountant generally participates. In this context, accounting must be recognized as an "information measurement system" requiring considerable use of judgment by both the preparer and the user of its output.

Education and training (including retraining) constitute critical elements in the privatization process. Accounting and auditing training, furthermore, warrant specific attention as accountants need to be updated in modern (international) standards of accounting and auditing, including sound management accounting concepts and techniques, and operational auditing procedures. Extensive training programs may have to be organized to update officers in modern methods. Banks and development banks, as well as government agencies (e.g., audit boards), could run special courses in privatization and the financial management issues involved.

SOME CONCLUSIONS

In general, the financial management issues of privatization on an international scale do not appear to have been extensively covered in the literature, and more elaborate appraisals may need to be carried out on the issues addressed in this research study. The soundness of privatization is highly linked to the level of a country's development in accounting and auditing. It may be necessary to pass adequate legislation concerning financial reporting and disclosure, audit requirements, feasibility studies, stock exchange legislation, and so forth. It is also necessary to address cost or management accounting issues, such as policies of transfer pricing, the costing of products and processes, and methods of valuing assets. It will be difficult to proceed with effective privatization efforts if the financial management issues are not properly catered to. In many countries, these include the concepts and methods of valuation of properties, issuance of privatization vouchers, presentation of financial statements, disclosure requirements, the measurement and classification of financial items, and so on.

In order for privatization to succeed, effective capital and finance market vehicles may have to be established, either in the form of a distinct share (stock) exchange market or other vehicles (e.g., financial institutions). The role of banks will be critical in the privatization process. Adequate regulations need to be in effect for "exchange markets" to flourish. Above all, governments may have to clearly set forth how privatization will be executed and what financial regulatory procedures will apply. Governments may also have to outline why and how privatization will occur—that is, the benefits to society. Adequate performance appraisals should be carried out on the entities to be privatized, and these appraisals should follow well-established accounting and auditing methods and procedures.

Education is needed not only to make the public aware of the aims and means of privatization but also to provide professionals with the specific "technical" and methodological concepts and procedures necessary to carry out effective studies of privatization. Education and training for countries in the process of privatization may involve, generally, a profound updating of the existing national body of knowledge in accounting, auditing, and finance. Gradually, these fields may have to be updated to include internationally accepted norms such as international standards of accounting and auditing.

APPENDIX A

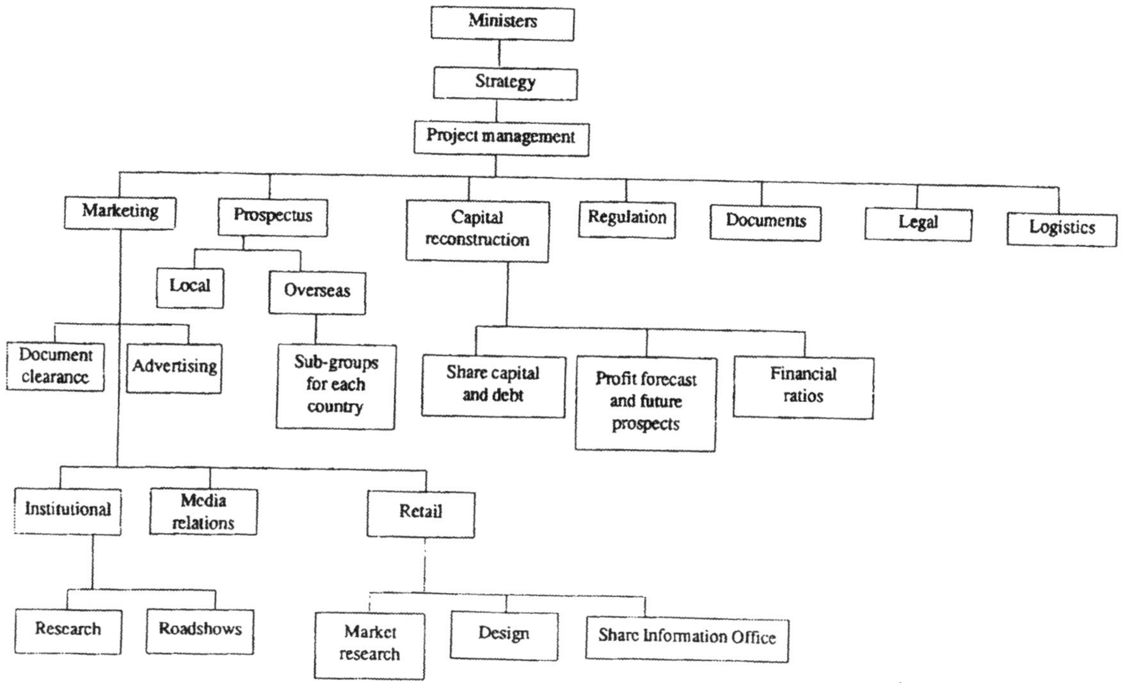

Figure A.1. A Major Share Offer: Strategy Management

Figure A.2. Outline of Typical Steps to Privatization

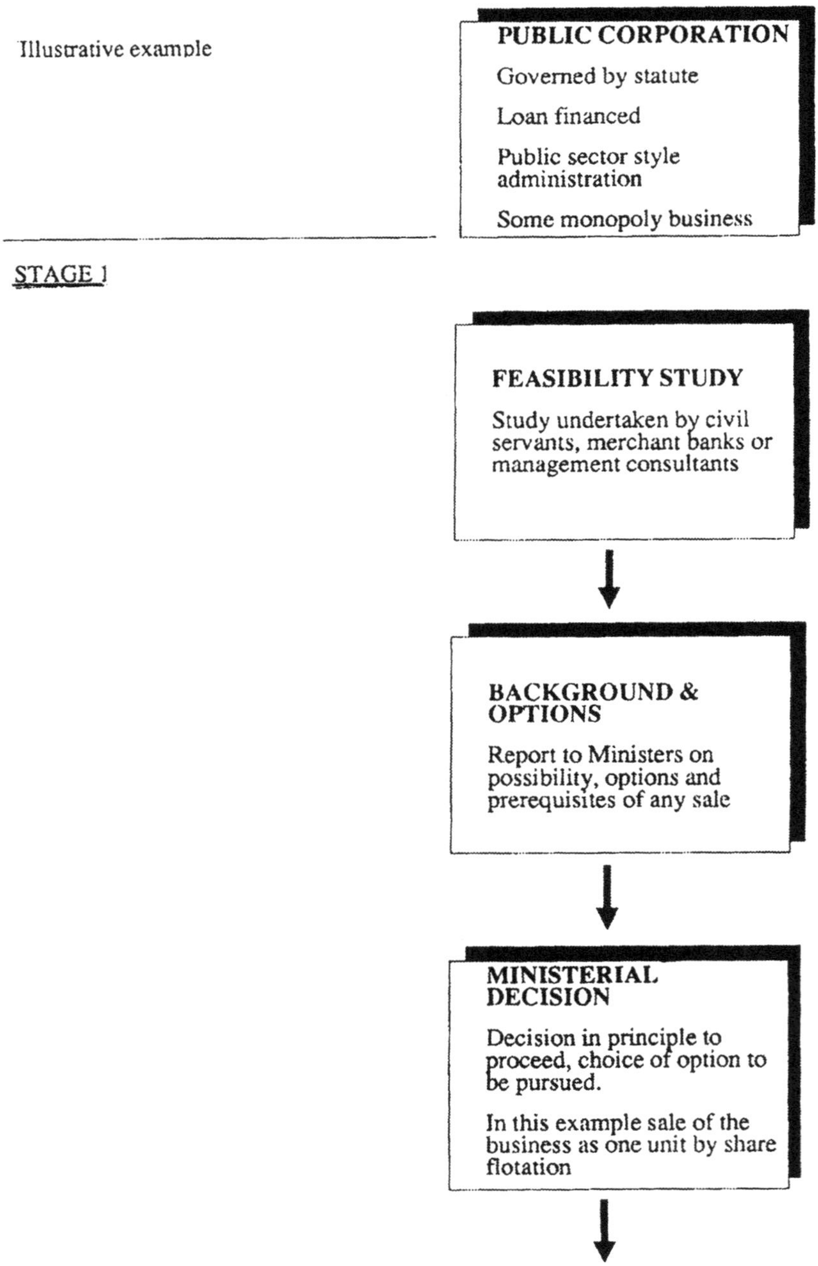

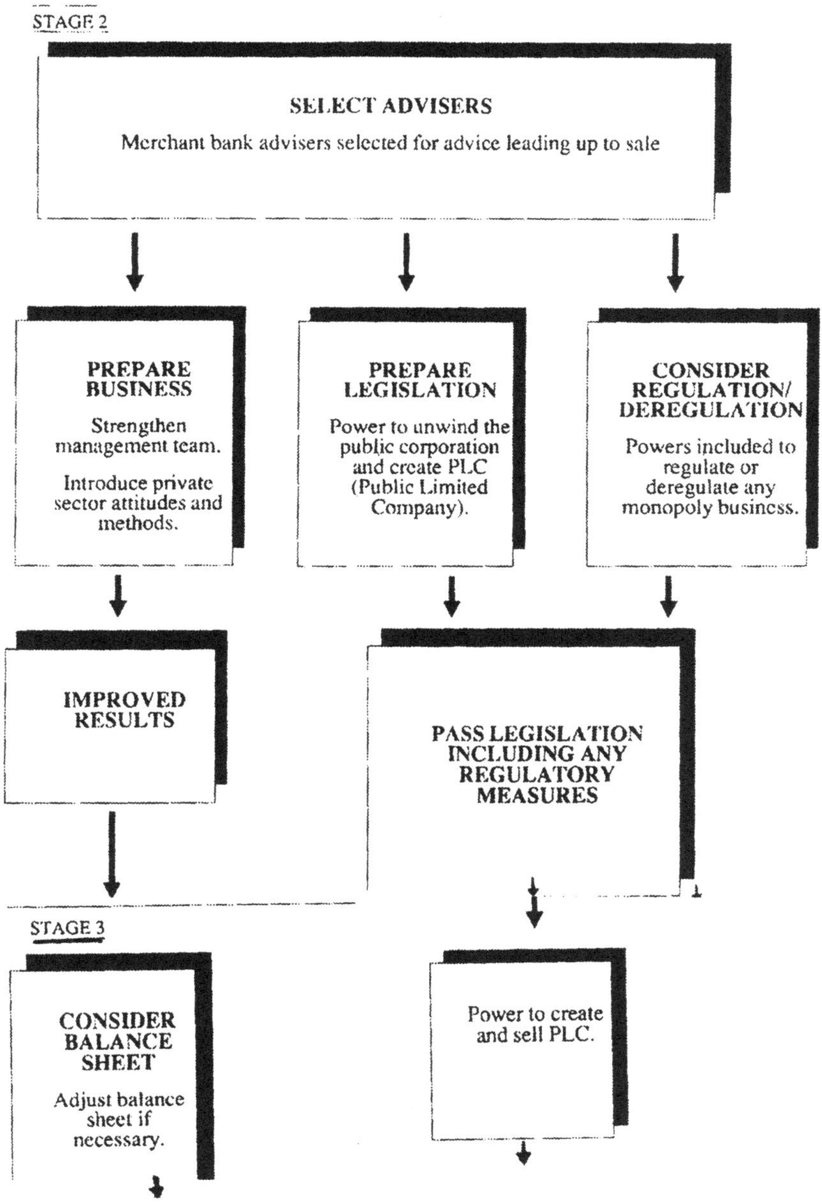
STAGE 2
SELECT ADVISERS
Merchant bank advisers selected for advice leading up to sale
PREPARE BUSINESS
Strengthen management team.
Introduce private sector attitudes and methods.
PREPARE LEGISLATION
Power to unwind the public corporation and create PLC (Public Limited Company).
CONSIDER REGULATION/ DEREGULATION
Powers included to regulate or deregulate any monopoly business.
IMPROVED RESULTS
PASS LEGISLATION INCLUDING ANY REGULATORY MEASURES
STAGE 3
CONSIDER BALANCE SHEET
Adjust balance sheet if necessary.
Power to create and sell PLC.

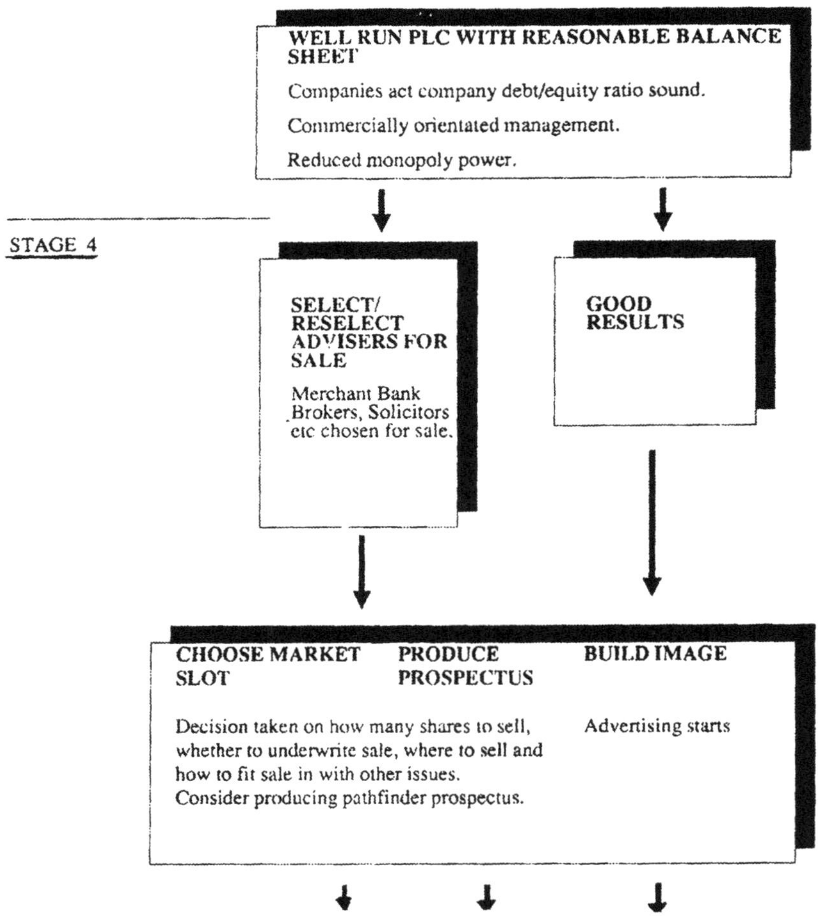
WELL RUN PLC WITH REASONABLE BALANCE SHEET
Companies act company debt/equity ratio sound.
Commercially orientated management.
Reduced monopoly power.
STAGE 4
SELECT/ RESELECT ADVISERS FOR SALE
Merchant Bank Brokers, Solicitors etc chosen for sale.
GOOD RESULTS
CHOOSE MARKET SLOT
PRODUCE PROSPECTUS
BUILD IMAGE
Decision taken on how many shares to sell, whether to underwrite sale, where to sell and how to fit sale in with other issues.
Consider producing pathfinder prospectus.
Advertising starts

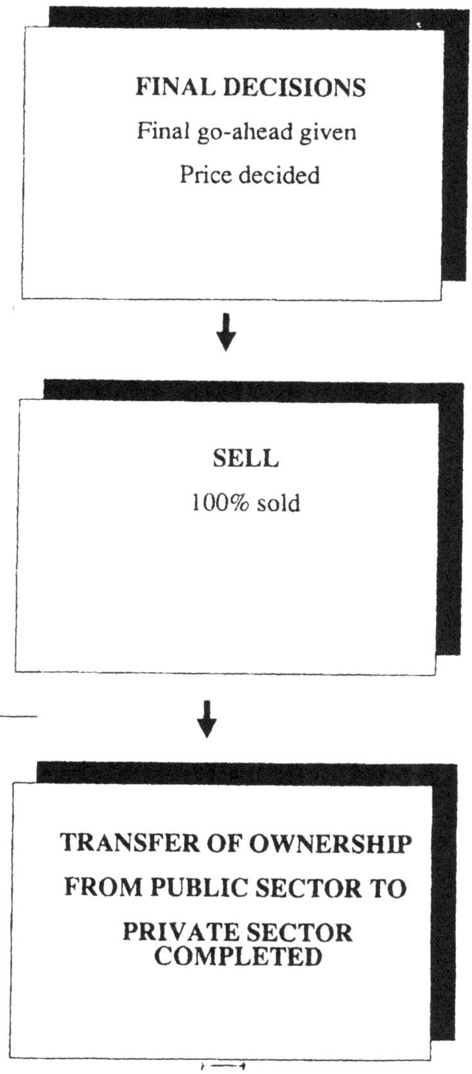
FINAL DECISIONS
Final go-ahead given
Price decided
SELL
100% sold
TRANSFER OF OWNERSHIP
FROM PUBLIC SECTOR TO
PRIVATE SECTOR
COMPLETED

PART III

A LOOK AT INTERNATIONAL ACCOUNTING STANDARDS AND THE PROBLEMS OF PRIVATIZATION IN TRANSITIONAL ECONOMICS

RUSSIA IN SEARCH OF ACCOUNTING PRINCIPLES

Joëlle Le Vourc'h

INTRODUCTION

Accounting is often called the language of business. As soon as a person, an entity, or a country is willing to develop business, it must develop its accounting according to the business needs. Therefore, the accounting system depends on the business environment (political, economic, and legal), which is the user of financial information, and on the types of decisions that are being made, the way the decisions are being made, and so on. This explains why accounting systems differ from one country to another, just as language differs from one country to another, and why an accounting system cannot be changed overnight or simply through passing a law. The development of accounting through the centuries has been linked with the development of the national culture. Hofstede's study *Cultural Differences in Management* is easily applied to accounting. The different variables shaping accounting development are

Advances in International Accounting, Supplement 1, pages 149-157.

ISBN: 0-7623-0461-8

not discussed here but should be kept in mind to understand better the pace of reform in Russia. Therefore, the first reason for accounting reform in any country is change in the national business environment.

This paper examines the evolution of accounting in Russia, analyzes this evolution, and, based on this, concludes with a discussion of the general difficulties faced in the development of accounting.

EVOLUTION OF ACCOUNTING IN RUSSIA

Before 1987

Until the Russian Revolution in 1917, the development of accounting in Russia was quite similar to its development in other European countries. Some accounting books published in the 1910s show that in some cases, Russian accounting was probably ahead of that in other countries.

Accounting was an important item in Lenin's agenda. He believed that the development of accounting was a way for the workers to get more information on the company they were working for. His basic ideas were adopted in the Basic Regulations on State Bookkeeping and Reporting (1920). They included the following:

1. *Openness*. There is no space for commercial secrets; all registers must be accessible for everyone.
2. *Mass character*. All of the adult population of the country must participate in the process of accounting.
3. *Responsibility*. Not only values themselves and the process of creating and circulating them, but also the activities of executives responsible for them, must be under control.
4. *Simplicity*. Accounting must be clear to every literate person (Enthoven, Sokolov, and Petrachkov).

Very quickly, especially under Lenin's successor, Stalin, accounting became a tool for reporting on the followup of the GOSPLAN. During the period of New Economic Policy (NEP), there were serious discussions on whether planning was to be directed by market forces or by the will of the planners: the latter approach prevailed (Radebaugh, Rahman, and Krylova). Therefore, the Soviet accounting system developed mainly for the purpose of providing the statistical information necessary to control the economy. It has been an instrument for central planning.

Progressively, the main objective of accounting became the fulfillment of the plans. The Soviet system continued to be based on double entry, but a number of other features were introduced. As in a number of European countries, the Soviet accounting system was based on a mandatory chart of accounts and very standardized accounting rules and regulations.

In the 1930s, accountants were considered as "bourgeois," and those who were accused of bringing harm to the national economy were physically eliminated. The role and specific duties of the chief accountant were defined by the law. The chief accountant became the person in charge of financial discipline and of the enforcing the strict application of accounting rules and inspection. Thus, for decades, the accounting profession was not well regarded and accounting was mainly performed by women.

During Perestroika

Accounting for Enterprises

In 1987, the Union of Soviet Socialist Republics began to move toward a market economy. Laws and regulations were liberalized to attract foreign investments, especially through East-West joint ventures. It quickly appeared, however, that the accounting and reporting system, oriented as it was toward providing statistical information, was not adapted to joint ventures. In June 1989, a conference was organized jointly by the United Nations for Transnational Corporations (UNCTC) and the Soviet Chamber of Commerce and Industry with the participation of the Ministry of Finance and the high-ranking Russian academics. One of the resolutions of the conference was to create a task force on accounting for joint ventures. This task force was cochaired by the UNCTC representative and by the representative of the Supreme Soviet (the head of the budget commission). The task force worked on the revision of the chart of accounts, which was supposed to be applied only to joint ventures. This work was finalized at the end of 1991. It was then decided to apply this revised chart of accounts to all enterprises (except financial institutions), not only to joint ventures.

The revised chart of accounts was approved by the USSR in November 1991 (just a few weeks before its dissolution); it was approved by Russia in December 1991. This chart of accounts introduced a number of changes but was not sufficient to bring Russian accounting in line with international standards. In addition, it was not applicable to financial institutions. Due partly to the unclear situation in Russia during the breakup of the USSR, the revised chart of accounts was not generally implemented.

Accounting in the Banking Sector

In July 1991, President Gorbatchev applied for USSR membership in the International Monetary Fund (IMF) and the World Bank. Due to the fact that membership generally takes time to be finalized and that quick actions were needed, the World Bank's Board decided to allocate out of annual income a fund of U.S.$30 million for immediate technical cooperation. This fund was used in different areas, including the development of "bank accounting" (less than 1%). An International Advisory Board (IAB), cochaired by the Central Bank of Russia and the World Bank, was created in January 1992 (after the breakup of the USSR). In addition to the cochairs, the members of this Advisory Board were: (1) on the Soviet side—the Ministry of Finance, the committee on banking in the Supreme Soviet of the Russian Parliament, and a few commercial banks, a few academics; and (2) on the foreign side—the UNCTC, the IMF, the European Union (EU), the Organization of Economic Cooperation and Development (OECD), the European Bank for Reconstruction and Development (EBRD), and the so-called Big Six audit firms, each representing one industrialized country. The objective of the Board was to coordinate the reform on accounting for financial institutions over two phases.

Phase 1 was to begin immediately and included the following steps:

- Develop, based on the Soviet chart of accounts for banks, financial statements in line with international standards, called broadly adjusted financial statements (BAFS);
- Write detailed instructions on how to prepare the BAFS;
- Test the instructions with about 10 to 15 banks;
- Make the necessary amendments; and
- Generalize the amended instructions.

Phase 2 was also to be started immediately, but its objectives were medium-term. This phase included two steps:

- Develop a new chart of accounts and new financial statements; and
- Implement them.

The European Commission agreed to cofinance the project with the World Bank.

The first draft of the BAFS was prepared and discussed by the Board in May 1992. It was tested in 10 banks and due to be implemented in September 1992. A second meeting took place in November 1992, when the first draft of a revised chart of accounts was distributed, but discussion concentrated mainly on the implementation of the BAFS. Changes took place in the Central Bank of Russia soon afterward, and the BAFS and their instructions were signed and made mandatory only in July 1993.

At the end of December 1992, the World Bank Fund closed, and the European Commission took over the accounting project for the banking sector.

Since the Breakup of the USSR

In July 1992, the former task force on the reform of accounting for enterprises was replaced by an International Advisory Board (different from the one on bank accounting). The board was chaired by the representative of the Committee on Budget and Taxes of the Supreme Soviet of the Russian Parliament. The members included representatives of the Ministry of Finance, the OECD, the European Commission, the World Bank, the International Federation of Accountants, and the International Accounting Standards Committee. Their objectives included the following undertakings:

- Further improvements in the chart of accounts for enterprises and to such standards as were relevant;
- Formats for balance sheets, profit and loss accounts, notes to the accounts, and the development of cash flow statements;
- Accounting law (including general accounting principles);
- Current draft auditing law; and
- Future standard-setting processes.

The European Union agreed to finance the technical assistance provided by the foreign experts. At the end of 1992, everything was in place to further develop the accounting reform and bring Russian accounting into line with international standards.

ANALYSIS OF THE RECENT EVOLUTION

A comparison of what was achieved before 1992 with the current position provides disappointing results. However, it would be unfair to say that nothing has been done since 1992. In addition to the two projects financed by the European Union, through Technical Assistance for the Commonwealth of Independent States, many other projects have been financed by different donors. If we compare what was accomplished with minimum funds between 1989 and 1993 to what has been achieved since 1993 despite greater funding, the result may be surprising.

This following sections analyze the reasons for such slow progress. This analysis may be controversial and may even be considered exaggerated, but it is my belief that the slowdown in progress was caused by the factors discussed below.

Political Environment

During 1993, relations between the Russian government and the Supreme Soviet of the Russian Federation on the one side, and the central bank, government, and Supreme Soviet on the other side were quite difficult. Disagreements arose on any decision taken by any body, even decisions about accounting and auditing regulations. It seems that each body (Duma, Ministry of Finance, Central Bank) worked separately with one (or more) multilateral or bilateral donors but without coordination. For instance, when the auditing law was approved by the Duma, it was vetoed by the President's office, and then an auditing regulation, quite different in substance, was issued by the Ministry of Finance.

Economic Environment

The development of privatization, foreign investments, and multilateral and bilateral technical assistance created an enormous market for the major consulting and auditing firms. These firms expanded rapidly in Russia, charging fees that were enormous in comparison to what Russian firms normally charged and what Russian companies were accustomed to paying. Russians thus discovered that they could make a great deal of money from this type of activity. (Incidentally, accounting became more and more a man's job!) Russian experts and academics thought that they could do at least as well as the foreign experts on projects financed by multilateral or/and bilateral donors, especially given their native understanding of the country and the language. But this was probably true only for the small number of Russians who have been exposed to foreign systems.

Due to the political environment and the uncertainty about the future, many intellectuals tried to make as much money as possible, preferably being paid abroad. It seems that they were more interested in their own wealth than in the development of the country. This is easily understandable considering the difficulties of day-to-day life in Russia.

Role of the Foreign Experts

The international consulting firms invested a great deal to develop their business in Russia. Due to the cost of implementation in Russia and probably to the need to have a good return on investment, they are more focused on profit making than on the development of the country. Most of these firms have hired young Russians, newly graduated from the top universities and institutes. Nevertheless, these firms, even when part of a project on the reform of accounting and auditing, did not contribute to the country's development, and in some cases, they may have contributed to slowing down the development process.

In addition, most of the foreign experts (individuals or members of firms) are experts on their own national accounting systems and on international accounting standards, but very few have experience in different national systems or are able to advise on the development and implementation of an accounting system based on the actual needs of the country and on the accounting culture of the country.

It seems also that accounting regulation opens up a market for accounting software, books, training, and so on. The Russian market is so huge (e.g., the country has about two million accountants) that the by-products of accounting reforms have inevitably had an important impact. Therefore, bilateral donors are often interested in the adoption of a system similar to their own. This would, of course, provide a competitive advantage for their own national products. This could explain why most of the attempts to coordinate the reforms did not work as well as expected.

A number of parallel projects were undertaken. There was much confusion, and three years later it is difficult to achieve an overall assessment of the situation: what the status of accounting for enterprises and in the banking sector is; who the players are; what the objectives are; what really has been implemented; and so forth.

Role of the Multilateral Donors

As mentioned previously, there was insufficient coordination to avoid overlapping or maintain consistency between different projects. This could be explained as follows:

- For most multilateral organizations, accounting is not considered a priority in the macroeconomics of a country. Too often, economists say something like, "Why not take the German system, translate it into Russian, and implement it in Russia as it has been done in Eastern Germany?" Accounting is too often considered a mere technique, capable of being changed overnight.
- The Russian authorities did not want to borrow funds from the Financial Institutions for Technical Assistance, especially when so many donors (multilateral, bilateral, and even private) were offering grants. But the funds available through individual grants are smaller and, therefore, need much more coordination.
- The Advisory Boards (accounting for enterprises and accounting for banks) created in 1992 could not completely play their coordinating role because they were chaired by different Russian authorities (either the Duma or the Central Bank of Russia) and were not fully recognized by the Ministry of Finance (which was developing yet another project with another bilateral donor).

CONDITIONS FOR ACCOUNTING DEVELOPMENT

The situation in Russia can in different ways seem similar to the situation in a developed country, a developing one, or another country in transition. In the case of Russia, the major difference is probably the number of players involved (on both the Russian side and the international side).

In conclusion, the following factors are necessary to the development and implementation of an accounting reform.

1. A commitment by the highest decision-making level in the country;
2. A standard-setting body with the authority to coordinate the reform;
3. A deep understanding by the standard-setting body of the priorities for the country;
4. A limit to the number of decision makers;
5. The use of foreign experts as advisers, not decision makers;
6. The design of implementation at the time of design of the reform; and
7. Recognition of the difference between what the country needs to have and what would be nice to have, and a focus on meeting the needs.

REFERENCES

Enthoven, Sokolov, and Petrachkov. 1992.
Hofstede, G. 1980. *Cultural Differences in Management.*
Radebaugh, Rahman, and Krylova. 1992.
Union of Soviet Socialist Republics. 1920. *Basic Regulations on State Bookkeeping and Reporting.*

PROBLEMS AND RECENT PROGRESS IN ACCOUNTING REFORM IN RUSSIA

Victoria Krivogorsky and John W. Eichenseher

THE CURRENT ECONOMIC ENVIRONMENT

In every society, accounting provides a service function. It must respond to the constantly changing needs of a society and reflect that society's legal, political, and economic conditions. Current changes in the generation and use of accounting information in Russia must be viewed in the context of the ongoing radical transformation of the Russian economy. This transformation has stressed the role of private (privatized) enterprises since 1991, but while ultimate success in transforming the Russian economy may rest primarily on the economic behavior of private entities, the government still has a role to play in establishing the microeconomic conditions (infrastructure) to support microeconomic adaptation. Thus, our study of current changes in Russian accounting must consider changes in the use of accounting information at the enterprise level, as well as changes in the accounting "rules" promulgated by the

Advances in International Accounting, Supplement 1, pages 159-177.

ISBN: 0-7623-0461-8

state. Both types of change must be positioned within a broad understanding of the major alterations in the Russian economy in recent years.

The current state of the Russian economy is both heavily influenced by developments in the command economy over the past 75 years and highly heterogeneous. Twentieth-century history has left Russia in a relatively unique economic condition. Technologically, its economy is quite unbalanced, containing "preindustrial," "industrial," and "postindustrial" elements to an extent not experienced in the West. Huge differences in production technologies combine with fundamentally autarkic tendencies to create perceptions of instability in the current Russian economy.

As the Russian economy enters a period of forced rapid transformation, it is naturally plagued by the forces of inertia. Organizationally speaking, it remains an amalgam of state capitalist, degenerating socialist, and clearly extralegal forms. Property rights are weakly and ambiguously delineated. And, perhaps most important, these various forms of economic organization tend to commingle in the activities of individual economic agents. Unlike the classical world of a mixed economy, no clear division between "modern" rational economic agents and "traditional" agents is possible. The informal relationships so important in a "traditional" society remain important to the managers of even the most organizationally advanced (market-oriented) enterprises in Russia today.

The natural behavioral (and organizational) inertia that constrains economic transformation in any society is reinforced by Russia's totalitarian bureaucratic tradition. There remains a tendency for managers to view markets not as objective reality but as bureaucratic forms that can be manipulated to achieve preset goals. The hierarchical totalitarian tradition further subordinates individual decision makers to a "system," making it very difficult to analyze economic behavior along the lines of traditional Western economic paradigms.

Finally, to fully understand the current state of the Russian economy, one must step outside the bounds of typical Western analysis. Economic analysis in the West focuses on the description and management of basically stable systems of economic relations. In contrast, it is necessary to understand that the Russian economy currently operates in a "crisis" state, that is, under conditions of extreme uncertainty. This condition alters the "rational" calculus of various economic actors. Among other effects, it makes transaction costs much more salient in a wide variety of economic decisions and lends a sense of urgency to information system (accounting) reforms.

The remainder of this chapter consists of four sections. The next section expands on the historical condition of the Russian economy, stressing the nature of the accounting system that evolved to service this economy. The following section, drawing heavily on recent survey results, describes the changes in the use of accounting information evident today within the Russian economy. The third section analyzes the various changes in Russian (and former Soviet) accounting law in recent years. The final section includes a brief summary and conclusion.

THE HISTORICAL CONTEXT: ACCOUNTING IN THE COMMAND ECONOMY

The Soviet system of central economic planning, with an emphasis on heavy industry and collectivized agriculture, had a profound influence on the evolution of Russian accounting. Until 1987, state-owned enterprise was the only legal form of business organization. Central planning stressed output targets (in physical and monetary units), which were handed down from above and used to evaluate the performance of enterprise managers. Performance in excess of plan targets was rare because it typically resulted only in higher targets in subsequent years. The Soviet central planning system, combined with other social systems, provided meager incentives for individual effort because both monetary rewards for extra effort and employment termination were rare. It became characterized over time by low productivity and employee motivation.

Accounting at the enterprise level within this system was control (as opposed to decision-support) oriented. Individual enterprise accounting systems were designed to provide reliable information on the fulfillment of plan targets, not on the efficient use of economic resources. At higher levels—that is, at Gosplan, the central Soviet planning agency, as well as its branches and counterparts at the Republic level—accounting systems were needed for both control and decision-making purposes. Gosplan, the top management in the Soviet planning system, used the combined output from enterprise-level accounting systems in setting output targets. It was assisted in this endeavor by scholars from major scientific (economic) institutes such as the Soviet Academy of Sciences.

Although accounting information was clearly used in some ultimate fashion in this system for decision-making purposes, the level of decision making encouraged an emphasis on uniformity rather than relevance (as understood in Western terms) in the design of accounting systems. The resulting control-oriented accounting system stressed fulfillment of a multidimensional array of physical targets, one for each product or group of products produced by the enterprise. Access to inputs was also controlled by the plan, and the entire output of the various enterprise accounting systems remained "confidential," not subject to public scrutiny.

The Soviet accounting system, with all of its centralizing and potentially disfunctional attributes, was inherited by the independent Russian state. Key elements of this system include: (1) mechanisms for "operative" control—largely, accountability for physical assets; (2) standard double-entry accounting records for transactions; (3) "statistical" accounting or financial reporting to top enterprise management and higher state organs; and (4) the entire range of planning mechanisms to support the central plan. The dominant role of accounting information in price setting within the old Soviet system should be noted. Lacking market-based (price) indicators for demand, higher-level Soviet officials were dependent on accounting information to establish the prices for individual products.

The Soviet accounting system stressed uniformity in both account structure and reporting format. An exhaustive and detailed list of accounts was provided to cover all sectors of the Soviet economy. Reporting formats (forms) were prespecified for the numerous reports flowing upward from individual enterprises, with standardized terminology and requirements for periodic reporting. In recent years, the number of accounts and reports required of an enterprise has gradually decreased, but the legacy of Soviet uniformity remains within Russian accounting systems.

From a broad historical perspective, the extreme uniformity (with attention to detail) witnessed in the Soviet accounting system has two sources. Clearly, this characteristic was and had to be stressed in an economic system that centralized decision making. But from another point of view, one can see it as the result of Soviet (Russian) preferences for the tradition of Roman (codified) law over that of English common law. In this sense, historical differences between the Soviet and U.S./U.K. accounting systems can be seen as similar to, albeit more extreme than, the differences between American/English and Continental (Western) European accounting models. One of the ironies of the current reform of the Russian economy is the fact that recent advances in information technology might have partially mitigated the obvious "accounting" problems in the old Soviet system; that is, "uniformity" in information in the modern computer age can be refined to accommodate much greater sensitivity to specific conditions in individual economic sectors or enterprises. (Of course, the same changes in information technology can also facilitate greater market efficiency.)

RECENT CHANGES IN THE USE OF ACCOUNTING INFORMATION

The Public Policy Background

This section focuses on accounting changes at the enterprise level in Russia over the past five years. The subsequent section provides extensive detail on changes in accounting "law" over the same time frame. Nonetheless, at this point, we briefly consider the public policy changes that have made microlevel accounting change possible.

Substantial reform in accounting practice began in 1987, when legislation was passeed that allowed for the formation of cooperatives, joint ventures, and joint stock companies within the Soviet economy. At this time, it became obvious that the existing distribution networks were inhibiting horizontal relationships among these new business entities and between them and the existing state-owned enterprises. This realization led to greater contracting flexibility for all enterprises, with the obvious need for greater flexibility in accounting to facilitate decentralization in decision making. Official directives and initiatives in the area of accounting from 1987-1989 focused on reducing the differences between Soviet and Western accounting practices. Work on harmonization of the Soviet accounting system with existing international standards, beginning with a workshop in Moscow in June 1989, stressed the need for revised Soviet practices in the areas of revenue recognition, profit recognition, production cost allocation, asset and liability valuation in general, depreciation methods, and inflation accounting.

Many of these issues were adequately addressed in Instruction Number 74, issued by the Soviet Ministry of Finance in June 1990 (*Bulleten Normativnich* 1992–1995). This instruction, however, was limited in scope to accounting by (foreign) joint ventures, reducing the number and simplifying the content of required financial reports. The Moscow workshop mentioned above was also instrumental in forming an international task force, which included representatives of the United Nations Center for Transnational Corporations (UNCTC), to aid the Ministry of Finance in improving the Soviet accounting system.

Accounting reform initiatives begun in the Soviet era accelerated in Russia upon the dissolution of the USSR. Such reforms were viewed as a vital and integral part of Russia's acceptance into the community of developed market economies. The ability of Russian enterprises to compete on equal terms with foreign competitors became a paramount concern, requiring a regulatory environment roughly equivalent to those in the rest of Europe. In this context, the Fourth Directive of the European Community (EU)—calling for individual enterprise financial statements that provide a "true and fair" view of financial position and changes therein—along with the standards of the International Accounting Standards Committee (IASC) became obvious focal points for accounting reform (harmonization).

Russian accounting must be currently viewed as in transition from a model suitable for a centrally planned economy to one more appropriate for a market-based economy. The various accounting pronouncements of the Russian Ministry of Finance since 1991 are intended to serve this process. They cover a broad range of measurement and reporting issues, including compliance with current tax laws. They tend to be global in application—that is, suitable for all sectors of the economy (except for certain financial institutions and governmental agencies) and all legal forms of business enterprise, although full success in universal applicability has yet to be achieved in many areas.

Changes in Economic and Accounting Behavior

Progress in changing the content and usage of accounting information in Russia has obviously not been uniform over the past five years. Various factors contribute to variations in the acceptance of accounting reform. One can, in general, point to three primary impediments to accounting reform in Russia today. First, full legislation of appropriate new accounting laws is far from complete, given the short period of time that has elapsed since reform began in earnest. Second, time limitations have constrained the reeducation of the millions of preparers of accounting information trained under the old Soviet system. Finally—and probably most important—many potential users of accounting information are simply not yet prepared or willing to utilize the new forms of this information.

To more fully explore the variations in current accounting usage in Russia, we summarize in some detail the findings of a 1994 survey conducted by the Institute of Economic Expertise (IEE) in Moscow (*Voprosy Ekonomiki* 1995). This survey explored the economic behavior (including the use of accounting information systems) of managers of business enterprises. Contrary to initial expectations, it found that the majority of Russian enterprises continued to follow the old (Soviet) patterns of economic behavior. In summary, it divided enterprises into three categories: conservative, active (in changing managerial behavior), and mixed.

Enterprises categorized as conservative in behavior tended to retain old contractual relationships and production patterns. They shied away from market participation and awaited directions from governmental officials. In supporting the importance of this style of behavior, the IEE pointed to the following survey results (among others):

1. A virtual absence of market research in many cases; for example, 20% of enterprises had experienced no change in suppliers or customers since 1992;
2. A similar lack of change in production; for example, 28% of enterprises neither introduced any new products nor altered their product mix during 1993–1994;
3. Very limited sensitivity to market demand; for example, 58% of enterprises continued to price their products solely according to production costs;
4. A strong tendency to maintain existing programs without regard for long-standing inefficiencies; and
5. A similar strong tendency not to analyze factor inputs in terms of value added but to employ factors of production solely on the basis of their availability.

In stark contrast to this "conservative" model of behavior, the IEE also found a substantial number of enterprises that could be labeled active in their response to economic reform measures. These enterprises had comprehensively altered their marketing, financing, and accounting systems to support a new style of management. Survey results that support the importance of such enterprises included (*Statisticheski otchet Rosiiskogo Statisticheckogo Uprayleniya Moscow* 1995):

1. Continuous change in the identity of suppliers and customers, for example, 33% and 39% of enterprises, respectively, had substantially changed their lists of suppliers or customers since 1992. Many of these changes involved a geographical expansion of relationships, including entry into international markets;
2. Substantial change in product mix for existing product lines, observed in 26% of the enterprises surveyed;
3. The introduction of major new products, observed in 46% of enterprises, 17% of which now claim the new products to be primary sources of revenue;
4. Pricing strategies based on "what the market will bear" (28% of enterprises) or the direct sale of output in auction markets (3% of enterprises);
5. Willingness expressed to eliminate inefficient (unprofitable) product lines and production departments and to shift existing capital into new investment projects;
6. Adoption of new forms of cost analysis and allocation, for example, activity-based costing, with changes in employee compensation to provide incentives for productivity; and
7. Major changes in enterprise organizational structure, including decentralization of existing units and the creation of new subsidiaries (28% of enterprises).

Enterprises characterized as active have significantly limited the importance of informal relationships among enterprise managers (directors). Such relationships had often helped enterprises avoid bankruptcy during the unstable early days of independence and reform. But given the growth of market relationships and high levels of nonpayment (default) by many former customers, especially state-owned enterprises, reliance on these relationships as a focal point for business transactions has often become disfunctional. Newly found competition among many formerly noncompeting enterprises has also limited the importance of informal relationships. (The recent creation of large corporations—associations of several formerly independent enterprises—is also partially driven by the desire to restrain competition in domestic markets.)

The third mixed category of behavior is reserved for enterprises somewhere between these two categorizations. These enterprises have begun to alter their behavior in response to economic reform but in relatively insignificant ways. For example, 47% of surveyed enterprises had made only minor changes to their set of suppliers, while 41% had made minor changes to their customer base. Of surveyed enterprises, 10% indicated a mixed approach to product pricing, including old cost-based approaches as well as newer demand-based approaches.

In short, enterprises characterized as conservative or mixed have shown preferences for the traditional (Soviet) management style and a reluctance to undertake major changes in their operations. This is, of course, an oversimplification. In some sense, all Russian enterprises have been mixed in their response to economic reform. It is important in this context to avoid normative connotations to these labels. A given enterprise's disposition toward reform depends largely on objective conditions: its size, type of ownership, ability to compete in export markets, former dependence on other Soviet republics, the degree of current government intervention in its economic sector, and so on. On the other hand, of course, many of these "objective" conditions also have a "subjective" element; that is, they are subject to change based on management attitude.

When one explores the "subjective" side of change in enterprise behavior, several factors that condition management's attitude toward change become salient. First, in a general sense, many enterprises—particularly those without domestic competition and those involved in the export of raw materials—have little need for reform of their management policies and accounting systems. Of the respondents to the IEE survey, 38% indicated satisfaction with their current (historical) operations, seeing little reason for change since their ongoing product line was quite saleable.

Second—and probably more important—one cannot ignore the risks faced by enterprise managers in economic and accounting reform. Some of these risks are sector-specific; for example, enterprises in high-tech industries are vulnerable to foreign competition and are likely to cling to traditional economic behavior, if possible, to avoid bankruptcy. This type of strategy is possible because of the great uncertainty facing Russian enterprises. In short, they all face a magnitude of (domestic) political risk largely incomprehensible in Western economies. Future government policies have been quite difficult to predict in recent years.

This makes "conservative" behavior in enterprise management quite "rational" in many situations, not just the product of inadequate training for managers (and accountants). Particularly in the area of accounting systems, it can be argued that change has been slow because managers are unwilling to give up the potential for disguising taxable income inherent in the traditional accounting systems.

NEW ACCOUNTING STANDARDS IN INDEPENDENT RUSSIA: AN OVERVIEW

A new comprehensive umbrella for accounting standards in Russia was provided by the *Uchetnaya Politica Predpriyatiya* (UPP), Accounting Policies for Enterprises (*Ekonomika i Zhizn* 1995). This legislation is designed to be supplemented by subsequent laws and governmental instructions and to be applicable to all types of business enterprises. It is intended to further the primary goals in economic reform—enhanced enterprise profitability, financial independence, and cost minimization, as well as macroeconomic growth in general. Its scope goes beyond accounting standards per se to include broader issues such as the organization of accounting departments within enterprises, internal control policies, and procedures for the selection of accounting policies when alternative approaches are possible.

Recognizing differences in the goals and problems faced by various business enterprises, the UPP provides room for accounting policy alternatives left to management discretion. Unfortunately, despite the "optional" features of this law, there is a noticeable absence of both theoretical and practical guidance today in Russia as to what accounting policies are optimal under what circumstances. Among the issues that should be important to an enterprise in this regard are: (1) legal form (partnership, joint stock company, state-owned enterprise, etc.); (2) industrial sector (trade, light industry, or heavy industry); (3) relative size (in terms of both turnover and employees); (4) potential for payment of income taxes; (5) autonomy in price setting; (6) current state of information technology; (7) existing accounting expertise; and (8) employee compensation contracts.

The UPP does articulate the right of enterprise managers to make various accounting choices. These choices are to be made based on two rudimentary assumptions: (1) that the enterprise is a relevant free-standing economic entity whose assets and liabilities need to be separated from those of its owners and other units (an entity assumption), and (2) that the enterprise will continue to exist for the foreseeable future (a going concern assumption). The latter of these two assumptions may often prove problematical, as official reports indicate that one-third of Russian manufacturing firms are on the verge of bankruptcy.

Analysis of new accounting rules under the rubric of the UPP shows a strong focus on income tax reporting. With only minimal adjustments, the enterprise's accounting records are to be used in determinating taxable income. This, of course, creates tensions between potentially conflicting objectives in accounting and seems at variance with the expressed desire to bring Russian accounting closer in line with Western practices. (One must recognize variations in "Western" practice in this regard; for example, traditional German financial reporting has similar tax-oriented features.) The priority given to income tax reporting tends to reinforce the notion of accounting as simply an exercise in compliance with very specific, and often arbitrary, externally imposed rules and inhibits conformity with current internationally accepted (IASC) accounting standards.

The following subsections look in some detail at the current state of Russian accounting rules in various areas (technical accounting topics).

Balance Sheet Format

Balance sheets or statements of financial position, both for individual enterprises and on a consolidated basis when one enterprise controls another, represent a key element of Russian financial reporting. The Ministry of Finance bears primary responsibility for specifying their form and content.

The form of the traditional Soviet balance sheet differed from that of Western models primarily in the presentation of owners' equity and the related results from recent operations. Current losses appeared in the asset section of the balance sheet, and current (net) profits appeared as liabilities. This treatment reflected Soviet ideology. The 1917 revolution abolished the notion of private property and, hence, the concept of (private) owners' equity. Profits or losses came to represent amounts to be transmitted to or reimbursed by higher public authorities. In the process, interest in their "objective" valuation was lost. The focal point for decision making became revenues, not profits. The accounting system, however imprecisely, measured expenses; then prices (revenues) had to be set to cover these expenses plus required profit. "Profit" in this context included many elements that in the West might be considered expenses, including certain payments to employees and governmental units.

New pronouncements of the Russian Ministry of Finance—Instruction Number 48 of June 1993 and Letter Number 91 of July 1994 (*Bulleten Normativnich* 1992–1995)—strive to change the presentation of operating results in enterprise financial statements. The current plan of accounts calls for "capital and reserves" to replace "funds and reserves." The equivalent of retained earnings should now be shown in the balance sheets of individual enterprises, capturing cumulative undistributed profits (and losses).

Valuation Principles

Asset valuation was not a contentious issue in Soviet accounting. Historical costing, with administratively set and quite stable prices, was the valuation norm. Western notions of conservatism in valuation—that is, the use of the lower of historical cost or market value—were not viewed as relevant because investors (the state) and creditors were virtually guaranteed predetermined payments. The price liberalization that began in Russia in 1992 obviously changed all of this. Not only did prices begin to change in response to market demand, but high levels of inflation served to render old historical costs quite irrelevant. The government, therefore, began as early as 1992 to allow for asset revaluation procedures, although these have yet to be followed by many Russian enterprises.

Accelerated privatization (and continued inflation) made the need for asset revaluation obvious. Law Number 967, issued in August 1994 and effective as of January 1, 1995 (*Ekonomika i Zhizn* 1995), addressed this need by calling for comprehensive adjustments in asset values. In practice, this has most commonly been implemented in a direct (current cost) form. Market values for assets as of January 1, 1995, replaced old historical costs. The procedure has not been costless. The law requires verification of new asset values in the form of price certification by suppliers, substantial price information from wholesale and retail trade organizations, or appraisal certificates from officially recognized experts.

Inventory Verification and Valuation

Given its control orientation at the enterprise level, the Soviet accounting system stressed accountability for inventories. Year-end discrepancies in inventories were handled in a rather detailed fashion. Both surpluses and deficiencies discovered in the audit process were typically traced to responsible parties. Write-downs due to inventory "shrinkage" beyond predetermined norms frequently led to the recording of receivables due from managers responsible for inventory maintenance. Little has changed in this area in recent years. Regulations of the Russian Ministry of Finance still call for annual inventory observation, with more frequent observation left to management discretion.

Current norms in inventory valuation call for the use of full historical cost without allowances for reductions in market value. Average cost has become the norm for both financial and tax accounting given recent changes in input prices. A law issued in 1994, The Regulation on Accounting and Reporting in the Russian Federation (*Ekonomika i Zhizn* 1995), now permits the use of LIFO and FIFO flow assumptions, but their use does not appear common so far.

The detailed attention to inventories in Russian (Soviet) accounting is reflected in the recognition of many low-value "working assets," that is, items such as special workplace clothing and incidental office equipment, which would be immediately expensed under standard Western accounting practices.

Fixed Assets and Depreciation

Under Soviet accounting rules, fixed assets were defined and originally valued in a manner quite similar to Western practices. Historical costs related to the creation of long-term productive investments, including those for leasehold improvements and identifiable intangibles, were capitalized and subsequently amortized.

Soviet accounting differed from Western practices in the linkage created between accumulated depreciation (amortization) and cash fund creation. Conceptually, depreciation was viewed as not only an expense but also the amount of funds that needed to be set aside to repair or replace the existing asset base. Therefore, depreciation in the Soviet world was clearly not a "source of funds," as is often claimed in Western enterprises. Segregated investment funds, frequently beyond the control of enterprise managers, were required in tandem with accumulated depreciation. The requirement for such funds was actually relaxed for foreign joint ventures as early as 1990. For domestic enterprises, it was retained until 1995, at which time new legislation—consistent with the notion of greater enterprise autonomy—eliminated this requirement, in general, for Russian enterprises.

Depreciation rates and methods remain complex and potentially troublesome in Russian accounting. Not unlike in the West, a wide range of useful lives is used for fixed and intangible assets, frequently depending on an enterprise's industry. The use of accelerated depreciation methods—up to double declining-balance—is also seen in certain circumstances. However, the use of these accelerated methods is often limited to only a portion of the fixed asset base—those assets employed in an "active" manner, for example, to create new product lines, to produce products for export, or to upgrade the technology used in producing standard products.

The use of accelerated depreciation methods can become troublesome for an enterprise, given certain current uses of accounting information. If the enterprise continues to price its output in a cost-plus manner, additional depreciation can trigger price increases that put the enterprise at a comparative disadvantage. Also, to the extent that depreciation charges have been (and perhaps continue to be) linked to the need for the creation of special investment funds, extra (accelerated) depreciation has real cash outflow implications for the enterprise. (It should be noted in this regard that amounts not properly set aside for fixed asset replacement have been viewed as elements of taxable income.)

Recent changes in Russian accounting rules have yet to fully address problems associated with depreciation methods, although inflation-adjusted depreciation is now permitted in many cases.

Cost Allocation Procedures

Soviet accounting procedures led to an extreme form of "full" (as opposed to "variable") costing. The traditional cost accounting system was used to set prices that fully covered all enterprise costs. In this context, there was little need for many of the cost distinctions prevalent in Western capitalist countries—for example, differences between actual and standard costs, fixed and variable overhead costs, and even production and administrative and marketing costs. The use of differential cost analysis was confined to scientific institutes.

Market-based economic reform with its accompanying decentralization in decision making has radically changed enterprise managers' need (demand) for more differentiated cost analysis. Legal changes in 1995 now also permit different costing procedures for product pricing and performance evaluation. One now sees the use of two types of cost accounting systems in Russia: the traditional system described above and a much more articulated (typically direct) costing system made acceptable under 1995 law. As described in some detail in the section on recent changes in the use of accounting information, the former (traditional) system is still dominant in many smaller enterprises. Under the more articulated (Western-style) cost accounting system, distinctions can now be drawn between direct and indirect costs and product and period costs.

One of the first users of a more articulated, Western-style costing system was the largest truck producer in the former Soviet Union, KamA3, which has decentralized decision making to the point where individual plant managers are responsible for planning and controlling operations. The company has, however, encountered several problems in attempting to implement their new cost accounting system fully. In particular, directives from the Russian Ministry of Finance call into question the income tax deductibility of amounts now accumulated in several distinct accounts. For example, overhead costs related to employee retirement and health benefits are largely disallowed or severely limited as expenses in the calculation of taxable income. Also, an October 1993 pronouncement on "Individual Expenses Included in the Cost of Production" (*Bulleten Normativnich* 1992–1995) allows for quite limited tax deductions for employee training costs (not to exceed 2% of compensation), business entertainment (0.02% of sales revenue), advertising (0.5% of sales revenue), and business travel expenses in general. Obvious conflicts arise between the use of accounting information for internal decision making and its use by taxing authorities. To the extent that taxing authorities have access to an enterprise's cost accounting system, that system may logically be suboptimally designed for strictly internal decision making.

Revenue Realization

Revenue and associated profit recognition were more constrained in Soviet accounting practice than in standard Western practice. When goods were shipped to buyers, their cost was merely recorded in a suspense (Dispatched Goods) account. Selling prices were recorded in revenue accounts only when payment was received. This procedure delayed the recognition of revenue beyond the "point of sale" used in Western practices and eliminated the recording of accounts receivable in enterprise balance sheets.

This approach to revenue recognition was modified for foreign joint ventures in 1990 to allow them to record revenues upon shipment of products and invoices to customers, although they may still defer recognition until the enterprise or a bank receives payment from the customer. The 1990 reform (Instruction Number 74; *Bulleten Normativnich* 1992–1995) allowed foreign joint ventures, even those operating in domestic markets, to use a form of accounting unavailable to purely domestic enterprises. Accompanying any change in the timing of revenue recognition, the joint ventures also had to begin accounting for the possibility of uncollectible receivables. Practices in this area have largely followed Western examples.

The Structure of Enterprise Equity

The evolution of accounting for enterprise equity (net assets) as Russian enterprises move away from standard Soviet fund accounting reflects elements quite similar to those seen in the West and elements that remain uniquely Russian. Similar to accounting procedures in several Western European countries (for example, Germany and France), Russian enterprises now show statutory reserves of up to 25% of contributed capital in their balance sheets. These reserves are designed to provide some security for creditors and are generally accumulated out of pretax profits and carried over from year to year. Their magnitude appears to be based on agreements internal to the enterprise, not dependent on government regulations.

After-tax (and statutory reserve) profit is typically allocated to two types of equity accounts, accumulation funds and consumption funds. The accumulation funds are analogous to appropriated retained earnings in the U.S./U.K. tradition. They are to be used to transform assets within the enterprise—for example, to support future research and development or tangible asset acquisition. Consumption funds are designated for "welfare" usage, such as employee bonuses or various social and cultural activities.

New accounting rules have technically eliminated the need for the dual distinction between accumulation and consumption funds, allowing enterprise managers to apply the total after-tax undistributed profits to just one account, Profit to Be Utilized for Various Purposes. This approach is currently being used by many, if not most, small and medium-size enterprises, which often have little profit to allocate. Government officials, however, continue to urge the use of separate accumulation and consumption funds for large joint stock companies, presumably to discourage the overuse of after-tax profits for "welfare" purposes. In practice, the use of a single or dual fund approach should lead to virtually the same result as long as enterprises and their managers retain full discretion in the overall allocation of after-tax profits.

It should be noted that the term retained earnings, a key element in Western accounting, is not currently used in Russia. Distributions to shareholders are common, but profits not so distributed must be built into the fund structure described earlier. Although in some sense, fund balances carried over can indirectly support future distributions to shareholders, an ideological bias against private property remains visible. Earnings not immediately withdrawn by shareholders appear to go into a public or semipublic domain and are not to be used for private (individual shareholder) consumption in the future.

Some features of these procedures for allocating income to enterprise equity accounts can create problems for Russian enterprises in the context of income taxation. Basically, any productive expenditure that is viewed as coming from after-tax profits (e.g., research and development) has the potential for creating future expenses that are not deductible for tax purposes. This does seem to be a problem because Russian taxing authorities create income tax accounting rules designed to maximize governmental revenues. (It also can create distortions in pricing if the enterprise still sets prices according to tax-based cost accounting allocations.)

A similar problem has emerged in the context of interest expense deductibility for tax purposes. Current income tax rules limit deductible interest expense to interest costs within three percentage points of rates quoted by the Central Bank of the Russian Federation. Interest deductibility is further limited to debt used to support "operating" activities. Thus, many Russian enterprises are not able to fully deduct their interest costs for tax purposes.

CONCLUSION

Russian and Western accounting systems have been and still remain quite different, being the products of different social, political, and economic environments. The Russian system builds on the Soviet system, which stressed highly centralized decision making and lower-level control. Rapid change in the Russian economy now brings in its wake the need for rapid accounting change or development. To the extent that economic change tends toward convergence with Western conditions, accounting change should naturally flow in the same direction, although it must be recognized that the West is far from homogeneous in terms of economic and accounting systems.

Analysis of recent changes in accounting rules and the use of accounting systems highlights the partial, at times even cosmetic, nature of accounting reform to date. But even the limited changes accomplished so far have not been easy, requiring substantial expenditures of time and money. This was to be expected. Complete accounting reform in support of full economic reform will take a massive redeployment of human capital—a retraining of literally millions of bookkeepers, accountants, auditors, and users of financial information both inside and outside business enterprises—while the private benefits to be derived from retraining still appear subject to substantial political risk.

The accounting "model" implicit in current accounting rules and practices in Russia is obviously transitional. Not totally unlike Western experience, it lacks a strong theoretical base. Basic contradictions remain in the general use of the same accounting system for management decision making, external investor evaluations, and income taxation. Greater theoretical articulation of the relative importance of these various end uses of the accounting system would foster more efficient accounting reform, perhaps with accounting "subsystems" being developed for different information purposes.

It should be noted in passing that many of the key issues currently faced in Russian accounting, such as human asset and social responsibility accounting, remain contentious in the West. Thus, although in many areas Russian accounting reform may appear primarily as a process of borrowing from the West, in other areas Russian and Western accounting "reformers" should be working in tandem.

The development of a reformed accounting profession in Russia will be a long-term process. Experience in other areas of the world where economic privatization is proceeding rapidly indicates the likely need for the creation of independent professional accounting bodies that can consult with and often guide the work of government agencies such as the Russian Ministry of Finance. Clearly, future accounting research should consider the development of accounting institutions, as well as the substance and use of accounting information, in rapidly transforming economies.

ACKNOWLEDGMENTS

The authors acknowledge the financial support of the Accounting Department of the School of Business of the University of Wisconsin, Madison, in executing the research reported in this paper.

ANNOTATED REFERENCES

This research draws on various Russian language sources for the details of official accounting pronouncements and the current accounting activities of Russian enterprises. The following (annotated) list of references is quite summary in nature. Detailed information on specific reference points for specific issues is available from the authors upon request.

Bulleten Normativnich Actov Ministerstv i Vedomstv Souza S.S.R., nos. 5–10 (1992–1995). This journal provides the text of various official pronouncements, in particular those of the Ministry of Finance.

Voprosy Ekonomiki. nos. 2 and 8 (1995). The results of the Institute of Economic Expertise's survey are contained in these two issues of this journal.

Statisticheski otchet Rosiiskogo Statisticheckogo Upravleniya, Moscow (1995). This annual statistical yearbook provides various statistics descriptive of the Russian economy and was used to supplement the survey results reported in *Voprosy Ekonomiki*, nos. 2 and 8.

Ekonomika i Zhizn, nos. 7–36 (1995). This periodical is used to publish the text of new laws passed by the Russian parliament (Duma).

THE EFFECTS OF APPLYING INTERNATIONAL ACCOUNTING AND AUDITING STANDARDS TO THE ACCOUNTING PROFESSION IN JORDAN

Ziad K. Al-Rai and Naim Dahmash

A HISTORICAL BACKGROUND

At the beginning of the twentieth century, the Jordanian economy was very simple and composed mainly of agricultural business. Accounting practices, therefore, were limited or nonexistent. But when Jordan was established as a nation, commerce and finance became more significant. This created a need for basic accounting techniques, and double-entry bookkeeping was introduced. Many commercial businesses started to apply basic accounting techniques.

Advances in International Accounting, Supplement 1, pages 179-193.

ISBN: 0-7623-0461-8

After the Arab Israeli war in 1948, the West Bank became a protectorate of the Hashemite Kingdom of Jordan. The new link between the West Bank and East Bank created a new structure in the Jordanian society. New ideas were exchanged and the need for more economic development emerged. The Jordanian government took several steps to satisfy the increasing needs of economic modernization and development. It established a state university, made education mandatory until the ninth grade, and created the Central Bank. In 1961, the Jordanian government passed income tax laws, companies laws, and laws regulating the public accounting profession.

The first formal recognition of public accountancy as a profession occurred in 1961, when the government established a Jordanian board of accountancy. The board's main responsibilities are to issue licenses to practice in the public accounting profession and to take disciplinary action against unethical or illegal practices. Since the board's inception,it has issued more than 450 licenses to public accountants.

During the period 1961 to 1990, the accounting profession in Jordan applied generally accepted accounting principles (GAAP) regardless of their origins—that is, whether based on U.S. or U.K. practice. There were not (and still are not) any private or governmental bodies in charge of issuing accounting and auditing standards and regulations. Accountants applied the basic accounting knowledge learned during their university education, in addition to meeting the requirements of Jordanian tax laws and companies law. As a result, the information produced was not comparable across firms or across industries. This accounting information did not help investors interested in making efficient investment decisions.

During the 1980s and early 1990s, the need for an efficient set of accounting and auditing standards became urgent for the following reasons:

1. The creation of the Amman Financial Market (AFM) in 1978 led to increased demand for useful financial information, which would help investors in making informed investment decisions.
2. The number of Jordanian firms increased significantly. The total capital of public shareholding companies grew by 151.41% from 1984 to 1994 (see Table 1).
3. The level of international debt led to economic policies that would attract foreign investments, encourage domestic private investments, and expand international exports.
4. The need for political stability, which depends among other factors on economic stability, became increasingly evident.

Table 1. Number of Companies and Their Total Capital for Different Sectors in Jordan, 1984–1994

	Number of Compaines		Total Capital		
Sector	1984	1994	1984	1994	Percentage
Banks and financial companies	23	18	272,972,678	743,365,244	172.32
Insurance companies	22	17	20,085,816	39,377,799	96.05
Service companies	32	36	76,648,130	156,857,716	104.65
Industrial companies	52	77	350,126,052	880,267,653	151.41

In 1985, a law was passed allowing the establishment of a 12-member council responsible for licensing new members, administering disciplinary action against accountants, and administering a written exam as one of the requirements for practicing accounting in Jordan. In 1987, the government permitted accountants in Jordan to establish a society of public accountants. Before 1988, the accounting profession in Jordan was not developed or efficient enough to achieve the goals of accounting. This meant that accountants did not supply reliable or relevant financial information for those who needed to make decisions within the Jordanian economy.

In 1988, as a result of the devaluation of the Jordanian dinar, companies did not know which accounting standards to follow in treating the foreign exchange losses that resulted from the devaluation. The need for consistent accounting standards became more urgent. Therefore, the accounting profession recommended the adoption of both international accounting and auditing standards, to take effect as of January 1990.

INTERNATIONAL ACCOUNTING AND AUDITING STANDARDS

Due to the diversity in accounting standards across different countries, which produced a general lack of comparability in financial reporting across different countries, a harmonization of accounting and auditing standards was recommended. In 1973, the International Accounting Standards Committee (IASC) was formed by an agreement of the leading professional bodies in Australia, Canada, France, Netherlands,

Japan, Germany, Mexico, the United States, the United Kingdom, and Ireland. The major goal of the committee is the development of worldwide accounting and auditing standards that will lead to the harmonization of accounting standards throughout the world.

Applying these standards is optional, not mandatory. The IASC does not include government representatives because it is a private-sector body with representatives from professional accounting organizations. The IASC consists of representatives from 13 countries, including the founding member countries mentioned above.

Since its creation, the IASC has issued 38 accounting standards. In 1977, the International Federation of Accountants (IFAC) was founded to develop a worldwide accountancy profession. The IFAC's international auditing practices committee issues international auditing standards designed to harmonize the way audits are conducted worldwide.

THE CURRENT STUDY

Methodology and Results

The research reported in this paper was carried out by a questionnaire (see Appendix A), which was delivered to professional auditors and university professors in accounting. Of the questionnaires delivered to auditing offices, all but one were returned, 18 questionnaires were delivered to university professors; all were returned.

Results of the Survey of Auditors

Table 2 summarizes the results of the survey of auditors, which include the following:

- More than 55% of the sample have more than 10 years of experience in the auditing field;
- More than 95% have at least a university degree in accounting;
- Approximately 38% of the auditors surveyed hold a professional certification in accounting;
- Over half (59.52%) attended training courses to prepare for accounting proficiency exams; and

- Over half (57.14%) attended seminars on the international accounting standards.

These results indicate that the auditing staff in Jordan has the required educational background and practical experience to practice and advance the accounting and auditing profession in Jordan. Approximately 95.24% of the sample auditors apply international accounting and auditing standards (IAAS) in performing their audits, and 95.24% of their clients apply IAAS. These large percentages indicate the great need for reliable and relevant accounting information in the Jordanian economy, even though application of IAAS is not required by any governmental or private accounting body.

In addition, more than 83% of the auditors questioned believe in the usefulness of the information produced as a result of applying IAAS and the positive impact it will have on the Jordanian economy.

The results of questions 5–8 in the survey, which deal with the involvement of the Government Accounting Bureau (GAB) and the Jordanian Accounting Society (JAS) in applying and enforcing IAAS, revealed an unsatisfactory situation:

- Approximately 64% of the auditors sampled believe there is a lack of monitoring in applying IAAS;
- Three-quarters (76%) of the sample believe there is a lack of monitoring by the GAB;
- Over half (52%) of the auditors indicated that the JAS informs them of any changes in amendments to IAAS; and
- A lack of any practical training sponsored by JAS in the application of IAAS was reported by 23% of the auditors.

These results further indicate that the application of IAAS is not enforceable or monitored by any private or governmental accounting bodies in Jordan.

The professional accounting examination in Jordan does not always include questions about IAAS, which are not even covered in most Jordanian universities. Approximately 93% of the auditors in our sample believe that IAAS are similar to U.S. accounting standards. International auditing standards have been translated into Arabic. A significant percentage of the auditors say they have both Arabic and English versions of the standards, which facilitates applying IAAS without any lan-

Table 2. Results of the Questionnaire

Auditors.							*Percentage*				
Question No.	*A*	*B*	*C*	*D*	*E*	*Sum*	*A*	*B*	*C*	*D*	*E*
1	4	7	9	15	0	35	9.52	16.67	21.43	35.71	0.00
2	8	5	0	16	0	29	19.05	11.90	0.00	38.10	0.00
3	0	30	3	3	2	38	0.00	71.43	7.14	7.14	4.76
	Yes	*No*					*Yes*	*No*			
4	16	20				36	38.10	47.62			
5	25	10				35	59.52	23.81			
6	24	12				36	57.14	28.57			
	Rarely	*Usually*	*Always*				*Rarely*	*Usually*	*Always*		
1	2	6	34			42	4.76	14.29	80.95		
2	2	28	12			42	4.76	66.67	28.57		
3	1	6	35			42	2.38	14.29	83.33		
4	0	6	36			42	0.00	14.29	85.71		
5	27	11	3			41	64.29	26.19	7.14		
6	3	17	22			42	7.14	40.48	52.38		
7	32	4	0			36	76.19	9.52	0.00		
8	9	23	10			42	21.43	54.76	23.81		
9	1	28	12			41	2.38	66.67	28.57		
10	10	28	1			39	23.81	66.67	2.38		
	Yes	*No*					*Yes*	*No*			
11	39	2				41	92.86	4.76			
	A	*B*	*C*	*D*	*E*		*A*	*B*	*C*	*D*	*E*
12	0	1	18	16	4	39	0.00	2.38	42.86	38.10	9.52
	Yes	*No*					*Yes*	*No*			
13	38	2				40	90.48	4.76			
14	37	4				41	88.10	9.52			
15	23	17				40	54.76	40.48			
16	16	25				41	38.10	59.52			

Professors

Question No.	A	B	C	D	E	Sum	Percentage A	Percentage B	Percentage C	Percentage D	Percentage E
1	4	7	3	15		17	22.22	38.89	16.67	16.67	
2	5	5	0	5		15	27.78	27.78	0.00	27.78	
	Yes	*No*					*Yes*	*No*			
3	4	12				16	22.22	66.67			
4	13	4				17	72.22	22.22			
	Rarely	*Usually*	*Always*				*Rarely*	*Usually*	*Always*		
1	2	5	11			18	11.11	27.78	61.11		
2	2	10	6			18	11.11	55.56	33.33		
3	3	2	13			18	16.67	11.11	72.22		
4	1	4	13			18	5.56	22.22	72.22		
5	8	8	2			18	44.44	44.44	11.11		
6	4	6	8			18	22.22	33.33	44.44		
7	17	1	0			18	94.44	5.56	0.00		
8	7	7	4			18	38.89	38.89	22.22		
9	4	10	4			18	22.22	55.56	22.22		
10	9	8	1			18	50.00	44.44	5.56		
	Yes	*No*					*Yes*	*No*			
11	17	1				18	94.44	5.56			
	A	*B*	*C*	*D*	*E*		*A*	*B*	*C*	*D*	*E*
12	0	0	7	9	1	17	0.00	0.00	38.89	50.00	5.56
	Yes	*No*					*Yes*	*No*			
13	14	4				18	77.78	22.22			
14	16	2				18	88.89	11.11			
15	8	10				18	44.44	55.56			
16	9	9				18	50.00	50.00			

guage difficulties. Furthermore, 60% indicated that they face no difficulties in applying these standards.

In the past, accounting firms applied a wide variety of accounting standards. Some used foreign standards from the United States or the United Kingdom. Other firms used accounting standards that were accepted in Jordan and in the Middle East. Still others relied on traditional accounting, practical experience and knowledge, and individual interpretations.

There is now a greater reliance on IAAS, which can be expected to lead to a positive impact on the efficiency of accounting information. This will improve the investment decision-making process and hopefully attract foreign investment.

Results of the Survey of University Professors

Table 2 summarizes descriptive statistics relating to the professors included in the survey. Their replies show that:

- Of the professors surveyed, 28% have 10 or more years of experience in the academic field;
- Another 38% have between five and 10 years of experience; and
- Only 28% have fewer than three years of experience.

These results indicate that Jordanian universities have as many recent graduates teacher accounting as they do professors with significant teaching experience. About 22% of the university professors hold a professional certificate, although teaching in Jordan does not require these certificates; this shows that professors are willing to continue their professional development.

Over 72% of the university professors reported attending training courses and seminars on international accounting standards. They believe that applying international standards will lead to the production of useful accounting information, and therefore they encourage the teaching of these standards as well as their application in the practical work of accountants and auditors. Most of the professors indicated that they found a high degree of similarity between international accounting standards (IAS) and U.S. accounting standards; the similarity was estimated as covering 70% to 90% of the standards.

Difficulties in Applying IAAS to Jordan

Certain difficulties face those willing to apply IAAS in Jordan. These difficulties stem from the fact that Jordan has unique laws and a unique economic environment. Specific difficulties mentioned by our respondents included:

- Some Jordanian rules and regulations are not compatible with IAAS, such as taxation law, insurance laws, and banking regulations and laws;
- Jordanian corporations face a different environment than other international corporations. They also differ in size;
- Costing systems do not exist in most industrial companies in Jordan;
- Interference by company owners with the work of management is prevalent in Jordan;
- Applying IAAS standards is not legally mandatory;
- Most clients do not apply IAAS either because the client's accounting staff is not familiar with the standards or the company fears that losses may occur which are not tax deductible under Jordanian tax. In addition, clients perceive auditors as lacking the experience and knowledge to apply these standards;
- Accounting associations, whether public or private, lack basic services. There are no associations that translate these standards into Arabic or conduct open discussions. None of the associations provides training courses for accountants and practitioners or follows up on changes and updates that may occur; and
- In general, the public and the users of financial statements are unaware of the importance of applying these standards.

Advantages of Applying IAAS to Jordan

Applying IAAS standards would have many advantages for Jordan. Respondents listed some of the following:

- IAAS provide accounting basics that would lead to the uniformity of accounting and auditing procedures within Jordan and therefore diminish individual interpretations;
- The use of IAAS would increase the ability to compare financial statements for different companies locally and internationally;

- The use of IAAS would enable analysts to extract comparable and accurate information from the financial statements of different companies;
- The use of IAAS would advance the accounting profession in Jordan by adding stability to the profession and improving the quality of information contained in financial statements;
- Useful external financial reporting would lead to more confidence in stock prices on the Amman Financial Market. This would encourage investment in Jordan, which in turn would boost the economy in general.
- The use of IAAS would result in the production of useful, reliable, and accurate information for investment decision making and research;
- The use of IAAS would foster the development of independent Jordanian and Arabic accounting and auditing standards;
- The use of IAAS would improve communication between local accountants and their counterparts throughout the world;
- The use of IAAS would provide more protection for the public and shareholders;
- Management would become more responsible for its performance;
- Areas of conflict in accounting practice would diminish; and
- IAAS would be easy and flexible to use.

Disadvantages of Applying IAAS to Jordan

The respondents mentioned a few disadvantages to applying IAAS in Jordan. Their main concern involves the fact that Jordan is still a small developing economy and applying these standards might not always be beneficial. Among their concerns were the following:

- Jordan has an economic environment, which is smaller and less dynamic than that of most larger countries;
- Some standards cannot be applied appropriately in some accounting areas;
- There are many small companies and corporations in Jordan. These firms have a small volume of repeat transactions, and could find it prohibitively costly to implement IAAS; and

- Some IAAS do not fully cover the treatment to accounting problems within a specific standard. For example, the standards covering leases and pensions do not provide full information on how to handle certain problems.

CONCLUSION AND RECOMMENDATIONS

Respondents encouraged the use of IAAS but only after taking the Jordanian economy and environment into consideration. This will foster creativity in the sense that IAAS will have to be adapted to fit the Jordanian situation. The quality of financial reporting will reach higher levels.

Some respondents indicated that government interference is necessary because corporations will not apply these standards unless they are obligated to do so. Official bodies must try to organize the accounting profession by providing training courses, seminars, and discussions.

The Jordanian Accountants Association (JAS) should be strengthened and become more active in the development of written accounting guidelines and concepts suited to the Jordanian economic environment. One way to try to narrow the gap between IAAS and local standards would be for the JAS to form an IAAS committee to update and adapt accounting principles according to economic and technological innovations. This would save time, money, and effort compared to trying to develop local standards from scratch.

APPENDIX A: THE QUESTIONNAIRE

Basic Information

(1) Years of practical experience in the field of Auditing:
  (a) less than 5 years
  (b) 5 years to less than 10 years
  (c) 10 years to less than 15 years
  (d) 15 years and more

(2) Years of practical experience in the field of Accounting:
  (a) less than 3 years
  (b) 3 years to less than 7 years
  (c) 7 years to less than 10 years
  (d) 10 years and more

(3) Education:
  (a) less than Baccalaureate in Accounting
  (b) Baccalaureate in Accounting
  (c) Baccalaureate in majors other than Accounting
  (d) Graduate studies in Accounting
  (e) Graduate studies in other field. Identify__________

(4) Do you have a professional certificate in accounting:
  (a) Yes
  If yes, name the certificate__________
  (b) No

(5) Did you attended any review courses which qualify you to sit for the Accounting Professional exam in Jordan:
  (a) Yes
  (b) No

(6) Did you attended any training programs in the International Accounting Standards:
  (a) Yes. How many (   )
  (b) No

Survey Questions

Circle the rank which reflects your opinion for the following questions:

(1) Does your firm apply the International Accounting and Auditing Standards in performing the audit of its clients?
Rarely Usually Always
1 2 3 4 5 6 7 8 9 10

(2) Do the clients of your firms apply the International Accounting Standards?
Rarely Usually Always
1 2 3 4 5 6 7 8 9 10

(3) Do you think that the application of the International Accounting Standards will lead to the production of useful information for the purpose of making rational economic decisions?
To a small degree To some extent To a large degree
1 2 3 4 5 6 7 8 9 10

(4) To what extent do you think that the application of International Accounting standards will have a positive impact on the accounting profession in Jordan?
To a small degree   To some extent   To a large degree
1 2 3 4 5 6 7 8 9 10

(5) Does the Jordanian Accounting Society follow up and monitor the auditing firms in applying the International Accounting and Auditing Standards?
Rarely   Usually   Always
1 2 3 4 5 6 7 8 9 10

(6) Does the Jordanian Accounting society inform you of any changes and or amendments in the International Accounting and Auditing Standards?
Rarely   Usually   Always
1 2 3 4 5 6 7 8 9 10

(7) Does the Accounting Governmental Bureau in Jordan follow up and monitor your firm in applying the International Accounting and Auditing Standards?
Rarely   Usually   Always
1 2 3 4 5 6 7 8 9 10

(8) Does the Jordanian Accounting Society or other accounting professional bodies in Jordan conduct practical training and seminars in the International Accounting and Auditing Standards?
Rarely   Usually   Always
1 2 3 4 5 6 7 8 9 10

(9) Does the Jordanian Professional Exam in Accounting cover the International Accounting Standards?
To a small degree   To some extent   To a large degree
1 2 3 4 5 6 7 8 9 10

(10) In your opinion, do the academicians at Jordanian Universities emphasize the International Accounting Standards in their teaching?
To a small degree   To some extent   To a large degree
1 2 3 4 5 6 7 8 9 10

(11) Are there any similarities between the International Accounting and the American Accounting Standards?
(a) Yes
(b) No

(12) If your answer to question (11) is Yes; to what extent is the similarity?
(a) less than 20 percent
(b) 20 percent to less than 50 percent
(c) 50 percent to less than 70 percent
(d) 70 percent to less than 90 percent
(e) more than 90 percent

(13) Does your firm have the International Accounting Standards?
(a) Yes
(b) No

(14) Does your firm have the International Accounting Standards in Arabic language?
(a) Yes
(b) No

(15) Does your firm have CPAs?
(a) Yes
(b) No

(16) Do you face any difficulties in applying the International Accounting and Auditing Standards?
(a) Yes
(b) No

(17) If your answer to question (16) is Yes, then list what are these difficulties:
1. ________________
2. ________________
3. ________________
4. ________________
5. ________________

(18) Which accounting and auditing standards was your firm applying before applying the International Accounting Standards?

____
____
____

(19) What are the positive aspects that result from applying the International Accounting and Auditing Standards?

1. ______________________
2. ______________________
3. ______________________
4. ______________________
5. ______________________

(20) What are the negative aspects that result from applying the International Accounting and Auditing Standards?

1. ______________________
2. ______________________
3. ______________________
4. ______________________
5. ______________________

REFERENCES

Dahmash, N. 1993. On challenges facing Arab accountants. Paper presented at the Third Arab Accounting Conference, Manama, Bahrain.

El-Issa, Y.A. 1984. *Financial Reporting Environment in Jordan: The Need for Change.* Unpublished manuscript.

Mueller, H., and G. Meek. 1994. *Accounting: An International Perspective*, 3rd edition. Chicago, IL: Richard D. Irwin.

Shair, W.A. 1988. *The Development of the Accountancy Profession in Jordan.* Unpublished manuscript.

Zeff, S.A. 1984. The international harmonization of accounting standards: The forces to play. Paper presented at the International Conference, Kuwait, December.

THE DEVELOPMENT OF ACCOUNTING STANDARDS IN THE KINGDOM OF SAUDI ARABIA:
AN INTERNATIONAL ACCOUNTING STANDARDS PERSPECTIVE

Mohamed Ali Mirghani

INTRODUCTION

The Kingdom of Saudi Arabia, as one of the world's largest producers of oil, has used its oil wealth to develop the country through a series of five-year development plans aimed at maximizing the economic and social welfare of the Saudi people. The current (sixth) development plan places major emphasis on diversification of the country's economic base, rationalization of government expenditure, and improving operational efficiency.

Advances in International Accounting, Supplement 1, pages 195-206.

ISBN: 0-7623-0461-8

The government's achievements have included building the infrastructure and institutional support for industrial development, a system of education at the general and higher levels, a health care system, self-sufficiency in agricultural products and certain industrial products, establishing an export- oriented petrochemical industry, and enacting laws and regulations providing strong incentives for the private sector to invest in all sectors of the economy.

The Saudi government has implemented policies, rules, and regulations to motivate Saudi nationals to invest in the stock of Saudi corporations. Moreover, the country's economy is open to the world, and international business activities are quite significant. Many multinational corporations operate in Saudi Arabia through either general agencies or joint ventures.

Before 1985, financial reporting and accounting practices were characterized by diversity in concepts, principles, and standards applied. Accountants and/or reporting entities practicing in Saudi Arabia came from different regions of the world and brought with them the accounting technology of their respective countries. Therefore, investors trying to analyze or compare financial statements faced formidable task.

Before 1986, stock in Saudi corporations was traded through brokerage offices, dealing mainly in real estate, without any kind of financial analysis and in a purely speculative manner. This resulted in fictitious increases in stock prices, creating a conducive environment for a market crash. These conditions created a great need to organize the accounting profession in Saudi Arabia to play its proper role in supporting the country's economic and financial activities.

The formation of corporations and the licensing of certified public accountants in Saudi Arabia is under the umbrella of the Ministry of Commerce. In 1985, the Ministry issued Ministerial Resolution No. 692, which established the objectives and concepts of financial accounting in Saudi Arabia as guidelines for professional accountants and business organizations licensed in Saudi Arabia. These objectives and concepts were also intended to provide a conceptual framework for setting accounting standards in Saudi Arabia. At the same time, the Ministry of Commerce issued two documents, *Requirements of General Presentation and Disclosure Standard* and *Bylaws for Setting Accounting and Auditing Standards* (1995a, 1995b). These standards were issued as an official guide and reference for accounting and auditing practices in Saudi Arabia.

The Ministry of Commerce invited comments and observations with regard to the objectives and concepts of financial accounting, the general presentation and disclosure standard, and the auditing standards during the guidance period (five years). The Ministry also mandated the general presentation and disclosure standard and auditing standards by Ministerial Resolution No. 852 (May 2, 1990), effective for fiscal years ending after August 11, 1990. The general presentation and disclosure standard applies to all types of business organizations, regardless of their legal form or nature of business. The provisions of the new standard do not contradict the International Accounting Standards (IAS). The new standard does not provide guidelines on accounting principles, policies, and practices that may be adopted by business organizations (Atieh, 1995).

Issuing these objectives and concepts of financial accounting presented a conceptual framework for financial reporting and accounting standards and a justification for accounting standards, techniques, and methods they use. Without such a conceptual framework, accounting practice would operate in a vacuum.

Issuing these two guidance documents was a prudent first step toward organizing an accounting profession characterized by significant diversity in accounting and auditing practices. The state of the accounting profession at that time made it virtually impossible to enforce any set of accounting and auditing standards, whether they were U.S., British, or international. Further, issuing these standards for guidance was necessary to prepare the accounting profession to be organized through a systematic approach.

Almost two years after these two documents became mandatory, the Saudi Organization for Certified Public Accountants (SOCPA) was formed by Royal Degree No. M/12 in 1992 as part of the Certified Public Accountants Regulations. These regulations defined the licensing requirements, professional responsibility and legal liability, and educational and continuing professional development requirements of Saudi certified public accountants. These regulations specified the following objectives for SOCPA:

1. Reviewing, developing, and approving of accounting and auditing standards;
2. Developing rules and regulations for the Saudi CPA examinations;

3. Organizing short courses for continuing education and professional development in accounting and auditing;
4. Conducting research studies in accounting and auditing;
5. Issuing periodicals, monographs, and books about accounting and auditing; and
6. Establishing appropriate mechanisms for monitoring the implementation of Saudi accounting and auditing standards and the Certified Public Accountants Regulations.

SOCPA has a 13-member board of directors chaired by the Minister of Commerce. SOCPA's Secretary General executes and follows up the board's decisions and has delegated authority of executive management.

SOCPA carries out its technical responsibilities through the following committees:

- The Accounting Standards Committee;
- The Auditing Standards Committee;
- The Training and Education Committee;
- The Quality Review Committee;
- The Professional Ethics Committee;
- The Professional Examinations Committee; and
- The Nominations Committee, which nominates candidates for SCOPA's board of directors and technical committees.

The rest of this chapter focuses on the work of SOCPA's Accounting Standards Committee and the standard-setting process and its interface(s) with IAS.

THE ACCOUNTING STANDARDS-SETTING PROCESS

This section provides a brief overview of the different phases of the accounting standards-setting process, according to SOCPA's by-laws, along with an analysis of each phase and its relationship to IAS.

Phase 1: Selection of a Proposed Accounting Standard

1. After coordination with the Accounting Standards Committee, SOCPA's Secretary General conducts a periodic survey of the accounting standards that need to be developed.

2. On the basis of the survey results, the Secretary General prepares a list of the needed accounting standards and presents it to the Accounting Standards Committee.
3. The Accounting Standards Committee rank-orders the accounting standards it intends to issue in terms of their importance to the accounting profession. The list is reviewed and updated on the basis of periodic reviews conducted by the Secretary General.

Discussion: This approach makes the standards-setting process responsive to the needs of the accounting profession and business organizations.

Phase 2: Consultant Selection

1. The Secretary General presents a list of the names of individuals interested and specializing in the topic of the proposed standard. The Accounting Standards Committee invites consultants to submit a study proposal of the proposed standard in accordance with SOCPA's general conditions and contractual requirements. The proposal should include: (1) the scope of the study, (2) methodology, (3) timetable, and (4) estimated fees.
2. The Secretary General studies submitted proposals and presents a summary report to the Accounting Standards Committee so that it can select a consultant to carry out the required study.
3. It is possible to accept contributions (from individuals or organizations) for the preparation of accounting standards provided that the donor complies with SOCPA's by-laws in this matter.

Phase 3: Preparation of the Study

1. The Secretary General communicates to the selected consultant the Accounting Standards Committee's decision and asks him to prepare a study that includes the following:

    - The conceptual and theoretical aspects of the proposed standard from all relevant sources including company law and regulations, *zakat* and income tax law, SOCPA's accounting standards, and the accounting standards of the United States, the United Kingdom, and the International Accounting Standards Committee;

- A summary of current practice in five business organizations expected to adopt the accounting standard upon approval. These business organizations represent an experimental sample for testing the efficiency and effectiveness of the proposed standard upon its practical application;
- Justification of the need for the proposed standard and expected problems upon its application;
- Identification of the expected regulatory, technical, and other problems related to the proposed standard and identification of alternative solutions so that the committee could establish guidelines for handling subsequent implementation problems; and
- Identification of the proposed standard alternatives and application methods and their respective merits and demerits in view of the objectives and concepts of financial accounting issued in the Kingdom of Saudi Arabia.

Discussion: The study's conceptual framework explicitly recognizes the International Accounting Standards Committee as one of the relevant sources. Hence, international accounting standards do play a role in the accounting standard-setting process.

2. The consultant presents the study project to the Secretary General within 90 days after being charged with the task.
3. Upon receipt of the study project, the Secretary General circulates copies of it to the committee members for their comments and observations.
4. The committee meets within 15 days of the end of the consultation period specified by the Secretary General, to discuss the study project and to lay the ground rules for subsequent work. The committee may call upon the consultant if there is a need.
5. The Secretary General transmits the committee's findings to the consultant within a week after their approval.
6. The consultant revises the study in view of the committee's comments and observations and resubmits it to the Secretary General within 21 days from the date of receiving the committee findings.
7. The Secretary General transmits the revised study to the committee members.
8. If there are significant comments, the Secretary General calls the Accounting Standards Committee for a meeting.

Phase 4: Surveying the Opinions of Interested and Specialized Parties

1. The Secretary General transmits copies of the study to members of SOCPA's board and technical committees, accounting faculty members, management of business organizations, and other users of financial statements. These parties are requested to provide their comments on the study in accordance with prescribed formats within 30 days.
2. The Secretary General prescribes the rules for safeguarding the responses against partial or total loss and for easy referencing. The Secretary General keeps the originals and turns over copies to the consultant.
3. The consultant tabulates and analyzes the responses in accordance with a scientific methodology that facilitates comparison and cross-referencing and presents the results of the analysis within 21 days from the date of receiving the response data. The Secretary General immediately transmits the analysis results to the committee members.
4. The Accounting Standards Committee convenes a meeting within 15 days of receiving the analysis results to be attended by the consultant. The purpose of the meeting is to present and discuss the points of view, comments, and significant observations received from interested and specialist parties.
5. The consultant prepares a summary of the discussion that transpired at this meeting, identifying basic conclusions and their expected benefits or lack thereof. Within 15 days of the meeting, the consultant submits a report to the Secretary General, who in turn submits it to the committee.
6. Each committee member studies the consultant's summary report and sends observations and/or comments to the Secretary General within one week. The Secretary General summarizes the comments and/or observations in a report and sends it to the committee within one week.
7. The committee meets within 15 days after receiving the summary report to resolve all issues prior to preparation of the exposure draft.
8. The Secretary General delivers the committee's resolutions to the consultant within one week after the meeting.

Discussion: Through this approach, wide participation in setting accounting standards is encouraged and consensus for the proposed standard can be built.

Phase 5: Preparation of an Exposure Draft

1. The consultant prepares and submits to the Secretary General an exposure draft, taking account of the committee's decisions and within 15 days after receiving them. The Secretary General sends the exposure draft to the committee on receiving it.
2. The committee members study the exposure draft and send their observations and/or comments to the Secretary General within one week. The Secretary General prepares a summary report and sends it back to the committee within one week.
3. The committee meets within 15 days after receiving the report, to resolve all pending issues before revising the exposure draft. It may invite the consultant to the meeting, if there is a need.
4. The Secretary General delivers the committee's resolutions to the consultant within a week after the meeting.
5. The consultant revises the exposure draft in view of the committee's resolutions and presents it to the Secretary General within 15 days.
6. The Secretary General submits the revised exposure draft to the committee and sends a copy to each committee member.

Discussion: The exposure draft, in addition to providing details of the proposed accounting standard, identifies the similarities and differences between it and the U.S., British, and international standards. This indicates that the focus is on developing accounting standards relevant to the circumstances of Saudi Arabia while benefiting from the experience of advanced accounting professions.

Phase 6: Publication of the Exposure Draft and Its Discussion in a Public Seminar

1. The Secretary General sends copies of the exposure draft to members of SOCPA's board and technical committees for their review and comments within 30 days according to prescribed format.

2. The Secretary General prescribes rules for safeguarding the responses against partial or total loss and for easy referencing. The Secretary General keeps the originals and turns over copies to the consultant.
3. The consultant classifies and analyzes the responses in accordance with a scientific methodology that facilitates comparisons and easy referencing to raw data and presents the results of the analysis and comments to the Secretary General within 21 days from the date. The Secretary General sends the report to the committee members as soon as it is received.
4. The committee meets within one week after receiving the report to approve the exposure draft for publication and may invite the consultant to the meeting if there is a need.
5. The Secretary General publishes the exposure draft as soon as it is approved by the committee and sends copies to interested and specialist parties.
6. Within three weeks of publication, the committee chairman organizes a public seminar, announced in local newspapers, to hear and discuss relevant comments and observations.
7. The committee chairman acts as the seminar's moderator. The Secretary General and the consultant prepare a summary of the comments made and the ensuing discussion and provide committee members with copies of it.

Discussion: This again indicates consistency in the approach of encouraging wide participation and consensus-building for proposed accounting standards. This would have a direct impact on the general acceptability of accounting standards.

Phase 7: Preparation of Final Exposure Draft

1. The consultant prepares the final exposure draft in view of the comments, opinions, and suggestions made in the public seminar and submits it to the Secretary General with comments about the observations and suggestions that were considered or disregarded. This is done within 15 days after the public seminar.
2. The Secretary General sends the final exposure draft to the committee members within one week after receiving it from the consultant.

3. The committee members study the final exposure draft and send their responses to the Secretary General within one week from receiving it.
4. The Secretary General summarizes the responses and sends copies of the summary report to the committee and the consultant.
5. The committee meets within 15 days from the date of the report to discuss the committee members' comments about the final exposure draft. The consultant is invited to the meeting, where the consultant is charged with preparing the exposure draft in its final form, as prescribed by the committee, and submitting it to the Secretary General within one week from the date of the meeting.
6. The Secretary General sends copies of the revised final exposure draft to the committee members. If significant comments are made, the Secretary General calls on the committee to make a final decision.

Phase 8: Approval and Issuance of the Standard

1. The committee chairman sends the final exposure draft to the Secretary General for presentation to the board of directors.
2. The Secretary General puts the final exposure draft on the agenda of the next (or closest) board meeting.
3. The committee members are invited to the board meeting. If the board approves the final exposure draft without modification, then the Secretary General informs the committee of the board's decision and completes the necessary steps to issue the accounting standard.
4. If the board has observations, the committee will look into them and may ask the consultant to revise the exposure draft to incorporate the board's observations.
5. After incorporating the board's observations, the consultant submits the standard to the committee within two weeks.
6. The committee approves the modified final exposure draft, submits it to the board for final approval, and then completes the necessary procedures for issuing the accounting standard.

Phase 9: Assessing Compliance with the Standard

1. The Secretary General keeps a record of observations received after issuance and application of the standard. The Secretary Gen-

eral also prepares a quarterly summary report accompanied by opinions to the committee for consideration if the standard needs amending.

2. In periods subsequent to the issuance of the financial statements of business organizations, the appropriate SOCPA department selects a sample and assesses the extent of compliance with the standard. Its findings are reported to the committee semi-annually.

Phase 10: Amendment of the Standard

1. The same procedures used to prepare a standard should be followed to amend it.

CONCLUSIONS

International accounting standards have an influence over the accounting standard-setting process in Saudi Arabia because they are explicitly considered in: (1) the conceptual study that precedes preparation of an exposure draft; (2) the exposure draft, which points out similarities and differences between the proposed Saudi standard and international, U.S., and British accounting standards; and (3) the Saudi general presentation and disclosure standard, which is not in conflict with international accounting standards. International accounting standards are relevant for setting accounting standards as long as they can be modified to suit local circumstances. Finally, a country like Saudi Arabia has national, regional, and international priorities for harmonization of accounting standards.

ACKNOWLEDGMENTS

The author gratefully acknowledges the research support received from King Fahd University of Petroleum and Minerals as well as travel support from Saudi Arabian Airlines.

REFERENCES

Atieh, S.H. 1995. *World Accounting*. Saudi Arabia: Mathew Bender.

Saudi Arabia. 1992. *Certified Public Accountants Regulations* (issued by Royal Decree M/13, 1992).

Saudi Arabia, Ministry of Commerce. 1995a. *General Presentation and Disclosure Standard.*

Saudi Arabia, Ministry of Commerce. 1995b. *By-laws for Setting Accounting and Auditing Standards.*

Saudi Organization for Certified Public Accounts. 1994. *SOCPA Objectives, Responsibilities, and Profession Development in Saudi Arabia.*

RECENT CHANGES IN THE ACCOUNTING PROFESSION AND FINANCIAL REPORTING IN TURKEY

Nasuhi I. Bursal

INTRODUCTION

The accounting environment in Turkey has been experiencing drastic changes since the early 1980s (Bursal 1984). Transition from a substantially state-controlled to a free market economy is making rapid progress. Strict regulations concerning interest and foreign exchange rates are being eliminated. Businesses accustomed to customs protection for many decades are opening up to foreign markets. Especially since Turkey joined the European Customs Union in 1996, its domestic industry is being confronted with global competition. Privatization of state-owned enterprises is proceeding despite the opposition of the Social Democratic parties. In addition, the modernization of the telecommunication system of the country has laid a solid foundation for sophisticated information system applications.

Advances in International Accounting, Supplement 1, pages 207-237.

ISBN: 0-7623-0461-8

These promising developments were not achieved, however, without some serious economic drawbacks. Inflation could not be brought under control for many years (75% in 1995). Interest rates were approximately 80% in 1995. The value of the Turkish lira is falling against foreign currencies. All of this is detrimental to a climate for sound business decisions.

One important result of the economy's rapid transition has been the remarkable development of the capital market. The number of corporations raising their capital in the capital market and the volume of transactions are steadily increasing (Appendix A). High interest rates for borrowed capital are forcing the old family-owned corporations to open up to the capital market. The Istanbul Stock Exchange has become a central point for the business world and the public with its modern communication and information systems.

These rapid changes in the economic environment, especially in the capital market, have moved the importance of the accounting profession and financial reporting to the foreground. Fundamental changes in the regulation of the capital markets, the accounting profession, and financial reporting have been carried out over the last 10 years. One interesting aspect of these changes seems to be the search for a compromise between continental European and Anglo-Saxon approaches to the main objectives of financial reporting. The purpose of this paper is to present an overview of basic developments in this field during the last decade.

LEGAL FOUNDATION OF THE CAPITAL MARKETS

Securities have been traded on the Istanbul Stock Exchange for many decades. As a capital was practically nonexistant until the 1980s, no need was felt for comprehensive legal regulation until then. A large sector of the economy was dominated by state- owned enterprises. Most of the emerging private corporations were family-owned, with no stock offerings or with only a few shares on the market. Some of the larger corporations later became holding companies, with diversified investments including financial institutions and insurance companies. These banks represented an important source for satisfying the financial needs of these corporations.

The low-interest-rate policy of the government also had an impact on the capital structure of the corporations. When the inflation rate reached 100% during the late 1970s, the Central Bank was still holding the official discount rate at 12%. This discrepancy enabled corporations to profit from high leverage. Especially because of the relatively high tax rates, financing by borrowed capital became more attractive than offering stock to the public.

The lack of comprehensive legal regulation of the capital market prior to the 1980s does not imply the lack of any regulation concerning corporations and their financial reporting. Two fundamental laws, the Turkish Commerce Law (1956 revision) and the Turkish Income Tax Legislation (1949, later revised in 1960 and 1961) constituted the main legal framework for corporations and their accounting and auditing requirements over many decades. Both laws were largely affected by the corresponding Swiss and German legislation.

The Turkish Commerce Law (TCL) regulated all procedures for corporations from their formation until their liquidation. Balance sheets and profit-and-loss statements were prescribed as two mandatory financial statements. Proper accounting records had to be kept according to the practices of "prudent businessmen." Protection of the interests of third parties (lenders and vendors) and the maintenance of the invested capital were the basic underlying concepts and concerns for these requirements. Without a need for financial disclosure to the capital market, auditing was confined to internal statutory auditors. The appointed auditors generally enjoyed close relations with the owners or management. They had other administrative assignments in addition to their auditing function.

Financial reporting of corporations, however, was heavily influenced by the regulations of the Turkish Income Tax System (TITS), consisting of Income Tax Law (for individual taxpayers), Corporation Tax Law, and Tax Procedures Law, which dominated accounting and reporting practice for many decades. Net income had to be calculated in accordance with the overriding requirements of the tax laws. The same income figures were used to measure the financial performance of corporations.

The most important milestone in the legal regulation of the capital market was the Capital Market Law (CML) and the establishment of the Capital Market Board (CMB) in 1981 (Bursal 1984). The design of the new system is similar to the U.S. Securities Act and Securities Exchange Act, which created the SEC. As a special law, CML overrides other regulations. In cases not covered by CML, other regulations, especially those of the TCL, should be observed.

The introduction of this legislation represented a fundamental shift from a continental European to a U.S. approach to the regulation of the capital market, financial reporting, and public auditing. Corporations that issue securities to the public or that have more than 100 shareholders are subject to this legislation.

As a framework law, CML established the CMB and set broad objectives, principles, and rules concerning the instruments, institutions, and transactions of the capital market. It further contains general provisions for securing confidence, transparency, and control in the capital market, especially as related to financial reporting and public auditing. Detailed regulations for the implementation of the law are left to the authority of the CMB, which fulfills its task by releasing instructions in the form of regulations or communiqués on topics covered by the CML. Regulations include general requirements for the achievement of certain goals of the CML. Communiqués prescribe more detailed procedures for the interpretation and implementation of these requirements. One important regulation (no. 19663) issued in 1987 contains the basic requirements concerning the external auditing of corporations by independent auditors. Communiqués are classified by serial numbers, each series pertaining to a specific topic. Examples are Series I: stocks; Series II: bonds; Series IV: corporations; Series V: intermediary institutions in the capital market; Series VII: investment funds; Series X: independent auditing; and Series XI: financial reporting. More detailed instructions of the CMB are issued as circulars.

In covering the legal foundation of the regulations concerning the capital market, several other special regulations, notably those issued by the Ministry of Finance (MF) and the Turkish Central Bank (TCB), should be mentioned. An important example of this is the communiqué (no. 21447) first issued by the MF in 1992 and revised in 1993 (no. 21790) and 1994 (no. 22055) concerning the implementation of the new accounting system. These communiqués have set the stage for the practice of financial reporting since 1994.

The CML law represents the first important impact of U.S. legislation on the Turkish legal system. However, the new requirements of this law will be implemented in a legal environment based on that of continental Europe. The requirements of the CML must be coordinated smoothly with the existing legal system, especially TCL and TITS. The differences between the terms of the regulations and the background and experience of the people in charge of interpreting and implementing the old and new legislation might create some areas of conflict, at least for the next few years.

LEGAL FOUNDATION OF THE ACCOUNTING PROFESSION

Without mandatory independent external auditing, there was practically no need for a separate accounting and auditing profession until the 1980s. There were no qualification requirements for the statutory auditors of the private corporations. Financial institutions such as banks and insurance companies had their own internal auditors. State economic enterprises (SEE) also had their special auditing system, under the High Auditing Board (HOB) (Bursal 1984). The only external auditors examining companies were tax auditors or accounting experts of the Ministry of Finance (MF).

It should be noted, however, that several auditing firms were already established in the market before public auditing became mandatory and that the multinational corporations and foreign financial institutions operating in Turkey had been subject to independent audit for many years. The large U.S. auditing firms had already set up their branch offices in Turkey. Large Turkish corporations, closely associated with foreign companies and those securing loans from the World Bank or other foreign financial institutions, were among the clients of these auditing firms.

The first legal step for the establishment of an independent audit profession came with a communiqué of the MF (January 16, 1987) introducing the external audit requirement for banks. In December 1987, the TCB issued further guidelines for the implementation of this requirement.

Another important step in this direction was a regulation of the CMB (no. 19633) concerning the independent external audit requirements for public corporations. According to this regulation, the independent audit firms had to be established in the form of corporations with a minimum capital of 100 million Turkish lira, with at least 51% of their shares held by their managing partners and auditors. The existing Turkish and foreign auditing firms adapted themselves to these requirements.

The real breakthrough for the establishment of an accounting profession, however, came with the enactment of the Independent Accountancy, Independent Accounting Financial Consultant, and Certified (sworn) Financial Consultant Law (no. 3568) in 1989. An educational background in accounting, a certain number of years' job experience, and passing professional exams are the basic requirements at each stage of the profession. Special requirements to qualify to take the exams are:

1. *Independent Accountant (IA):* Two years of college education or vocational high school for commerce and finance, four years of on-the-job training for college graduates, and six years for high school graduates.
2. *Independent Accounting Financial Consultant (IAFC):* B.A. degree and two years of training with an IAFC or CFC.
3. *Certified Financial Consultant (CFC):* B.A. degree and 10 years of experience as a IAFC.

A rather generous provision of the law allowed the automatic granting of CFC certificates without taking the qualification exams to persons with certain backgrounds and practical experience, including that gained in government and academia. At the time of the introduction of the law, this was largely due to another provision stipulating the formation of a chamber of accountants in each province with more than 25 members of the profession. These provincial chambers then had to be united into a nationwide union of chambers of accountants. This union would be in charge of organizing the qualification exams and, most important, have the authority to set up national standards for financial reporting and auditing.

This law evoked some serious criticism in the profession and among academics at the time of its initiation. The heaviest criticism was directed against the continuing dominance of the profession by the MF. In fact, large numbers of MF tax controllers and auditors had been automatically granted CFC certificates. This also led to domination of the committees set up for the introduction of the law by MF members.

Another criticism was directed at the automatic granting of CFC certificates to a large number of persons without sufficient background and experience in accounting. In fact, not only accounting and auditing professors but also senior professors in public finance, banking, public administration, and political science were among the recipients of these certificates. It was argued that this might eventually turn the profession into retirement positions and discourage young people from joining it.

The most important criticism directed at the law, however, has involved a provision holding the certifying auditors mutually responsible for the eventual tax liabilities of audited clients. This nurtured the belief that the CFCs were essentially tax auditing agents of the MF rather than independent external auditors safeguarding the public interest.

Although not enough time has passed for a final evaluation, the first few years of the implementation of the law have been rather encouraging. The heavy impact of the MF on accounting and financial reporting is gradually shifting to greater influence by the profession. The Union of Chambers of Certified Public Accountants of Turkey (TURMOB) is making important contributions with its efforts toward the development of the profession. In addition to its organizational activities, TURMOB is trying to improve the competency level of the profession by holding continuous educational programs, providing high-level qualification exams, and issuing a series of supporting publications. From 1990 until 1995, only 129 of 620 applicants for the CFC certificate passed the exams. The number of the members of the profession reached 23,750 IAs, 12,021 IAFCs, and 2,400 CFCs by the summer of 1995.

One critical issue still on the agenda is the mandatory signing requirement of companies' tax returns by certified public accountants. TURMOB favors this to enhance the importance of the profession and to open more job opportunities for its members. Companies oppose it because of the additional cost implications. The responsibilities and eventual tax liabilities of the attesting accountants are another area of concern. Efforts are presently being made to find a compromise that will satisfy the interests of the profession, the tax authorities, and the taxpayers.

Another important topic covered by TURMOB is the establishment of national accounting and auditing standards. A special accounting and auditing standards board (TMUDESK) that has been constituted for this purpose will certainly have lasting impact on the development of financial reporting and auditing in Turkey.

ACCOUNTING AND FINANCIAL REPORTING SYSTEM

The new accounting and financial reporting system officially took effect early in 1994. Detailed instructions for its implementation are issued by the MF, as mentioned. The issuance of these instructions by the MF also implies permission for taxpayers to use the new system; they had been accustomed to the guidance of the tax authorities for decades. The system represents a radical shift from a tax-dominated accounting tradition to a financial reporting system providing relevant, reliable, and comparable information to internal and external users.

The new system has been largely influenced by the U.S. model, especially with respect to the underlying concepts and principles. However, the requirements concerning the formal structure of the accounting system, with its uniform framework of accounts and standard general plan of accounts, indicate that the European, especially German, accounting approach also had an impact on the design of the system.

Underlying Concepts and Principles

The basic concepts and principles of the new system are largely inspired by the FASB's Conceptual Framework. A comparison of the similarities and differences between it and the Turkish system is shown in Table 1. It can be seen that It can be seen that 10 of the 12 assumptions and principles of the new system are identical with the U.S. system, although some of them appear in different subsets. Consistency is included in the basic assumptions, but it represents a qualitative characteristic. On the other hand, economic entity and monetary unit are considered as principles, not as basic assumptions. Revenue recognition,

Table 1.

New Turkish System	*FASB's Conceptual Framework—United States*
Basic assumptions	Basic assumptions
1. Going concern	1. Going concern
2. Periodicity	2. Periodicity
3. Consistency	3. Economic entity
	4. Monetary unit
Principles	Principles
1. Conservatism	1. Historical cost
2. Full disclosure	2. Revenue recognition
3. Materiality	3. Matching
4. Social responsibility	4. Full disclosure
5. Neutrality	
6. Substance over form	Qualitative characteristics
7. Economic entity	1. Relevance
8. Monetary unit	2. Reliability
9. Historical cost	a. Verifiability
	b. Representational faithfulness
	c. Neutrality
	3. Comparability
	4. Consistency
	Constraints
	1. Cost-benefits
	2. Materiality
	3. Industry practice
	4. Conservatism

matching, and comparability principles are not included in the conceptual framework of the new system. These are cited later among the instructions pertaining to the preparation of financial statements.

Social responsibility is instituted as a separate principle. It is defined in such a way that it rather implies a combination of the European "true and fair view" and the U.S. "representational faithfulness" principle. It expresses the responsibility of the management to disclose true or reliable information to the public.

Substance over form, another novelty of the system, is used in a sense quite close to relevance. Its definition indicates that in interpreting economic transactions, more attention should be given to their substance than to their external legal form.

These basic concepts must be used in defining and disclosing the accounting policies of enterprises. As an additional source for concepts, reference is made to generally accepted accounting principles (GAAP). International accounting standards, industrial practices, and opinions accepted by academic circles are included in GAAP. Some references also are made in other communiqués to the Fourth Directive of the European Community.

Uniform Classification of Accounts

The new system uses a uniform framework for the classification of accounts to enhance the comparability in financial reporting. The final format of this framework was set by the CMB in 1989 (communiqué of January 29, 1989, series XI, no. 1), and consists of a three-step classification:

1. Uniform framework of accounts.
2. Uniform group of accounts.
3. Uniform plan of accounts.

The uniform framework comprises the following seven accounts:

1. Current assets;
2. Long-term assets;
3. Short-term liabilities;
4. Long-term liabilities;
5. Equities;

6. Income statement accounts; and
7. Cost accounts.

Each item within this framework represents a basic group of accounts.

The group accounts are then further classified into subaccounts. The restriction of the number of subaccounts to 10 at each stage indicates that the decimal system is to be used for more detailed breakdowns.

An example of the subclassification of an group account follows:

2: Long-term assets
  - 2.2 Long-term trade receivables
  - 2.3 Other long-term receivables
  - 2.4 Financial long-term investments
  - 2.5 Tangible fixed assets
    - 2.5.1 Land
    - 2.5.2 Superstructures and infrastructures
    - 2.5.3 Buildings
    - 2.5.4 Plant, machinery and equipment
    - 2.5.5 Motor vehicles
    - 2.5.6 Furniture and fixtures
    - 2.5.7 Accumulated depreciation
    - 2.5.8 Construction in progress
    - 2.5.9 Deposits on purchase orders
  - 2.6 Intangible fixed assets
  - 2.7 Assets subject to special expiration
  - 2.8 Prepaid expenses and accrued revenues for over a year
  - 2.9 Other long-term assets

This uniform classification approach reflects the impact of the European, especially German, accounting system on the new regulations. This impact can be felt to a larger extent in the classification of cost accounts.

The cost accounting part of the new system also was regulated by the CMB in 1989, within a separate communiqué (January 29, 1989, series XI, no. 2) concerning the standard general plan of accounts (SGPA). According to this regulation, costs must be recorded in the following steps:

1. On a functional basis in the related general ledger account.
2. On the basis of their nature in the related cost accounts and at the same time.
3. On the basis of their allocation in the related cost center accounts.

Using a flexible approach, the regulation provides two options for the practice, one for larger (A) and another for smaller (B) companies. In option A, cost recordings occur simultaneously at functional, nature of cost, and cost center levels. In option B, the costs are first recorded according to their nature and later recapitulated for functions and cost centers, depending on the special needs of the business.

The cost accounts classification includes the following group accounts:

7: Cost accounts
- 7.0 Cost accounting connection accounts (for the application of predetermined costs)
- 7.1 Direct raw material expenses
- 7.2 Direct labor expenses
- 7.3 General manufacturing expenses
- 7.4 Cost of production of services
- 7.5 Research and development expenses
- 7.6 Marketing, sales, and distribution expenses
- 7.7 General administration expenses
- 7.8 Fiancing expenses
- 7.9 Costs classified by their nature (for option B)

This classification demonstrates how divergent approaches to accounting may lead to a rather inconsistent compromise with respect to terminology. Five of the group accounts (7.4, 7.5, 7.6, 7.7, and 7.8) are classified on a functional basis, whereas three group accounts (7.1, 7.2, and 7.3) are classified according to the nature of expenses. These three manufacturing expenses are subsequently allocated to products as cost expenses.

The use of the term *expense* for manufacturing costs reflects the impact of the German approach, which dominated Turkish practice for many decades. Expense here does not imply an expired cost but a production factor consumption, as in the corresponding German term *Aufwand.* The definition of the expenses allocated to products as *cost expense*, a term widely used in practice for many years, should therefore be interpreted as a consumption factor during the manufacturing process.

FINANCIAL REPORTING

The type of financial statements to be filed and disclosed, their format, and their content have been regulated for the capital market corporations and intermediary institutions by the CML and subsequent instructions of the CMB and the MF. Large, noncapital market companies must also comply with the disclosure requirements.

The new reporting system comprises the following financial statements:

1. Balance sheet;
2. Income statement;
3. Funds flow statement (optional);
4. Cash flow statement;
5. Profit distribution statement;
6. Cost of sales statement; and
7. Statement of changes in owners equity (optional).

The statements must disclose the financial results of two accounting periods in a comparable setup. The balance sheet and the income statement constitute the basic financial statements and must be prepared in two different formats, one comprehensive and the other condensed. Those in condensed format are published in three newspapers; the comprehensive ones are filed with the CMB.

The other five statements are supplements to the basic statements. Large capital market corporations must submit these statements to the CMB together with the basic statements. Most of the financial statements (1, 2, 4, 5, 6) also have to be disclosed and filed by the intermediary institutions operating in the capital market, some of them (the income statement and the profit distribution statement) in a slightly changed format.

CMB regulations also include requirements for additional information to be disclosed at the end of the financial statements in the form of footnotes. Inventory valuation methods, revenue and expense recognition principles, contingencies, and prior period gains and losses are among the important additional information. Furthermore, the regulations require the disclosure of supplementary information concerning important investment, financing, and administrative activities in the annual management reports.

Examples of two basic financial statements, one Turkish and one U.S., are shown in Appendix B. These statements allow a comparison of typical formats in U.S. and European practice. As can be seen from the formats of the balance sheet and income statement, the new reporting system follows the U.S. model, rather than the European approach. Balance sheet items are classified on the asset side according to their liquidity, and on the financial sources side by the terms of the liabilities, ending with owners' equity. Similarities also exist in the grouping of the accounts on both sides.

The income statement basically uses the multiple-step format. The main difference from the U.S. approach is that the intraperiod tax allocation is not applied in the Turkish system. Extraordinary income and profits and the extraordinary expenses and losses stated after the operating profit are not net of taxes as in the U.S. system. Taxes are calculated based on total taxable income at the end of the statement.

The disclosure of earnings per share not in the body of the income statement but in the footnotes is another difference from the U.S. practice. This information is also disclosed as the last item in the profit distribution statement.

The content of financial statements must be determined according to the instructions of the CMB and the MF. The instructions include detailed definitions for the items to be disclosed in financial statements. They are heavily influenced by the standards of the IASB and FASB and by the directives and practices of the European Community. GAAP must be observed when making judgments in selecting among available alternatives.

The new regulations have led to important changes in the content of financial statements during recent years. Other issues are still under consideration. The main objective of these changes has been the conversion of financial reporting from being primarily an instrument for taxation to being a powerful tool for reflecting the real economic performance of business entities. Most of the changes also attempted to reflect ongoing developments in the legal, economic, and social environment of accounting. Important changes are summarized here:

1. To alleviate the distortion of financial statements, an inflation adjustment with fixed weights was introduced in the early 1980s. This was transformed to a new system in 1987, allowing wholesale price indexes of less than 10% as the basis for reevaluating fixed assets. The difference between the historical costs and adjusted values must be assigned to a revaluation fund account. Corporations are allowed to convert this fund into equity by issuing additional stock. Beginning in 1994, corporations have been able to depreciate the reevaluated fixed assets (except buildings) within five years using 40% accelerated depreciation rates.

2. Another change in connection with high inflation has been the acceptance of the LIFO inventory valuation method. This surely will lead to a more realistic income determination. Sufficient disclosure about the undervalued inventories on the balance sheet would, however, be needed in footnotes to enable a more reliable analysis of the financial statements.

3. Marketable securities must be valued at acquisition cost. Net realizable value must be used and an allowance set up if a permanent decrease in the market value of these securities exceeding 10% can be "objectively and reasonably" predicted. In valuing the trade receivables, an allowance for doubtful accounts must be used based on the percentage of sales method.

4. Most of the employees working in a state or private organization are covered by a state-run health and retirement plan (Governmental Retirement Fund and Social Insurance Fund). Therefore, a pension accounting problem does not exist in Turkey as in the United States. One of the most important issues in this area over the last decades, however, has been the seniority indemnity issue. According to the Labor Law (1975), employees laid off after a certain number of years may claim as seniority indemnity an amount equal to the product of the number of service years and the average monthly gross pay over the last three years (e.g., 20 years × 25,000,000 = 500,000,000 TL). Although the maximum amount of this indemnity was later capped, the accounting and financing of this payment represented a real issue for most enterprises. The Tax Procedure Law did not permit the recognition of special allowances for this indemnity during the service time of the employees. Expensing could occur only at the time of the actual payment. The new regulation, however, allows special provisions for seniority indemnity during the service time. Companies are also allowed to recognize provisions for services rendered before 1988 over a period of five to 10 years. Only the amount of the actual payment, however, is tax deductible.

5. New regulations introduced more flexibility in depreciation policies as compared with the rather rigid requirements for tax purposes. Companies are now allowed to determine the depreciation methods and the length of the depreciation periods. Full-year depreciation may be taken at the time of acquisition. The flexibility can be interpreted as an additional incentive to foster investment and to offset the effect of inflation. The concept of a useful life for fixed assets also has been intro-

duced into accounting practice. Tax laws prescribe the use of linear or digressive depreciation methods. This may lead in practice to discrepancies between accounting and tax depreciation policies. Also, research and development costs and purchased goodwill must, under certain conditions, be capitalized and expensed over five years. Organizational costs may either be directly expensed or written off over five years.

6. The ongoing deterioration of the Turkish currency has caused a serious problem, especially for the valuation of imported investment goods financed by long-term foreign credits. The regulations allow the inclusion of foreign currency differences into the acquisition cost of investments until they reach their final operational stage. It is left to the discretion of management to directly write off or capitalize any additional currency difference after this date.

7. The need for a clear distinction between accounting income to be disclosed as a measure of economic performance and income used only for tax purposes also has put the deferred tax problem on the agenda of Turkish accounting practice. This is presently one of the important issues under consideration by the CMB, MF, and TURMOB. Another issue pertains to the preparation of consolidated financial statements. No regulation for mandatory consolidation has been released thus far. Large corporations having to report to foreign markets regularly prepare consolidated statements. Yet another issue on the agenda relates to the treatment of leasing contracts, which have become common in Turkey recently. Having no specific requirement concerning their capitalization, they are presently treated as rental arrangements.

AUDITING

Turkey has not set its own accounting and auditing standards. Therefore, the accounting policy of corporations' must, in the first place, conform with the guidelines and requirements set up by laws and the subsequent regulations of the CMB and MF. On topics not covered by these regulations, GAAP must be observed. These include, in addition to the CMB regulations, the auditing standards issued by the IASB, FASB, and the European regulatory agencies. Generally, the "true and far view" is expressed in the final audit statements. The examples in Appendix C present show in detail the format and content of typical audit reports.

CONCLUSION

Turkey represents a typical case of how rapid changes in the economic environment of a country affect the development of the accounting profession and financial reporting practice.

The development of the free market economy, especially the capital market, during the last decade led to the establishment of a regulatory agency (CMB) in charge of the organization and control of this market.

This was followed by the development of a legal foundation for the accounting and auditing profession, so it could provide qualified services to the participants in the capital market.

The CMB in cooperation with the MF regulates the transactions on the Securities Exchange and issues guidelines and instructions concerning financial reporting and auditing. Still in the early stages, it largely relies on internationally accepted standards and practices. Standards set by the IASB and FASB and the directives of the EC have greatly influenced the new regulations.

These rather divergent sources of influence and the differences in the educational background and experience of the persons in charge of these regulations seem to have caused some inconsistencies in the formulation of the guidelines. Frequent changes in publications released may be considered a sign of uncertainties that still exist.

The financial reporting system is largely influenced by U.S. regulations, whereas the formal structure of the accounting system bears traces of the European approach. Audit reports commonly use the "true and fair" terminology for their certification.

Despite initial difficulties, the new system represents a fundamental breakthrough for the Turkish accounting profession and practice. For the first time, accounting has been separated from the sole domination of the Turkish Commerce and Tax Procedure Laws and has been transformed into a reporting system with the primary objective of disclosing to the public relevant and reliable information for better business decisions. It will also help to reflect the real economic performance of business entities and, by doing so, will contribute to a better utilization of economic resources.

The new system will certainly mature with time, especially with the contributions of the accounting profession and practice. The Joint efforts of TURMOB and academics, along with experience, will determine the future development of Turkish financial reporting and auditing.

APPENDIX A

Table A.1. Turkey: Equity Market Profile 1986–1994
(currency in millions; end-of-period level)

	1986	*1987*	*1988*	*1989*	*1990*	*1991*	*1992*	*1993*	*1994*
Number of listed companies, Istanbul Stock Exchange	40	50	50	50	110	134	145	152	176
Market capitalization in									
T. lira	708,801	3,181,715	2,048,999	15,553,000	55,249,665	78,906,566	84,809,001	546,316,238	836,117,601
U.S. dollars	935	3,221	1,135	6,783	19,065	15,703	9,931	37,496	21,605
Trading value in									
T. lira	8,703	98,701	142,867	1,668,609	15,028,176	35,487,077	55,855,578	255,224,182	650,846,098
U.S. dollars	13	115	101	798	5,841	8,571	8,191	23,242	21,692
Turnover ratio	5.1	5.5	19.0	42.2	52.9	68.3	80.9	94.2	
Local index									
ISE index*	170.9	673;0	370.9	2,217.1	3,255.8	4,369.1	4,004.2	20,682.0	27,257.1
Change in index (%)	293.9	–44.4	493.1	46.8	34.2	–8.3	416.0	31.8	
Economic data									
GDP in U.S.$	57,396	67,744	71,498	80,113	110,071	104,22	109,609	126,330	135,000
Exchange rate, U.S. $ in T. lira	758	988	1,805	2,293	2,898	5,025	8,540	14,750	38,700

Note: * Istanbul Stock Exchange.
Source: Source: International Finance Corporation, Emerging Stock Markets Factbook, 219.

APPENDIX B

Table B.1. Brisa Bridgestone Sabanci Lastik Sanayi ve Ticaret A.S.
Detailed Balance Sheet as of December 31, 1994 (TL 1,000)

Assets	*Current Period 31.12.1994*			*Previous Period 31.12.1993*		
I. Current Assets			3,433,245,621			1,103,708,206
A. Liquid Assets		719,028,361			9,389,707	
1. Cash	29,925			21,109		
2. Banks	718,988,436			9,368,598		
B. Securities		56,720,514			0	
1. Public Sector Bonds	56,720,514			0		
C. Short-term Trade Receivables		1,623,191,490			562,677,349	
1. Trade	1,052,338,370			188,632,586		
2. Notes receivable	598,409,875			393,125,178		
3. Discount of receivable	(22,608,337)			(19,287,776)		
4. Deposits and Guarantees	385,935			252,567		
5. Other short-term receivables	1,187,776			512,270		
6. Provision for doubtful receivables(*)	(6,522,129)			(557,476)		
D. Other short-term receivables		123,124,220			56,514,122	
1. Other short-term receivables	123,124,220			56,514,122		
1.1 Deferred export V.A.T.	80,003,627			32,790,516		
1.2 V.A.T. claimed back	19,150,586			9,936,172		
1.3 Other	23,970,007			13,787,434		
E. Inventories		898,697,984			472,596,714	
1. Raw materials	363,888,788			172,082,596		
2. Semi-finished goods	96,978,191			36,261,690		
3. Finished goods	363,766,425			226,064,259		

4. Goods for resale	24,355,581			21,516,125		
5. Other inventories	290,633			125,085		
6. Advances on purchase orders	49,418,366		16,546,959			
F. Other current assets		12,483,052			2,530,314	
II. Long-term Assets			2,346,390,163			1,172,188,813
A. Long-term trade receivables		6,215,251			1,052,547	
1. Trade receivables	6,160			477,743		
2. Notes receivable	1,203,291			878,984		
3. Discount of notes receivable (–)	(664,172)			(447,263)		
4. Deposits and guarantees	45,032			43,083		
5. Other long-term trade receivables	5,624,940			100,000		
B. Tangible fixed assets		2,330,053,503			1,160,239,531	
1. Lands	536,479			291,479		
2. Superstructures and infrastructures	63,600,606			33,804,262		
3. Buildings	811,799,611			389,220,544		
4. Plant, machinery and equipment	3,221,036,316			1,691,804,511		
5. Motor vehicles	40,774,062			26,998,873		
6. Furniture and fixtures	25,639,442			16,629,723		
7. Accumulated depreciation (–)	(1,933,781,619)			(1,081,811,410)		
8. Construction in progress	96,605,006			81,937,413		
9. Advances on purchase orders	3,843,600			1,364,136		
C. Intangible fixed assets		8,128,962			8,216,370	
1. Rights	8,128,962			8,216,370		
D. Other long-term assets	1,992,447			2,680,365		
Total Assets			5,779,635,784			2,275,897,019

(continued)

Table B.1. (Continued)

Liabilities	Current Period 31.12.1994			Previous Period 31.12.1993		
I. Current Liabilities			2,037,583,691			800,718,803
A. Financial liabilities		70,679,963			317,968,124	
1. Bank overdrafts	38,663,000			285,205,906		
2. Current year portion of long-loans	32,014,315			32,759,570		
3. Principal installment and interest of bond	2,648			2,648		
B. Trade payables		692,491,135			320,725,861	
1. Suppliers	596,312,077			180,035,674		
2. Notes Payable	103,986,605			158,475,740		
3. Discount of notes payable (–)	(7,807,547)			(17,821,553)		
4. Deposits and guarantees received	0			36,000		
C. Other short-term liabilities		233,663,742			95,957,857	
1. Amounts due to shareholders	581,625			352,131		
2. Accrued liabilities	6,775,682			5,050,108		
3. Taxes, charges and other deductions payable	86,923,080			37,483,172		
4. Short-term liabilities	139,383,355			53,072,446		
4.1. Deferred export V.A.T.	80,003,627			32,790,516		
4.2. Royalty	42,365,130			17,570,520		
4.3. Other	17,014,598			2,711,410		
D. Purchase orders received		709,949,077			7,232,952	

E. Provisions		330,799,774			58,834,009	
1. Provision for taxation	316,668,660			33,330,646		
2. Other provisions	14,131,114			25,503,383		
2.1. Provisions for warranties	0			7,800,000		
2.2. Provision for short-term loan interest	4,425,054			5,039,534		
2.3. Provision for medium-term loan interest	9,706,060			12,654,781		
2.4. Other	0			9,048		
II. Long-term Liabilities			235,390,557			220,091,952
A. Financial Liabilities		42,880,660			74,777,421	
1. Bank loans	42,880,660			74,777,421		
B. Other long-term liabilities		2,200			19,993	
1. Other long-term liabilities	2,200			19,993		
C. Provision		192,507,697			145,294,538	
1. Provision for termination indemnities	192,507,697			145,294,538		
III. Shareholders' Equity			3,506,661,536			1,255,086,264
A. Capital		1,063,125,000			151,875,000	
B. Share premium		4,194,327			2,602,153	
C. Revaluation reserve		1,507,665,120			810,612,853	
1. Revaluation of tangible fixed assets	1,507,665,120			810,612,853		
D. Reserves		181,051,418			92,745,584	
1. Legal reserves	51,083,549			28,293,251		
2. Extraordinary reserves	129,967,869			64,452,333		
E. Net income for the period		750,625,671			197,250,674	

Notes to the Financial Statements dated December 31, 1994
(TL 1,000)

1. Accounting Techniques and Valuation Procedures Applied
   a. *Accounting Techniques Applied*
   The company has prepared its accounting records and financial statements of financial terms after December 31, 1988 in accordance with announcement number XI/1, dated January 29, 1989, published in the Official Newspaper and the amendments and additions brought by announcements XI/4 and XI/5 dated December 29, 1989 and announcement XI/3 dated July 26, 1989 published in the same paper.
   b. *Inventories*
   Inventories are stated at the lower of cost or net realizable value. Cost is determined by the continuous mobile average method for raw materials, goods for resale and others, and by the monthly average method for semi-finished goods and finished goods.
   c. *Fixed Assets*
   Due to high inflation the Company does not consider to value its fixed assets by applying historical cost. So the Company values its buildings (excluding land), plant, machinery and equipment, superstructures and infrastructures, motor vehicles, furniture and fixtures by applying coefficients fixed by the Ministry of Finance. Revalued fixed assets are depreciated by the regular depreciation method and the following rates in accordance with the tax law are used:

Superstructures and infrastructures	4-10%
Buildings	2-4%
Machinery, plant, and equipment	10-25%
Motor vehicles and equipment	25%
Furniture and fixtures	10%

   d. *Intangible Fixed Assets*
   The Company applies a 10% depreciation on its intangible fixed assets. These are stated after amortization.
   e. *Revenues and Expenses*
   The accruals basis of accounting is applied for the recognition of revenues and expenses. Income is recognized at the

time of delivery of goods or termination of service. The price differences that may arise from sales made during prior terms are entered in the current period.

f. *Assets and Liabilities in Foreign Currency*
Assets and liabilities in foreign currency are translated into Turkish Lira at exchange rates issued by the Turkish Central Bank at balance sheet dates. Transactions in foreign currencies during the year are translated into Turkish Lira at the rates in effect on transaction dates. Exchange gains and losses resulting from such transactions are included in the statement of income.

g. *Termination Indemnities*
In accordance with the requirements of the Capital Market Board, the Company is making provisions for potential future payments to employees with rights to termination indemnities under the Turkish Employment Legislation.

h. *Provision for Defective Tire Indemnities*
Since 1994 the Company is not making provisions for defective tire indemnities. The sum of the provision made for 1993 has been entered as an income in 1994.

i. *Securities*
Securities are valued at their purchase cost.

j. *Net Assets Tax and Economic Balance Tax*
The Company has recorded as an expense all of the Net Asset Tax and Economic Tax within the year.

k. *Premiums for Freight Support Price Stability Fund*
The accrual date in entering the Freight Premiums is the accrual date used by the Turkish Central Bank.

2. Subsequent Events
As of January 1, 1995 the upper limit of termination indemnities has been increased to TL 16,726.

3. Conditional Events
The liabilities of the legal claims pursued against the company which are outstanding as of December 31, 1994 are estimated to be TL 1,995,908 (1993 TL 1,561,000). The amount of claims pursued by the company is TL 38,665,256 (1993 TL 10,017).

4. Changes in Accounting Estimates
There are no changes seriously affecting the Company's gross margin estimates.

5. Mortgages or Guarantees on Assets
   As of December 31, 1994 the total amount of mortgages outstanding on tangible fixed assets amounted to TL 224,350,000 (1993 TL 224,350,000).
6. Insurance Coverage
   As of December 31, 1994 the total insurance coverage on assets amounted to TL 4,392,750,507 (1993 TL 2,831,649,505).
7. Mortgages and Guarantees Received
   As of December 31, 1994 the total amount of letters of guarantee and mortgages obtained against short-term receivables amount to TL 421,162,864 (1993 TL 205,750,381).
8. Commitments and Contingent Liabilities
   Commitments and contingent liabilities of the Company as of December 31, 1994 are as follows:
   a. *Commitments*
      The Company has outstanding commitments of USD 12 million for 1995.
   b. *Contingent Liabilities*
      As of December 31, 1994 the outstanding contingent liabilities in the form of letters of guarantee given to banks and customs amount to TL 394,317,856 (1993 TL 167,430,571).
9. Blocked Deposit Account at Banks
   As of December 31, 1994 the blocked deposit accounts at banks amount to TL 96,059 (1993 TL 126,530).
10. Securities Below Stock Market Current Value
    There are no securities below stock market current value as of December 3, 1994 and 1993.
11. Balances with Related Parties
    (Table omitted)
12. Doubtful Receivables Related to Receivables due and not yet due
    A provision of 100% was made for doubtful receivables related receivables due amounting to TL 6,522,129 (1993 TL 557,476) for 1994 and the previous years. There are no doubtful receivables related to receivables not yet due.
13. Revaluation of Tangible Fixed Assets
    (Table omitted)
14. Foreign Currency and Liabilities in Foreign Currency
    (Table omitted)

15. Unaccrued Interests Payable

The portion of the unaccrued interest of loans pertaining to the financial period has been recorded in the income statement as a financing expense. The portion of the said loans pertaining to the next period is approximately TL 51,114,736 (1993 TL 104,574,473).

16. Capital

	(000 TL)
January 1, Opening Balance	151,875,000
Increase of Capital:	
Cash	450,625,000
Revaluation Fund	450,625,000
As of December 31, 1994	1,063,125,000

As of December 31, 1994, the highest limit of the registered capital of the Company is TL 607,500,000 (1993 TL 607,500,000). As of the same date the Company and 100 incorporator shares entitled to participate only in the profit and 5% of the period profit is distributed to the holders of such shares as stipulated by the Articles of Association.

17. Personnel Structure

The personnel structure as of December 31, 1994 is as follows:

	31.12.1994	31.12.1993
Salaried	331	379
Waged	999	1,073
Total	1,330	1,452

Note: Some detailed amount disclosures have been left out of the footnotes in order to shorten the format.

Table B.2. Brisa Bridgestone Sabanci Lastik Sanayi ve Ticaret A.S.
Detailed Income Statement as of December 31, 1994 (TL 1,000)

	Current Period 31.12.1994		*Previous Period 31.12.1993*	
A. Gross Sales		5,198,112,122		2,708,075,562
1. Domestic sales	3,245,383,918		1,796,905,893	
1.2. Export sales	2,672,728,204		911,169,669	
B. Sales Deductions (–)		(474,933,354)		(31,073,336)
1. Sales returns (–)	(14,608,164)		(6,637,081)	
2. Sales discounts (–)	(460,325,190)		(24,436,255)	
C. Net Sales		5,443,178,768		2,677,002,226
D. Cost of Sales (–)		(3,269,638,545)		(1,729,352,447)
Gross Profit		2,173,540,223		947,649,779
E. Operating Expenses (–)		(750,457,153)		(415,091,206)
1. Marketing, selling and distribution expenses (–)	(460,521,838)		(235,139,949)	
2. Administrative expenses (–)	(289,935,315)		(179,951,257)	
Trading Profit		1,423,083,070		532,558,573
F. Income and Profit from Other Operations		143,049,634		32,540,868
1. Interest income and other dividends	55,625,593		182,338	
2. Other income and profits relating to operations	87,424,041		32,358,530	
2.1 Agency income	3,041,059		1,955,227	
2.2 Investment incentive income	0		1,253,806	
2.3 Rediscount income	27,542,586		23,412,373	
2.4 Raw material sales	661,532		169,643	
2.5 Other sales	24,829,988		1,413,361	
2.6 Purchase discounts		5,515,058		
2.7 Other	25,833,818		4,154,120	

G. Expenses and Losses from Other Operations (–)		(139,578,444)		(48,455,279)
1. Termination indemnities (–)	(31,322,266)		(6,837,125)	
2. Taxes on real estate (–)	(2,622,183)		(392,166)	
3. Rediscount expense (–)	(41,094,063)		(23,741,060)	
4. Cost of sales of raw material (–)	(233,501)		(1,467,363)	
5. Cost of other sales(–)	(532,025)		(644,229)	
6. Exchange losses (–)	(53,385,830)		0	
7. Other (–)	(10,388,576)		(15,373,336)	
H. Financial Expenses (–)		(384,763,523)		(281,330,902)
1. Short-term borrowing expenses (–)	(334,527,180)		(218,627,816)	
2. Long-term borrowing expenses (–)	(50,236,343)		(62,703,086)	
Operating Profit		1,041,790,737		235,313,260
I. Extraordinary Income and Profits		133,210,336		13,414,820
1. Prior period income and profits	83,297,228		7,393,642	
2. Other extraordinary income and profits	49,913,108		6,021,178	
2.1 Exchange profits	46,418,387		0	
2.2 Other	3,494,721		6,021,178	
J. Extraordinary Expenses and Losses (–)		(107,706,742)		(18,146,760)
1. Expenses and losses relating no non-operating activity (–)	(3,244,048)		(8,847,801)	
2. Prior period expenses and losses (–)	(25,696,337)		(6,154,325)	
3. Other extraordinary expenses and losses (–)	(78,766,357)		(3,144,634)	
3.1 Exchange losses	(13,253,906)		0	
3.2 Doubtful receivables provision	(8,662,023)		(319,683)	
3.3 Additional taxes	(52,965,807)		0	
3.4 Other	(3,884,621)		(2,824,951)	
Income for the period		1,067,294,331		230,581,320
K. Taxes Payable and Other Statutory Obligations		(316,668,660)		(33,330,646)
Net Income for the Period		750,625,671		197,250,674

Notes of the Income Statement dated December 31, 1994
(TL 1,000)

1. Inventory Cost
Inventories are valued by using the process cost method. Cost is determined by the continuous mobile average method for raw materials, goods for resale and others, and by the monthly average method for semi-finished goods and finished goods.
2. Inventory Count
A physical inventory count was made on December 31, 1994. (A physical inventory count was made as of December 31, 1993)
3. Financing Expenses Concerning Related Parties Recorded as Expenses or Assets
Interest amounting to TL 35,175,918 (1993 TL 40,985,597) was charged to the Company by Akbank T.A.S. a member of the Sabanci Group of Companies. Furthermore, interest amounting to TL 6,418,135 (1993 TL 5,023,936) was charged to the Company in respect of a Truk Eximbank credit utilized by the Company through Exsa Export Sanayi Mamulleri Satis ve Arastirma A.S.
4. Transactions with Related Parties
   a. *Sales to related parties are as follows:*
      Bridgestone Corporation
      (table omitted)
      Exsa Export Sanayi Mamulleri Satis ve Arastirma A.S.
      (table omitted)
5. Financing Expenses
Short-term borrowing expenses include the TL 284,425,462 (1993 TL 2,176,877) exchange loss resulting in the value increase in foreign currency loans.
6. Non-Operating Period Expenses and Losses
Non-operating period expenses and losses refer to the portion of the depreciation applied to fixed assets for the said period when the fixed assets are not being actually physically used.
7. Prior Period Incomes and Expenses
   a. *Incomes related to previous period are as follows:*
      (table omitted)
   b. *Expenses related to previous years are as follows:*
      (table omitted)

8. Total and Ratio of Profit and Dividend per Share
Profit and dividend per share for ordinary and incorporator shares are as follows:
   a. *Profit per Share:*

	31.12.1994	31.12.1993
1,063,125,00 shares receiving 12 months' share from profit (1993: 151,875,000)	706 TL/70, 6%	1,223 TL/122.3%

   b. *Dividend per Share*

	31.12.1994	31.12.1993
1,063,125,00 shares receiving 12 months' share from profit (1993: 151,875,000)	330 TL/33%	620 TL/62%
100 incorporator shareholders	533,647,170 TL	115,290,660 TL

Note: The author is grateful to Brisa Bridgestone Sabanci Corporation for providing the financial statements used as examples.

APPENDIX C

Brisa Bridgestone Sabanci Lastik Sanayi ve Ticaret A.S. Independent Auditors' Report for the 1994 Accounting Period

1. We have examined the balance sheet (page 1 and 2) of Brisa Bridgestone Sanayi ve Ticaret A.S. ("Company") prepared as of December 31, 1994 and related income statement for the relevant period (page 2). Our examinations were made in accordance with generally accepted auditing standards and therefore, included such tests of the accounting records and such other auditing procedures as we considered necessary in the circumstances.

2. We were appointed company auditors in 1994. The financial statements pertaining to the period ending December 31, 1993 were examined by another independent auditing company and in the auditors'

report dated February 2, 1994 the said company presented an unconditional auditing opinion.

3. In our opinion the said financial statements present the actual financial position of Brisa Bridgestone Savanci Lastik Sanayi ve Ticaret A.S. for the period ending on December 31, 1994 fairly and that the results of its operations for the year then ended are in conformity with generally accepted accounting principles issued by the Capital Market Board applied on a consistent basis.

DRT YEMINLI MALI MUSAVIRLIK A.S.
Member Firm of DELOITTE TOUCHE TOHMATSU INTERNATIONAL
Derya OZALP
Responsible Partner
Istanbul, February 3, 1995

Eregli Demir ve Celik Fabrikalari T.A.S. (Eregli Iron and Steel Mills Corporation)

Auditors' Report: The following is an excerpt from the Report of Independent Auditors, Deloitte Touche Tohmatsu International, as it appeared in the 1994 Annual Report:

> 2. We were appointed auditors of the Company during 1994. The financial statements for the year ended December 31, 1993 were audited by another independent audit firm which issued an opinion dated February 22, 1994 on those statements, qualified in respect of the nonapplication of inflation accounting required by International Accounting Standard 29.
>
> 3. Social welfare supplements totaling TL 121,560 million (TL 168,739 million including delay interest) have not been paid to the Social Security Department and have not been expensed in he relevant accounts by the Company who are relying on Law No.: 4046 (the "Law Concerning Arrangements For The Implementation of Privatization And Amending Certain Laws and Decrees With The Force Of Law"), article 23.
>
> 4. As discussed in greater detail in note 1, International Accounting Standard 29 requires that financial statements prepared in the currency of a highly inflationary economy be stated in terms of the measuring unit current at the balance sheet date, and corresponding figures for previous periods be restated in the same terms. In common with most entities in Turkey, the Company has not applied this standard in the accompanying financial statements.
>
> 5. In our opinion, except for the effects of such adjustments as may be required in respect of the matters set out in the paragraphs above, the attached financial

statements present fairly, in all material respects, the financial position of the Company as at December 31, 1994 and its income and cash flows for the year then ended, in conformity with International Accounting Standards.

REFERENCES

Bursal, I.N. 1984. The Accounting environment and some recent developments in Turkey. *The International Journal of Accounting Education and Research* 19(2)(November): 93–127.

International Finance Corporation. 1995. *Emerging Stock Markets Factbook*. Washington, DC: IFC.

ACCOUNTING STANDARD-SETTING: A COMPARISON OF INDIA AND THE UNITED STATES

Bhabatosh Banerjee, Stanley C. Martens, and John E. McEnroe

INTRODUCTION

This paper describes the accounting standards-setting process in India and then briefly compares it with the U.S. process, which is implemented by the Financial Accounting Standards Board (FASB). The paper begins with a description of the promulgation process in India, continues with a brief discussion of the U.S. standard-setting process, and then compares the two systems.

Advances in International Accounting, Supplement 1, pages 239-251.

ISBN: 0-7623-0461-8

FRAMING ACCOUNTING STANDARDS IN INDIA

The motivation for, and explicit encouragement of, accounting standard-setting in India have come from external influences, such as the International Accounting Standards Committee (IASC), rather than from within the Indian accounting establishment. Before 1970, there was virtually no effort, systematic or otherwise, on the part of the accounting profession even to initiate the standard-setting process.

In 1976, as a result of impetus from the membership of the IASC, the Institute of Chartered Accountants of India (ICAI) decided to undertake seriously the task of setting accounting standards. Recognizing the need to harmonize the diverse accounting policies and practices in use in India and international developments in the field of accounting, the Council of the ICAI constituted the Accounting Standards Board (ASB) in April 1977 to formulate accounting promulgations. While formulating such promulgations, it considers the applicable laws, customs, usages, and business environment.

The ASB finalized the procedure to be followed in the formulation of its standards in its *Preface to the Statements of Accounting Standards*, issued in January 1979. The Preface outlines the ASB scope and functions and the procedure to be followed by the ASB in formulating the standards, as well as the scope of accounting standards and the manner in which compliance with the standards will be encouraged by the ICAI.

The ASB constitution gives adequate representation to all interested parties. At present, the ASB consists of members of the ICAI Council and representatives of industry, banks, the Company Law Board, Central Board of Direct Taxes, and the Comptroller and Auditor General of India.

The procedure for the formulation of accounting standards is designed to ensure the participation of all those who are interested in the formulation and implementation of those standards (ICAI 1990). However, a point worth noting is that academicians do not appear to have been given any role in formulating accounting standards. The ASB has invited no academic bodies, institutes, or organizations, such as the Indian Accounting Association, Indian Accounting Association Research Foundation, Indian Commerce Association, or departments of accounting and commerce of leading universities in India to take part in the process of framing accounting standards. Therefore, the standards generally lack academic input and perspective.

The preliminary drafts of the standards are prepared by study groups, which take up specific subjects assigned to them. A draft is then considered by the ASB and sent to various outside bodies, such as the Federation of Chambers of Commerce and Industries, Association of Chambers of Commerce, Company Law Board, Comptroller and Auditor General, Institute of Cost and Works Accountants of India, Institute of Company Secretaries of India, Central Board of Direct Taxes, and Securities and Exchange Board of India, among others. The representatives of these bodies are also invited to a meeting with the ASB to discuss the draft.

After considering the views of these organizations, the ASB issues an exposure draft (ED) for comments by members of the ICAI and the public at large. At this stage, the ED is sent to approximately 250 to 300 institutions for their comments. In addition, it is published in the Institute journal (about 70,000 copies). Comments on the ED are considered by the ASB. Then the final draft of the standard is submitted to the ICAI's Council for its approval and is issued as a definitive standard. These steps, the exposition of which relies to a great extent on accounting standards published by the ICAI from time to time, can be summarized as follows:

1. The ASB determines the broad areas in which accounting standards need to be formulated and priorities in regard to the selection thereof.
2. Study groups are constituted to prepare the draft of the standards on specific subjects allotted by the ASB. In the formation of study groups, a provision is made for wide participation by the members of the ICAI and others.
3. The study group prepares a point outline on the subject of the standard to be formulated and submits it to the ASB for its consideration. The ASB considers the point outline in broad terms and then settles the issues relating to the point outline, again requesting the views of the study group.
4. The ASB also communicates such issues to the ICAI Council members for their comments and holds a dialogue with representatives of the government, public sector, industry, and other organizations to ascertain their views on these issues.
5. The comments received from the Council members and the views expressed by the representatives of various interested parties are

communicated to the study group, which then prepares a draft of the standard along with background material and submits it to the ASB.

6. The draft of the standard prepared by the study group includes the following basic points:

   - The statement of the fundamental accounting principles and concepts relating to the standard;
   - Definitions of the terms used in the standard;
   - The manner in which the accounting principles have been applied for formulating the standard;
   - The presentation and disclosure requirements of the standard;
   - The class of enterprise to which the standard will apply; and
   - The date from which the standard will be effective.

7. The ASB then considers the draft of the standard and, after making suitable modifications, issues an exposure draft of the proposed standard for comments by the members of the ICAI and the public at large. The ED is published in *The Chartered Accountant*, the ICAI journal.
8. After considering the comments received, the ASB completes another draft of the proposed standard and submits it to the ICAI Council.
9. The ICAI Council then considers the final draft of the standard, and, if necessary, modifies it in consultation with the ASB. The accounting standard is then issued under the authority of the Council.

Accounting standards issued by the ICAI are intended for use in the presentation of the general purpose financial statements issued to the public by commercial, industrial, or business enterprises specified by the ICAI from time to time and subject to the attest function of its members. The general purpose financial statements include the balance sheet, profit-and-loss account (income statement), and statements and explanatory notes, issued for the use of shareholders, creditors, employees, and the public. It should be mentioned that the responsibility for preparation of the financial statements and for adequate disclosure is that of the management of the enterprise.

While discharging their attest functions, it becomes the duty of the members of the ICAI to ensure that the accounting standards are implemented in the presentation of financial statements covered by their audit reports. In the event of any deviation from the standards, it also becomes the duty of the members to make adequate disclosures in their reports so that the users of such statements may be aware of such deviations.

Standards are of little value unless they are observed. The real challenge, therefore, lies in their adoption. Accordingly, one of the major functions of the ASB is to publicize the accounting standards and persuade the concerned parties to adopt those concerning the preparation and presentation of financial statements. Generally, the preparers of financial statements need some time to familiarize themselves with the standards before implementation. The following additional measures have been taken by the ICAI for this purpose:

1. Discussions of the standards issued are included in the continuing education programs of its regional councils and branches, and student associations.
2. Companies are reminded that compliance with the standards is an important criterion in designating the awards for best presented accounts given by the ICAI every year.

ACCOUNTING STANDARDS ISSUED IN INDIA

The ICAI issued its first standard in November 1979 and has issued a number of accounting standards since then (see Table 1). Initially, all the standards were recommendatory. Once awareness had grown among users of financial statements and members of the ICAI regarding the usefulness of the accounting standards and the need for complying with them in the preparation of financial statements, steps were taken to make them mandatory.

As of 1997, the ICAI had revised AS3, AS6, and AS11. However, even the revised AS6 permits the use of "any method" for calculating depreciation. The comparability of accounting information will be affected greatly as long as "diversity" in inventory valuation and depreciation accounting is not narrowed. The other standards should be continuously reviewed and revised to make them "living statements." It is the opinion of the authors that there is a critical necessity to revise AS2.

Table 1. Accounting Standards Issued by the ICAI

Number	*Particulars*	*Date of Issue*	*Status*
AS 1	Disclosure of Accounting Policies	November 1979	Mandatory 1.4.1991*
AS 2	Valuation of Inventories	June 1981	Recommendatory
AS 3	Changes in Financial Position	June 1981	Recommendatory
AS 4	Contingencies and Events Occurring after the Balance Sheet Date	November 1982	Mandatory 1.4.1987*
AS 5	Prior Period and Extraordinary Items and Changes in Accounting Policies	November 1982	Mandatory 1.4.1987*
AS 6	Depreciation Accounting	November 1982	Mandatory 1.4.1995
AS 7	Accounting for Construction Contracts	December 1983	Mandatory 1.4.1991*
AS 8	Accounting for Research and Development	January 1985	Mandatory 1.4.1991*
AS 9	Revenue Recognition	November 1985	Mandatory 1.4.1991*
AS 10	Accounting for Fixed Assets	November 1985	Mandatory 1.4.1991*
AS 11	Accounting for Effects of Changes in Foreign Exchange Rates	June 1989	Mandatory 1.4.1991*
AS 12	Accounting for Goverment Grants and Disclosure of Goverment Assistance	August 1991	Mandatory 1.4.1995*
AS 13	Accounting for Investments	September 1993	Mandatory 1.4.1995*
AS 14	Accounting for Amalgamation	September 1994	Mandatory 1.4.1995
AS 15	Accounting for Retirement Benefits	September 1994	Mandatory 1.4.1995

Note: *Effective date.

COMPLIANCE WITH INDIAN ACCOUNTING STANDARDS

The real challenge lies in the adoption of the standards by the preparers of financial statements. From a study of the standards issued by the ICAI and the dates with effect from which they have been made mandatory (Table 1), the following features become discernible:

1. Initially, the standards were recommendatory.
2. They have been made mandatory in stages. For example, two were made mandatory in 1987, six in 1991, and five in 1995.
3. Two important standards (AS2 and AS3) are still recommendatory.

Another important aspect is that, even when many standards have been made mandatory, there is as yet no legal enforcement in the Companies Act to ensure compliance with them. In the Companies Bill 1997, however, an enforcement provision has been proposed. Under the circumstances, the only way to attempt compliance is through the audit function by members of the ICAI. That is, in the event of deviations from the standards, the auditors may make adequate disclosure in their reports so that users may be aware of such deviations.

Therefore, compliance with standards depends much on the willingness of management to do so and on the degree of value the users may attach to the disclosure of noncompliance by the auditors. This is again influenced by the usefulness of the financial information for making investment and credit decisions by the users.

Earlier studies (Banerjee 1991; Chakraborty 1994) indicate that compliance has been moderate. Banerjee's comparison of the situations in India, Bangladesh, and Pakistan shows that compliance is better in India than its two neighboring countries in spite of Pakistan's having some legal provisions for compliance in its Companies Ordinance 1984. Chakraborty's study shows that, by and large, public enterprises in India exhibit better compliance than do their counterparts in the private sector.

ACCOUNTING STANDARDS FOR PUBLIC ENTERPRISES IN INDIA

Public enterprises in India occupy a key position in the economy. While there are approximately 1,400 units comprising central and state enterprises, the central enterprises (240 operating companies as of March 31, 1996) represent about 60% of the total corporate capital in the economy. Because of the social responsibility attached to the functioning of these enterprises, they have been giving leadership to the corporate sector in many respects, including the preparation and presentation of accounts. The government of India appointed several ad hoc committees to make recommendations on the organizational and managerial problems of public enterprises. Among them, the Sengupta Committee is noteworthy. It suggested that a group consisting of representatives of the Comptroller and Auditor General of India (C&AG), professionals in the field including public enterprises, and the Bureau of Public Enterprises—now known as the Department of Public Enterprises (DPE)—should be formed without further delay to evolve accounting policies for public enterprises. In pursuance of the recommendation of the Sengupta Committee, a committee to formulate accounting policies for central public enterprises was set up under the chairmanship of K.V. Ramakrishnan. The Ramakrishnan Committee, while drawing up accounting policies for central public enterprises, evaluated various accounting standards, guidance notes, and statements issued by the ICAI. In December 1986, it recommended adoption of all standards on a compulsory basis, subject to certain "additions and amplifications," which the committee found necessary to make the standards more suitable for public enterprises. Thus, with respect to compliance with accounting standards, public enterprises are on better footing than enterprises in the private sector. This is the primary reason that we find more uniformity and disclosure in the financial statements prepared by the government companies than in those prepared by their counterparts in the private sector. With respect to some controversial issues, such as depreciation, valuation of inventories, and revenue recognition, public enterprise accounting has some definite and authoritative solutions. The directive issued in 1985 by the C&AG to auditors of public enterprises relating to accounting policy gave public enterprises another definite course of action relating to their accounting and reporting. Since these enterprises dominate economic activity in the country, corporate accounting as a whole has been influenced greatly by the accounting and reporting practices followed by them.

In summary, in India generally accepted accounting principles (GAAP) have not been defined by any private or government regulatory body. They are derived (following the British practice) from the provisions of the Companies Act 1956; statements on accounting matters, guidance notes, and accounting standards issued by the ICAI from time to time; guidelines issued by the Department of Public Enterprises (in the case of government companies); and sometimes court decisions. Construction of a cohesive set of accounting standards will be facilitated when a conceptual framework of accounting is developed. Alternatively, if the IASC standards are, in fact, to be adopted, India should first adopt the Framework for the Preparation and Presentation of Financial Statements so that adoption of and compliance with IASC standards become more meaningful.

ACCOUNTING STANDARD-SETTING IN THE UNITED STATES

In the United States, accounting standards for businesses and nongovernmental nonprofit entities are set by the Financial Accounting Standards Board (FASB). Accounting standards for state and local governmental entities are set by the Government Accounting Standards Board (GASB). The federal government sets its own accounting standards. Both the FASB and the GASB are constituted and supported by the Financial Accounting Foundation (FAF), a private foundation, whose trustees come from various professional associations including the American Institute of Certified Public Accountants (AICPA). The remainder of this section concentrates on the FASB, not the GASB, because the FASB has responsibility for setting business accounting principles.

As of December 1997, the FASB had issued 125 Statements of Financial Accounting Standards, numerous interpretations and technical bulletins, and six concepts statements. The FASB's Emerging Issues Task Force publishes consensus opinions on emerging issues or refers such issues to the FASB. In addition, the FASB deems as still effective certain promulgations of its two predecessor bodies, the Committee on Accounting Procedures (1938–1959) and the Accounting Principles Board (1959–1973).

The FAF and the FASB were created in 1973 as a result of a 1972 recommendation by the Wheat Committee, a group commissioned to study the accounting standard-setting process in the United States. The two predecessor bodies to the FASB were both committees of the AICPA, and the Wheat Committee believed that accounting standard-setting had not been sufficiently independent of the auditing profession and its clients.

The FASB follows a set procedure in its deliberations. It receives advice on setting priorities and on the suitability of tentative positions from the Financial Accounting Standards Advisory Council, a group of prominent persons appointed by the FAF trustees to represent a microcosm of the business community. The due process procedure consists of the following steps:[1]

1. A problem is identified and evaluated in a preliminary fashion. The FASB receives input on problem identification from the Emerging Issues Task Force, the Financial Accounting Standards Advisory Committee, letters from constituents, the press, and the SEC.
2. The FASB meets to admit an issue to its agenda.
3. The FASB engages in early deliberations, which include literature reviews and possible surveys of interested parties by the FASB staff, as well as the formation of a Project Task Force or Project

Advisory Group. The FASB may at this point issue a Discussion Memorandum or Invitation to Comment and hold public hearings.

4. The FASB reaches a tentative resolution. It may issue a Tentative Conclusions or Preliminary Views document and invite comments from the public. The FASB is required to issue an Exposure Draft for any project that is intended to result in a Statement of Financial Accounting Standards. Comments on the Exposure Draft are invited from the public.
5. The FASB then evaluates the responses to the Exposure Draft and decides to terminate the project, release a revised Exposure Draft, or move to a vote on the final statement.
6. The FASB then votes on a final statement. It currently has a supermajority voting rule, according to which five of the seven board members must approve the draft before a final statement is issued. All Statements of Financial Accounting Standards are mandatory, not recommendatory (in the sense used in the discussion of Indian standards setting). Each Statement of Financial Accounting Standards contains an effective date that gives businesses sufficient time to implement it.

COMPLIANCE WITH U.S. ACCOUNTING STANDARDS

Nearly universal compliance with statements promulgated by the FASB results from the nature of securities regulations in the United States and the nature of auditing there. The primary laws in the United States regulating the issuance of corporate securities and the trading of those securities on secondary markets are the Securities Act of 1933 and the Securities Exchange Act of 1934.[2] The 1934 Act created the Securities and Exchange Commission, a government commission with the power to enforce securities regulations. Companies whose shares are publicly traded must register with the SEC.

SEC registrants engage in a dual system of financial reporting: these companies issue quarterly and annual reports to shareholders, but they also file certain reports with the SEC, including a quarterly report (10-Q) and an annual report (10-K). The annual report to shareholders differs from the 10-K report in the nature of certain disclosures, even though in recent years the SEC has been creating incentives to make the reports more similar.

The 1934 Act gave the SEC the power to determine the accounting principles to be followed in preparing reports filed with it. Hence, the SEC has the power to prescribe accounting standards for preparation of the 10-K, but, in general, it has allowed the standards to be produced in the private sector. The SEC stated in *Financial Reporting Release No. 1* (section 101) that the standards promulgated by the FASB have substantial authoritative support. Hence, in preparing 10-Ks, SEC registrants follow the standards promulgated by the FASB, except where explicit pronouncements by the SEC dictate (minor) differences.

In preparing annual reports to shareholders, SEC registrants also follow the standards promulgated by the FASB. The reason for this is that the SEC requires annual reports to shareholders to be audited,[3] and the auditing profession (through the AICPA) is committed to compliance with FASB promulgations. Auditing standards in the United States are set by the Auditing Standards Board, a committee of the AICPA. Unlike the "give a true and fair view" audit opinion in the United Kingdom and India, the standard audit report in the United States attests that the financial statements "present fairly in accordance with generally accepted accounting principles." Since the phrase "generally accepted accounting principles" (GAAP) occurs in the standard audit report, the AICPA (through the Auditing Standards Board) had to define this concept. The AICPA (in Rule 203 of its *Rules of Conduct* and in *Statement of Auditing Standards No. 69*) defined GAAP in such a way that financial statements must comply with FASB standards to be considered as being in accordance with GAAP. Since the AICPA has defined GAAP in this way, the reports to shareholders of SEC registrants, as well as any reports of non–SEC-registered businesses audited by certified public accountants, must comply with FASB standards.

COMPARISON OF THE INDIAN AND U.S. SYSTEMS

Clearly, there are two major differences between the Indian system of standard-setting and the U.S. system. The first difference concerns the structural independence of the accounting standard-setting body from the auditing profession. In India, the Accounting Standards Board is a committee of the ICAI. The situation in India is comparable in this respect to the situation in the United States before the creation of the

FAF and FASB in 1973, when accounting standards were set by the Accounting Principles Board, a committee of the AICPA. Since the FASB is under the aegis of the FAF, a private foundation, it is structurally independent of the AICPA. Several FAF trustees come from the AICPA, but the majority do not. Perhaps the Indian system will move in the future toward establishment of a structurally independent standard-setting body. Before that happens, there would have to be a perception among interested parties in India similar to the 1972 perception by the Wheat Committee in the United States, that there was a problem of the auditing profession exerting too much power over accounting standards.

The second, and perhaps greatest, difference concerns the lack of widespread compliance with promulgated accounting standards in India. If standards are not being complied with, the problem of who controls the standard-setting body is not very important. In India, quite a few important standards are recommendatory in nature, there is no legal sanction to ensure that companies comply with the standards, and public enterprises, because of certain government initiatives, lead private enterprises in compliance. In the United States, the unique interplay among the FASB, SEC, and AICPA results in almost universal compliance with FASB standards. In India, if universal compliance is seen as a desirable goal, a solution must be found that is consistent with Indian politics and culture. India could not simply duplicate the situation in the United States. Perhaps compliance with promulgated accounting standards could be written into a future version of the Companies Act, but if this was done, an adequate enforcement mechanism would have to be created. Such an approach, however, would involve the problem of structural independence, because any such attempt to revise the Companies Act would grant considerable power to the ICAI through its committee, the Accounting Standards Board.

NOTES

1. This description relies to a great extent on Miller and Redding (1988).
2. For more information on the Acts and the SEC, see Skousen (1991).
3. Stockholders generally receive the annual report along with a stock proxy solicitation. The SEC has the power to regulate stock proxy solicitations and has required annual reports to shareholders to be audited under its stock proxy solicitation rules.

REFERENCES

Banerjee, B. 1991. Harmonization of accounting standards in some SAARC countries. In *Contemporary Issues in Accounting Research*, ed. B. Banerjee. Calcutta: Indian Accounting Association Research Foundation.

Chakraborty, D.K. 1994. *Development of Corporate Accounting in India*. New Delhi: Venus Publishing House.

Institute of Chartered Accountants of India. 1990. *Compendium of Standards*. New Delhi: ICAI.

Miller, P., and R. Redding. 1988. *The FASB: The People, the Process, and the Politics*. Homewood, IL: Irwin.

Skousen, K.F. 1991. *An Introduction to the SEC*. Cincinnati, OH: South-Western.

www.ingramcontent.com/pod-product-compliance
Ingram Content Group UK Ltd.
Pitfield, Milton Keynes, MK11 3LW, UK
UKHW020801290926
15470UKWH00003B/893

9 780762 304615